THE *InterActive* READER™ PLUS

TEACHER'S GUIDE

Active Reading Strategies for All Students

Grade 10

McDougal Littell

Evanston, Illinois   Boston   Dallas

ISBN 0-618-31029-0

5 6 7 8 9 10 – PBO –10 09 08 07 06 05

Table of Contents

Table of Contents (continued)

What is *The InterActive Reader™ Plus* ?

A book that allows students with different abilities to develop stronger reading skills by encouraging the use of a variety of comprehension strategies.

Every student is on the same page, but strategic help varies across three levels:

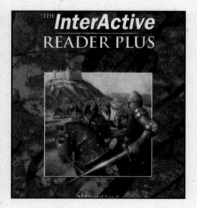

The InterActive Reader™ Plus

Includes

- Literature selections from the Grade 10 *Language of Literature* broken into short, manageable sections
- Reading support throughout
- A consumable format that allows students to mark the text with their notes and questions
- In-book activity sheets

The InterActive Reader™ Plus with Additional Support

Includes

- All of the features of *The InterActive Reader™ Plus*
- Special reading support for your struggling readers including
  - a brief summary with every section
  - more contextual background information
  - extra reading checks
- Page layouts that are the same across all books.

The InterActive Reader™ Plus for English Learners

Includes

- All the features of *The InterActive Reader™ Plus*
- Special support for English Learners including
  - a brief summary with every section
  - more contextual background information
  - special language and culture notes
  - extra reading checks
- Page layouts that are the same across all books.

The InterActive Reader™ Plus encourages students to write in their books!

Before Reading

During Reading

All levels of *The InterActive Reader™ Plus* provide students and teachers with a unique resource that fosters reading comprehension. *The InterActive Reader™ Plus* encourages students to engage or *interact* with the text. Activities before, during, and after reading a selection prompt students to make personal connections; ask themselves questions; clarify their ideas; and visualize objects, persons, and places—all thinking processes performed by proficient readers.

The following features help students interact with the text:

Connect to Your Life and **Key to the Selection** give students concrete ways to begin thinking about the selection they will read.

FOCUS Appearing before each "chunk" of text, the focus serves as a mini-preview and sets the purpose for reading.

Additional Support for Struggling Readers and English Learners

As the story begins . . . Every chunk of text begins with a brief summary of the section.

KEEP TRACK Using a system of stars, question marks, and exclamation marks, students monitor their understanding as they read.

Pause & Reflect Students read until the *Pause & Reflect* symbol appears, signaling them to stop and answer the questions in the margins. These questions allow students to follow up on the purpose-setting statement in the Focus and to learn and practice a variety of reading skills and strategies, including

- summarizing
- inferring
- questioning
- predicting
- visualizing
- connecting
- clarifying
- evaluating
- drawing conclusions
- stating opinions
- locating main ideas
- making judgments
- analyzing
- identifying cause-and-effect relationships
- understanding an author's purpose
- distinguishing fact from opinion

MARK IT UP At specific points in each selection, students are directed to underline, circle, or highlight key passages that help clarify meaning.

READ ALOUD Frequently, students are asked to reread a particular passage aloud and focus on some particular aspect of its meaning or intent.

WORD POWER As students read, they are encouraged to mark words that they don't know. They can then add them to their **Personal Word Lists,** found at the back of their books.

NOTES Extra space is provided in the side columns for students' personal notes about the literary selections and the ideas that spring from them.

Additional Support for Struggling Readers and English Learners

☑ **Reading Check** These questions at key points in the text help students clarify what is happening in a selection.

More About . . . These notes provide key background information, such as historical context, political situations, scientific background, needed for understanding the selection.

What Does It Mean? Possibly confusing words, phrases, references, and other constructions are clearly explained in these notes.

☆ **Reader Success Strategy** Specifically for struggling readers, these notes give useful and fun tips and strategies for comprehending the selection.

English Learner Support Support for English Learners involves a wide range of vocabulary, language, and culture issues that are covered in these special notes.

After Reading

✎ CHALLENGE At the end of most selections, a Challenge activity requires students to reenter the selection to analyze a key idea and to answer a higher-level question.

SkillBuilder Pages During and after reading a selection, students are encouraged to complete the SkillBuilder pages that follow each lesson. The three SkillBuilder pages help students practice and apply important skills.

• **Active Reading SkillBuilder** Comprehension skills are reinforced through graphics and other visual representations, requiring students to use their understanding of the selection to extend their reading skills.

• **Literary Analysis SkillBuilder** Literary elements are reinforced through graphics and other visual representations, requiring students to use their understanding of the selection to extend their literary skills.

• **Words to Know SkillBuilder** (for most selections) Words underlined and defined in the selection are reviewed, requiring students to use the words contextually and in original sentences.

Ongoing Assessment In addition to increasing students' involvement in the reading process, *The InterActive Reader™ Plus* offers you, the teacher, a window on students' progress and problems. Students' notes, responses, and other markings should be looked at regularly as part of the ongoing informal assessment process.

The InterActive Reader™ Plus helps students with differing abilities to access authentic text.

The InterActive Reader™ Plus
(for on-level and above-level students)

- On-level students will find appropriate support or scaffolding to hone their reading process strategies and skills. The interactive activities enable students to construct meaning and to recognize *how* that meaning was constructed.

- Above-level students will be able to sharpen their analytical reading skills using this level. Being able to write in the book allows these students to annotate authors' use of tone, mood, symbols, and other literary concepts addressed by the College Board.

The InterActive Reader™ Plus with Additional Support
(for below-level readers)

Struggling readers will achieve best in this level. Summaries, additional background information, extra vocabulary support, and extra interactive activities will provide the necessary help for these students. Allowing students to work in pairs or small groups and partner-reading followed by talking through their answers to questions in the side columns; will not only build reading competence but also reading confidence!

Three levels of books . . . Yet the SAME text on the SAME page . . . and all students receive the differentiated support they need for their reading abilities.

The InterActive Reader™ Plus for English Learners
(for students learning English)

Students learning English will achieve best in this level. Extra assistance to meet their specific needs will allow these students to break through the word-level barrier to focus on the meaning and ideas of the selection.

How is *The InterActive Reader™ Plus* best used in the classroom?

Because all three levels contain the *same* literary selections with the *same* page numbers, you can easily use them in a single classroom. As you introduce a selection or discuss a "chunk" of text, there will never be any confusion by students; for they will have their own customized side-column activities based on their reading abilities. *The InterActive Reader™ Plus* changes the level of support, not the literature.

Lesson Planning

You may wish to use the following sequence for a lesson using all levels of *The InterActive Reader™ Plus:*

Before Reading

- Assign the **Connect to Your Life** and **Key to the Story** activities for the whole class. Students may complete them independently or in partners before sharing their answers with the group.

During Reading

- Read aloud the **Focus** and **Mark It Up** to clarify the "reading with pen in hand" activity that is suggested.

- Read aloud or think aloud or model the thinking strategy required to complete the **Mark It Up** task for the first section.

- Encourage all students to read through the side column notes and to answer questions and mark anything that puzzles or confuses them. Struggling readers and English learners will find summaries and notes especially for them.

- At the Pause & Reflect, discuss as a group the questions listed in the side column or have students work with a partner to answer the questions.

- Beginning with the next section, again read the **Focus** and **Mark It Up.** At this point you may have some students working independently while you assist others with think-alouds or other strategies.

- Use the SkillBuilder pages along with the reading if appropriate. For example, an Active Reading SkillBuilder on predicting is best filled out while students read. They can then check the accuracy of their predictions as they finish the selection.

After Reading

- You may wish to work together as a whole class on the **Challenge** activity, or you may find pairs or small groups most effective.

- Use the SkillBuilder pages as an effective review and reinforcement of the vocabulary, reading and literary skills covered.

Suggested Reading Options

A variety of methods can be used with *The InterActive Reader*™ *Plus.*

The InterActive Reader™ *Plus* allows you to choose from a number of different reading options as you assign students work. Each Lesson Plan in this Guide suggests one of the following options, the suggestion being based on the nature of the selection itself. However, any reading options may be used at any time. Options marked with an asterisk (*) are especially effective with Students Acquiring English.

Independent Reading

Students can read independently, using the questions in the margins of their books for guidance and focus. Though most often this option is used with students who need little support, all students should have some opportunities to read independently. In this situation, *The InterActive Reader*™ *Plus* may be used as a take-home text.

Note: If *The InterActive Reader*™ *Plus* is being used in conjunction with *The Language of Literature,* you may wish to begin the prereading activities, such as Connect to Your Life and Build Background, in class; the main anthology can then be left at school while students carry home their smaller and less cumbersome readers.

Partner/Cooperative Reading*

Students can read in pairs, pausing at the indicated places to discuss the questions, write answers, and compare notations and highlighted passages. Alternately, students can read in small groups, pausing in the same manner to discuss the selection and respond to prompts. In either setting, encourage students to discuss the strategies they use as they read.

Teacher Modeling*

Read aloud the first part of a selection, discuss key events or concepts that are important for comprehension, and then have students continue reading on their own. For particularly challenging selections, reading aloud can continue farther into the selection, or there could be an alternating of silent reading and teacher read-aloud.

Oral Reading*

This option works well for plays, speeches, or selections that contain an abundance of dialogue. It can also work well with narrative passages, providing an aural dimension to the comprehension process.

Audio Library*

Recordings of almost all selections in *The InterActive Reader*™ *Plus* are provided as part of *The Language of Literature* core program. You may find it useful to have students read along with these recordings.

Note: In order to familiarize students with the lesson structure and format of *The InterActive Reader*™ *Plus,* you might consider reading aloud the beginning of each selection and modeling the *Focus* and *Pause & Reflect* activities provided.

Reciprocal Teaching

Reciprocal teaching refers to an instructional activity that teaches students concrete, specific, "comprehension-fostering" strategies they will need whenever they approach the reading of a new text. The activity consists of a dialogue between students and teacher, with each taking a turn in the role of the teacher or leader. Classroom use of this activity has been found to improve the reading comprehension of both good and struggling readers.

Step 1: Have everyone silently read a short passage (one or several paragraphs) of a new text. Model the following four thinking strategies using only the part of the reading that has been read.

- **Questioning** – Ask the class to think of a question that everyone can answer because everyone has read the same text. Model by generating a question for the class. Call on a student to answer your question. Ask that student to then generate a question for the class and to call on another student to answer her question. Repeat this procedure until you think all students are thoroughly familiar with the facts and details of the passage. (If students do not ask a question beginning with *why,* model one for them to move their thinking from literal to inferential comprehension.)

- **Clarifying** – Model for the class a confusion you need to clarify; for example, a word or a phrase that caused you to pause as you initially read the passage. Think-aloud as you discuss your mental engagement with this section, explaining to the class how you figured it out. Ask students if they found any confusing parts when they read the passage. Have a dialogue about the problem-solving methods used by students to make sense of confusing parts.

- **Summarizing** – After students have comprehended the passage as a result of the reciprocal questioning and clarifying strategies, ask them to think of a one-sentence summary for the passage. Ask a volunteer to share his summary statement. Encourage others to revise, if needed, the shared summary by elaborating and embellishing its content. Identify the best summary through a dialogue with class members.

- **Predicting** – Now that students know what the first passage in the reading means, ask them to predict what the author will discuss next.

Step 2: Ask everyone to silently read another portion of text. Have a student volunteer repeat Step 1, serving as the teacher/leader, over this new portion.

Step 3: In groups of four, have students silently read the next portion of text, taking turns role-playing the leader and following the 4-step procedure.

Teacher's Role: Guide students' practice by monitoring the student dialogue in each group during steps 2 and 3. Remind students of the procedure and give additional modeling of the steps.

Reciprocal Teaching training provides students with explicit ways to interact with new text. *The InterActive Reader™ Plus* extends this powerful technique by focusing on additional strategies: connecting, visualizing, and evaluating. You will notice that students connect and visualize while clarifying and evaluate in order to predict.

For each Lesson Plan in *The InterActive Reader™ Plus,* one of the above comprehension strategies is modeled. An on-going review of all of the strategies provides a helpful reminder to students and encourages their pursuit of independent reading.

Strategies for Reading

These strategies can help you gain a better understanding of what you read. Whenever you find yourself having difficulty making sense of what you're reading, choose and use the strategy that seems most likely to help.

PREDICT   Try to figure out what will happen next and how the selection might end. Then read on to see how accurate your guesses are.

VISUALIZE   Visualize characters, events, and setting to help you understand what's happening. When you read nonfiction, pay attention to the images that form in your mind as you read.

CONNECT   Connect personally with what you're reading. Think of similarities between the descriptions in the selection and what you have personally experienced, heard about, or read about.

QUESTION   Question what happens while you read. Searching for reasons behind events and characters' feelings can help you feel closer to what you are reading.

CLARIFY   Stop occasionally to review your understanding of what you read. You can do this by **summarizing** what you have read, identifying the **main idea,** and **making inferences**—drawing conclusions from the information you are given. Reread passages you don't understand.

EVALUATE   Form opinions about what you read, both while you're reading and after you've finished. Develop your own ideas about characters and events.

Developing Fluent Readers

Good readers are fluent readers. They recognize words automatically, group individual words into meaningful phrases, and apply phonic, morphemic and contextual clues when confronted with a new word. Fluency is a combination of accuracy (number of words identified correctly) and rate (number of words per minute) of reading. Fluency can be taught directly, and it improves as a consequence of students reading a lot of materials that are within their instructional range.

Understanding Reading Levels

Every student reads at a specific level regardless of the grade in which he or she is placed. Reading level in this context is concerned with the relationship between a specific selection or book and a student's ability to read that selection. The following are common terms used to describe these levels:

- **independent level**—The student reads material in which no more than 1 in 20 words is difficult. The material can be read without teacher involvement and is likely to be material students would choose to read on their own.

- **instructional level**—The student reads material in which no more than 2 in 20 words is difficult. The material is most likely found in school and read with teacher involvement.

- **frustration level**—The student reads material in which significantly more than 2 in 20 (or 89%) of the words are difficult. Students will probably get little out of reading the material.

If students read only material that's too easy, growth in skill, vocabulary, and understanding is too slow. If students read only difficult material, they may give up in frustration much too early.

Providing Reading Materials in the Student's Instructional Range

Most states have testing programs that provide information about each student's reading ability. Once you determine a student's general reading level, you can work with the library media teacher to identify reading materials that will be within the student's instructional level. To develop fluency, students should read materials that contain a high proportion of words that they know already, or can easily decode. Work with each student to develop a list of books to read, and have students record their progress on a Reading Log.

Repeated Oral Readings

Repeated oral readings of passages is a strategy that improves fluency. Oral reading also improves prosody, which is the art of sounding natural when you read, that is reading with appropriate intonation, expression, and rhythm.

Beginning readers sound awkward when they read aloud. They pause and halt at the wrong places; they emphasize the wrong syllables; they may read in a monotone. Repeated oral readings can increase fluency and prosody as students 1) identify words faster and faster each time they read; 2) correctly identify a larger percentage of words; 3) segment text into appropriate phrases; 4) change pitch and emphasis to fit the meaning of the text.

To improve fluency and prosody, select passages that are brief, thought provoking, and at the student's current independent level of reading. You may chose narrative or expository text, or have the student choose something he or she enjoys. Performing a play, practicing to give a speech, reading to younger students, and re-reading a passage to find evidence in support of an argument are all activities that provide opportunities to re-read. For the following exercise, you may chose to pair students together and have them read to each other, or use this as a one-on-one teacher-student or tutor-student activity.

1. Select an excerpt within the student's reading level that ranges from 50-200 words in length.

2. Have the student read the passage aloud to a partner. The partner records the number of seconds it takes to read the whole passage, and notes the number of errors. Reverse roles so that each student has a chance to read to the other.

3. Read the passage aloud to the students so that students can hear it read correctly.

4. As homework, or an in-class assignment, have students practice reading the passage out loud on their own.

5. After practice, have each student read aloud again to his or her partner, who records the time and the number of errors.

6. After repeated practice and readings the student will read the passage fluently, that is with a moderate rate and near 100% accuracy.

Example Excerpt

But soft! What light through yonder
    window breaks?
It is the East, and Juliet is the sun!
Arise, fair sun, and kill the envious moon,
Who is already sick and pale with grief
That thou her maid art far more fair
    than she.

from Romeo and Juliet
by William Shakespeare

Repeated Silent Readings

Having students silently read and re-read passages that are at their instructional level also improves fluency. As they practice, students will recognize words more quickly each time, will group words into meaningful phrases more quickly, and will increase their reading rate. One nice thing about repeated silent reading is that a student can do it individually. Many students enjoy timing themselves when they read, and seeing improvement over time. Have them keep a record on a piece of graph paper.

Modeling

Students benefit from repeated opportunities to hear English spoken fluently. By listening to live models or tapes, listeners can understand the rhythm of the language and the pitch and pronunciation of particular words and phrases. They can hear when to pause, when to speed up, and what words to emphasize. In addition, you can model, or ask an experienced reader to read passages aloud. At most advanced levels, this technique is particularly useful to introduce students to various forms of dialect. As you play the tapes aloud, have students read along silently or chorally, or pause the tapes after each paragraph and have the students try reading the same passage aloud.

Phrase-Cued Text

Less proficient readers may not know when to pause in text. They may pause in the middle of a phrase, or run through a comma or period. They may not recognize verb phrases, prepositional phases, or even phrases marked by parentheses or brackets as words that "go together." This makes their reading disjointed and choppy, or gives it a monotone quality. Some poems have essentially one phrase per line, and can be used to demonstrate to students how to phrase text. Or you may take a passage and have students re-write it with one phrase per line, so that they pause at the end of each line, after each phrase. Alternately, you can show them how a passage should be read by inserting slash marks or blank spaces at appropriate places to pause. Choose words of about 50-100 words in length from fiction or non-fiction selections. For example, you can take a passage like the following:

Example Modeling

When the man entered the room, he failed to notice the trembling brown fox crouching in the corner next to the refrigerator. When the man opened the door of the refrigerator to grab a cold soda, the fox leapt between his feet and the door and scrambled for a hiding place on the shelf behind the lettuce.

And present it to students in this way:

When the man entered the room,/he failed to notice/ the trembling brown fox/ crouching in the corner/ next to the refrigerator. When the man opened the door of the refrigerator/ to grab a cold soda,/ the fox leapt between his feet and the door/ and scrambled for a hiding place/ on the shelf /behind the lettuce.

Informal Reading Inventory

Have students read, and re-read the passage, stopping to pause at each slash mark.

An informal inventory can give an initial idea of a student's reading level. Teachers often use an Informal Reading Inventory (IRI) to place students in the appropriate textbook.

To conduct an IRI, you need at least one 100-word passage from the material in question, and 10 comprehension questions about the material. If you want more than one passage, select them randomly from every 30th page or so. Have the student read the same passage twice—the first

time orally to assess oral reading skills. The student should read the passage a second time silently, after which he or she answers questions for assessment of reading comprehension. Suggestions for administering an IRI.

1. Tell the student he or she will read the passage out loud, and then again silently, and then you will ask some questions.

2. Give the student a copy of the passage and keep one for yourself. Have the student read the passage. As the student reads out loud, note on your copy the number of errors he or she makes:

   Mispronunciations: Words that are mispronounced, with the exception of proper nouns.
   Omissions: Words left out that are crucial to understanding a sentence or a concept.
   Additions: Words inserted in a sentence that change the meaning of the text.
   Substitutions: Words substituted for actual words in the text that change the meaning of a sentence.

Use these criteria for assessing reading levels after oral reading:

   - Fewer than 3 errors—The student is unlikely to have difficulty decoding text.
   - Between 4 and 9 errors—the student is likely to have some difficulty, may need special attention.
   - More than 10 errors—The student is likely to have great difficulty, may need placement in less material.

3. Have the student read the passage again, silently.

4. When the student finishes, ask the comprehension questions you have prepared ahead of time. Tell the student that he or she can look back at the passage before answering a question.

5. Note the number of correct responses. Use these criteria for assessing reading level after silent reading.

  - Eight or more—The student should be able to interpret the selections effectively.

  - Five to seven—The student is likely to have difficulty.

  - Fewer than five—The student needs individual help or alternate placement.

6. Evaluate results from oral and silent reading to decide how good a match the material is for a student's independent or instructional level.

Another approach allows you to assess the student's choice for independent reading. Have the student independently select a book he or she would like to read. The student should open to a random page in the middle of the book (that has not been read before) and begin reading silently from the top of the page. Ask the student to extend one finger on one hand for each time he or she comes across an unfamiliar word. If, by the end of that page, the student has five or more fingers extended, the book is probably too difficult for that student. You may want to suggest that the student find a book more suitable to his or her reading level.

Research/Related Readings

The following research supports the philosophy and pedagogical design of *The InterActive Reader™ Plus:*

Beck, I. et al. "Getting at the Meaning: How to Help Students Unpack Difficult Text." *American Educator: The Unique Power of Reading and How to Unleash It* 22.1–2 (1996): 66–71, 85.

California Reading Initiative and Special Education in California: Critical Ideas Focusing on Meaningful Reform. Sacramento: California Special Education Reading Task Force, California Department of Education and California State Board of Education, 1999.

Carnine, D., J. Silbert, and E. J. Kame'enui. *Direction Instruction Reading.* Columbus: Merrill, 1990.

Langer, J. A. "The Process of Understanding Literature." Center for the Learning and Teaching of Literature. Report Series 2.1. Albany: State U of New York, 1989.

Langer, J. A., and A. N. Applebee. "Reading and Writing Instruction: Toward a Theory of Teaching and Learning." *Review of Research in Education.* Ed. E. Rothkopf. Washington, D.C.: American Educational Research Association, 1986.

Lapp, D., J. Flood, and N. Farnan. *Content Area Reading and Learning: Instructional Strategies.* 2nd ed. Boston: Allyn & Bacon, 1996.

Lyon, G. Reid. "Learning to Read: A Call from Research to Action." *National Center for Learning Disabilities.* 9 Nov. 1999. <http://www.ncld.org/theirworld/lyon98.html>

Palinscar, A. S. and A. L. Brown. "Interactive Teaching to Promote Independent Learning from Text." *The Reading Teacher* 39.8 (1986): 771–777.

Palinscar, A. S. and A. L. Brown. "Reciprocal Teaching of Comprehension-Fostering and Comprehension-Monitoring Activities." *Cognition and Instruction* 1.2: 117–175.

Pearson, P. D., et al. "Developing Expertise in Reading Comprehension." *What Research Says to the Teacher.* Ed. S. J. Samuels and A. E. Farstrip. Newark: International Reading Association, 1992.

Rosenshine, B., and C. Meister. "Reciprocal Teaching: A Review of the Research." *Review of Educational Research* 64.4 (1994): 479–530.

Simmons, D. C., and E. J. Kame'enui, eds. *What Reading Research Tells Us About Children with Diverse Needs: Bases and Basics.* Mahwah: Lawrence Erlbaum, 1998.

Tierney, R. J., J. E. Readence, and E. K. Dishner. *Reading Strategies and Practices: A Compendium.* 4th ed. Boston: Allyn & Bacon, 1995.

Tompkins, Gail. *50 Literacy Strategies: Step by Step.* Upper Saddle River: Merrill, 1998.

Lesson Plans

BEFORE READING

Connect to Your Life Ask students to identify a personal talent, skill, or ability and then imagine what life would be like without it. Have them write their ideas on page 3 and then share them with a partner.

Key to the Story Explain to students that the concept of equality is the subject of this story. For the **Key to the Story**, have students complete the word web on page 3 and share their responses with the class.

Build Background To help students understand the meaning of the term *handicap* as it is used in "Harrison Bergeron," have them read the Build Background information on page 20 of *The Language of Literature*.

COMPREHENSION FOCUS

KEY POINTS	STRATEGIES FOR SUCCESS
Target Skill: Cause and Effect In order to understand the special meaning of the word *equal* as it is used in the story, students must be able to recognize the cause-and-effect relationship between a character's special skills or strengths and the "handicaps" he or she is given.	• **MINI-LESSON** Before students read "Harrison Bergeron," you may wish to teach the **Cause and Effect** lesson on page 92 of this Guide. • As students read, have them use the **Cause-and-Effect Chart** on page 93 of this Guide to identify the special skills or strengths that each character possesses and the handicaps he or she is given because of these abilities.
Story Premise It is crucial to story comprehension that students understand that the government places physical burdens on individuals to create equality, a condition generally considered to be positive, but that the effect of their actions is negative.	• Read aloud lines 1 through 76. Have students identify details that show how the handicaps burden the characters' lives.
Shifts in Setting To follow the plot, students must recognize shifts in setting between the Bergerons' home and the television studio.	• Each time the setting shifts, have students write *home* or *studio* next to the sentence where the change takes place.

ADDITIONAL WORDS TO KNOW

resemblance
page 6, line 59

glimmeringly
page 6, line 68

uncertainly
page 7, line 108

extraordinarily
page 8, line 127

uncompetitive
page 8, line 136

realization
page 9, line 175

VOCABULARY FOCUS: Using Structural Analysis

Teacher Modeling Remind students that they can use prefixes, suffixes, and base words to figure out the meanings of unfamiliar words. Then use the following modeling suggestion for the word *unceasing* (page 4, line 11):

You could say I'm not sure what unceasing *means, but I do recognize the prefix* un-, *which means "not." I also see the word* ceasing, *which means "ending or stopping." By putting these parts together I can figure out that* unceasing *means "not ending."*

Student Modeling Now have students follow your lead. Ask a volunteer to model how to use structural analysis to determine the meaning of *graceful* (page 5, line 42):

A student might say I can try breaking graceful *into parts. I see the base word* grace, *which means "beauty or charm." Then I see the suffix* -ful, *which means "full of." So, a graceful gesture must be one that is full of beauty.*

MINI-LESSON See page 88 of this Guide for additional Work on **Using Structural Analysis**.

DURING READING

SUGGESTED READING OPTIONS

- An oral reading of "Harrison Bergeron" is available in *The Language of Literature* Audio Library. 🎧
- Partner/Cooperative Reading (See page 10 of this Guide.)
- Additional options are described on page 10 of this Guide.

RECIPROCAL TEACHING SUGGESTION: Visualizing

Teacher Modeling *Pause & Reflect, page 9*   Model using story clues and prior knowledge to visualize what Harrison looks like and how he affects others.

You could say   *I want to understand why people react to Harrison with such fear. When I picture Harrison, I see a seven-foot-tall young man wearing earphones and thick eyeglasses, and carrying three-hundred pounds of scrap metal strapped to his body. He has a red rubber ball on his nose, shaved eyebrows, and black caps on some of his teeth. He must look bizarre! Picturing him in my mind helps me understand why people are afraid of him.*

Student Modeling *Pause & Reflect, page 11*   Have several students model how they would visualize the dance between Harrison and the ballerina. Remind them to use details to help them visualize what is happening.

> Encourage students to use the other five reading strategies when appropriate as they proceed through the rest of the selection. (See page 12 of this Guide.)

AFTER READING

RECOMMENDED FOLLOW-UP

- **Thinking Through the Literature**, page 27, *The Language of Literature*
- **Choices & Challenges**, pages 28–29, *The Language of Literature*
- **SkillBuilders**, pages 12–14, *The InterActive Reader*

INFORMAL ASSESSMENT OPTIONS

Retell   Have students meet in small groups and take on the roles of the main characters. Ask them to tell what happened in the story, with each character giving his or her own view of the events. Offer these prompts:

- *Do you have a handicap? How does it affect you?*
- *Do you think handicaps are fair or unfair?*

Spot Check   Review the comments and responses students wrote in the margins, paying particular attention to their responses to the *Pause & Reflect* questions and to any predictions they made.

FORMAL ASSESSMENT OPTIONS IN *The Language of Literature*

Selection Quiz, page 9, Unit One Resource Book

Selection Test, pages 7–8, Formal Assessment Book

Students Acquiring English/ESL

1. Students might benefit from reading along with the recording of "Harrison Bergeron" provided in *The Language of Literature* Audio Library. 🎧

2. Make sure students understand these terms:

211th, 212th, and 213th Amendments to the Constitution, page 4

drove people crazy, page 4

like something the cat drug in, page 5

dark ages, page 7

under-handicapped, page 8

neutralizing gravity with love and pure will, page 11

Additional Challenge

1. Share Opinions   Ask students to explain why they would or would not like to live in the world described in "Harrison Bergeron." Have them cite story details to support their response.

⟋MARK IT UP⟍

2. Identify Sound Images Direct students to underline the descriptions of the sounds that George hears through the government transmitter. Then ask them to evaluate the effect of these images on both George and the reader.

BEFORE READING

Connect to Your Life

Define the term *rite of passage* and have students brainstorm examples of rites of passage. Have them complete the concept web on page 16 and then share their responses in small groups.

Key to the Story Ask students to discuss how their views of the world might differ from those of people who grew up before the creation of the first nuclear bomb. Ask students to silently read the **Key to the Story**.

Build Background To help students learn more about rites of passage and the meaning of the story's title, have them read the Build Background information on page 42 of *The Language of Literature*.

NEW WORDS TO KNOW

enchantments
   page 23, line 230

wilderness
   page 23, line 258

magical
   page 24, line 265

destruction
   page 28, line 437

unconquered
   page 29, line 472

COMPREHENSION FOCUS

KEY POINTS	STRATEGIES FOR SUCCESS

Target Skill: Making Inferences
Because John, the narrator and main character, has limited knowledge of the advanced civilization he is exploring, his descriptions of what he discovers are sketchy and superficial. Students must be able to make inferences in order to understand what places, objects, and events he is describing.

- **MINI-LESSON** Before students read, you may wish to teach the **Making Inferences** lesson on page 102 of this Guide.

- As students read, have them mark parts of the text in which John describes the Dead Places and the Place of the Gods. Then have them use this information along with what they already know to make inferences about the civilization he is exploring.

- Duplicate and distribute the **Inference/Judgment Chart** on page 104 of this Guide. Have students list on it inferences they make.

Internal Conflict Students need to be aware of the internal conflict the main character experiences between respect for society's laws and curiosity about the forbidden Place of the Gods.

- After students have read to the first *Pause & Reflect*, have them identify and read aloud details that illustrate John's internal conflict. Encourage students to predict how this conflict will influence his actions throughout the story.

VOCABULARY FOCUS: Using Familiar Words or Roots

Teacher Modeling Remind students they can often use familiar words or roots to figure out the meanings of new words. Then use the following modeling suggestion for the word *purified* (page 17, line 8):

You could say *I'm not sure what* purified *means, but part of it looks like the word* pure. *I know that* pure *is an adjective that can mean "containing nothing that does not belong." I think* purify *is a verb that probably means "to make clean" or "to free from unwanted elements."*

Student Modeling Now have students follow your lead. Ask a volunteer to model using familiar words or roots to determine the meaning of *ignorant* (page 18, line 54):

A student might say Ignorant *is probably related to* ignore. *I know that* ignore *is a verb that means "to disregard or refuse to notice something." Maybe* ignorant *is an adjective that means "unaware or lacking knowledge of something."*

MINI-LESSON See page 89 of this Guide for additional work on **Using Familiar Words or Roots.**

DURING READING

SUGGESTED READING OPTIONS

- An oral reading of "By the Waters of Babylon" is available in *The Language of Literature* Audio Library. 🎧
- Independent Reading (See page 10 of this Guide.)
- Additional options are described on page 10 of this Guide.

RECIPROCAL TEACHING SUGGESTION: Clarifying

Teacher Modeling *Pause & Reflect, page 22* Model the Clarifying strategy to help students who are unsure why John is so certain he should go east on his journey (page 16, lines 100–119):

You could say *I'm not sure how John decides he is supposed to go east. After all, such a journey is clearly forbidden by his people. However, when I reread what happens before he makes his decision, I remember that John finds signs in nature—the eagle and deer going east and his successful hunting of the panther. These signs seem to guide him.*

Student Modeling *Pause & Reflect, page 26* Have several students model how to clarify their understanding of what John discovers inside the "dead house." Remind them that rereading can help them make sense of parts that are unclear.

> Encourage students to use the other five reading strategies when appropriate as they proceed through the rest of the selection. (See page 12 of this Guide.)

AFTER READING

RECOMMENDED FOLLOW-UP

- Thinking Through the Literature, page 53, *The Language of Literature*
- Choices & Challenges, pages 54–55, *The Language of Literature*
- SkillBuilders, pages 31–32, *The InterActive Reader*

INFORMAL ASSESSMENT OPTIONS

Retell Have students work in small groups to retell the story. Assign each member of each group a different section of the story to summarize. Remind students that an oral summary is a brief statement of the most important events told in their own words.

Spot Check Read the notations students wrote in the margins, giving special attention to their responses to the *Pause & Reflect* questions and to the inferences they made.

FORMAL ASSESSMENT OPTIONS IN *The Language of Literature*

Selection Quiz, page 20, Unit One Resource Book

Selection Test, pages 11–12, Formal Assessment Book

Students Acquiring English/ESL

1. Students might benefit from reading along with the recording of "By the Waters of Babylon" provided in *The Language of Literature* Audio Library. 🎧

2. Make sure students understand these phrases:

my knowledge and my lack of knowledge burned in me, page 18

like the buzzing of bees in my head, page 19

a fire in my mind, page 21

Additional Challenge

1. Predict the Future Have students reread line 473 through to the end of the story. Ask: *How might what John has learned change him and his society forever?*

✏️ MARK IT UP

2. Identify Figurative Language John uses the simile "My heart was cold as a frog" to express how he feels. Locate and circle at least five other examples of figurative language used by John to express emotion. Explain the meaning of each.

BEFORE READING

Connect to Your Life Ask students to identify an era either in the past or in the future that they wish to visit. Ask them to write their choice and reason for choosing it on page 34. Have students share their ideas with the class.

Key to the Story Ask students to silently read the folk adage presented in the **Key to the Story** and then share their interpretations.

Build Background Have students read the Build Background information on page 71 of *The Language of Literature* in order to learn more about time travel as a subject of many science fiction films and stories.

COMPREHENSION FOCUS

KEY POINTS	STRATEGIES FOR SUCCESS
Target Skill: Sequence "A Sound of Thunder is set in the future—in the year 2055. To understand this story, students must follow the shift in time from this setting to the distant past and back to the year 2055.	• **MINI-LESSON** You may wish to teach the **Sequence** lesson on page 107 of this Guide. • After *Pause & Reflect* on page 38, call attention to the dates in line 76. Point out the descending order of numbers, which indicates that the time machine is traveling backwards in time. After the *Pause & Reflect* on page 47, reread lines 430–432 and 444–445. Make sure students understand that the men have now returned to their own time. • As they read, students can use the **Sequence/Flow Chart** on page 108 of this Guide to record story events.
The Story's Ending It is crucial that students understand why the world that the characters return to is so changed from the one they left at the beginning of the safari.	Remind students of Travis's obsession with leaving the past untouched. Then reread aloud from the Focus box on page 47 to the end of the selection. Ask students to name the changes that have taken place in the world. List them on the board. Help students conclude that Eckels's leaving the Path has had a tremendous effect on all of civilization.

ADDITIONAL WORDS TO KNOW

proportion
     page 40, line 175

disproportion
     page 40, line 179

correlate
     page 40, line 204

paradox
     page 41, line 213

remit
     page 43, line 292

VOCABULARY FOCUS: Using Letter-Sound Correspondences

Teacher Modeling Remind students that they can use letter-sound correspondences to help them figure out the meanings of unfamiliar words. Then model using letter-sounds to decode the word *subtle* (page 40, line 177):

You could say This word is unfamiliar to me. I tried pronouncing the first syllable as it is pronounced in the word submarine. I pronounced the second syllable like the second syllable in bottle. These two syllables together, sub′ əl, did not sound like a word I know. Then I remembered that in some words, the letter b is silent. I pronounced the word without the "b" sound: sŭt′ l. This sounded like a word I know. Subtle means "hard to notice."

Student Modeling Now have students follow your lead. Ask a volunteer to model using letter-sound correspondences to decode *throttled* (page 39, line 163):

A student might say The letters thr are pronounced as in the word three. The remainder of the word is pronounced as in the word bottled. I've heard of the word throttle before. It has something to do with choking. So throttled *must mean "choked."*

MINI-LESSON See page 90 of this Guide for additional work on **Using Letter-Sound Correspondences.**

DURING READING

SUGGESTED READING OPTIONS

- An oral reading of "A Sound of Thunder" is available in *The Language of Literature* Audio Library. 🎧
- Independent Reading (See page 10 of this Guide.)
- Additional options are also described on page 10 of this Guide.

RECIPROCAL TEACHING SUGGESTIONS: Predicting

Teacher Modeling *Pause & Reflect, page 38* Model making a prediction about whether Eckels will disobey any of the rules Travis has just listed.

You could say *Eckels seems both aggressive and insecure. When speaking to the official at the beginning of the story, he gets angry when the official suggests that he might be afraid. Now Eckels meets Travis, the Safari leader, who seems like a strong, no-nonsense person. He is definitely a match for Eckels. I predict that there will be a conflict between these two men.*

Student Modeling *Pause & Reflect, page 38* Have several students model making predictions about whether Eckels will go off the Path or shoot an animal that the guides do not approve. Remind them to use story clues and their prior knowledge about tone and foreshadowing to help them.

Encourage students to use the other five reading strategies when appropriate as they proceed through the rest of the selection. (See page 12 of this Guide.)

AFTER READING

RECOMMENDED FOLLOW-UP

- **Thinking Through the Literature,** page 82, *The Language of Literature*
- **Choices & Challenges,** page 83, *The Language of Literature*
- **SkillBuilders,** pages 50–62, *The InterActive Reader*

INFORMAL ASSESSMENT OPTIONS

Retell Have students imagine that Travis is explaining to his boss what occurred on the safari with Eckels and the others. Offer the following prompts:

- *When you first met Eckels, was there anything about him that made you think he would disobey the rules of Time Safari, Inc.?*
- *How did you feel when you first saw the Tyrannosaurus rex?*
- *Why did you send Eckels back to collect the bullets?*

Spot Check Read students' answers to the *Pause & Reflect* questions and the notations they wrote in the margins. Pay particular attention to the "X's" they marked to show examples of foreshadowing.

FORMAL ASSESSMENT OPTIONS IN *The Language of Literature*

Selection Quiz, page 26, Unit One Resource Book
Selection Test, pages 13–14, Formal Assessment Book

Students Acquiring English/ESL

1. Students might benefit from reading along with the recording of "A Sound of Thunder" provided in *The Language of Literature* Audio Library. 🎧

2. Make sure students understand these terms:

stiff penalty, page 36

bag the biggest game, page 31

stretching luck, page 37

it all boils down to this, page 39

weighed the evidence, page 43

met my match, page 43

Additional Challenge

1. Write a Description
Have students reread the description of the Tyrannosaurus rex (page 42, lines 262–280), noting the details that make the creature come alive. Then ask them to write a description of another prehistoric animal, mimicking Bradbury's style.

✏️ MARK IT UP

2. Analyze Writer's Style
Ask: *How does Bradbury create suspense in this story? Provide examples from the story to support your response.*

BEFORE READING

Connect to Your Life Ask students to list technologies developed during their lifetime. Ask: *How have these new technologies affected you? In the future, how might these technologies change?* Have students write their responses in the chart on page 54.

Key to the Essay Discuss the benefits and drawbacks of technological innovation. Ask: *Are new technologies always beneficial?* Have students silently read the **Key to the Essay.**

Build Background Have students read the Build Background section on page 107 of *The Language of Literature* to learn about Isaac Asimov.

COMPREHENSION FOCUS

KEY POINTS	STRATEGIES FOR SUCCESS

Target Skill: Fact and Opinion It is crucial that students are able to distinguish fact from opinion when reading any expository essay. This essay may prove particularly challenging because the author sometimes states opinions as if they were facts.

- **MINI-LESSON** You may want to teach the **Fact and Opinion** lesson on page 98 of this Guide.
- After the *Pause & Reflect* on page 57, guide students in identifying two facts and two opinions. Point out that in the third paragraph on page 56, the author states an opinion as if it were a fact.
- During or after reading, have students record the facts and opinions they find in the **Two-Column Chart** on page 99 of this Guide.

Synthesize Because it has been many years since students learned how to tell time, it may be difficult for them to understand the point Asimov makes on page 57–58 about the "unnecessary stumbling block" that the lack of dial clocks would cause in education.

After the *Pause & Reflect* on page 58, draw the outline of a dial clock on the board and demonstrate Asimov's observation that the position of the clock's hands at half-past and quarter-past the hour allows people to "see time as space and not as numbers." Discuss how this ability might help someone grasp the abstract concept of time.

NEW WORDS TO KNOW

retrograde
page 56, line 39

respectively
page 56, line 39

colleague
page 56, line 44

applications
page 57, line 71

irregularity
page 58, line 81

VOCABULARY FOCUS: Using Context Clues

Teacher Modeling Remind students that they can often use the words and sentences that surround a word to help figure out the meanings of an unfamiliar word. Demonstrate using this process to understand the word *conversion* (page 56, line 13):

You could say *I'm not sure what the author means by the phrase "the conversion of dial to digital" in line 13, but in the first paragraph of the essay Asimov states that the clock dial "is on the way out. More common today are digital clocks . . .". So the word* conversion *must mean "change."*

Student Modeling Now have students follow your lead. Ask a volunteer to model using context clues to determine the meaning of *consideration* (page 56, line 26):

A student might say *The word* consideration *sometimes means "kindness" or "attention." But here that meaning would not make sense. In the phrase "a consideration of your hands," the author must mean "a careful look at your hands," because this is what he goes on to describe in the next few sentences.*

MINI-LESSON See page 87 of this Guide for additional work on **Using Context Clues.**

DURING READING

SUGGESTED READING OPTIONS

- An oral reading of "Dial Versus Digital" is available in *The Language of Literature* Audio Library. 🎧
- Partner/Cooperative Reading (See page 10 of this Guide.)
- Additional options are also described on page 10 of this Guide.

RECIPROCAL TEACHING SUGGESTION: Clarifying

Teacher Modeling *Pause & Reflect, page 57* Model clarifying the meaning of a phrase:

You could say *I'm not sure what Asimov means by "location by o'clock" (line 50). I can clarify this by thinking about where "an object at 11 o'clock" might be located. If I imagine a giant clock face in front of me, I can visualize where the hour hand would be on the dial at 11:00—just to the left of the top. Now I understand what "location by o'clock" means.*

Student Modeling *Pause & Reflect, page 58* Ask a volunteer to demonstrate how to clarify Asimov's phrase "an odd conservatism among people" in line 88.

> Encourage students to use the other five reading strategies when appropriate as they proceed through the rest of the selection. (See page 12 of this Guide.)

AFTER READING

RECOMMENDED FOLLOW-UP

- Thinking Through the Literature, page 110, *The Language of Literature*
- Choices & Challenges, page 111, *The Language of Literature*
- SkillBuilders, pages 59–60, *The InterActive Reader*

INFORMAL ASSESSMENT OPTIONS

Retell Have students form groups of four. Ask one group member to paraphrase in general terms the problem Asimov is discussing in his essay. Then have each remaining member restate one of the three specific problems the author cites.

Spot Check Read the notations students wrote in the margins. Pay particular attention to the details they circled that reveal Asimov's feelings about the conversion from dial to digital clocks. Ask students who used the ? notation what questions they had, and whether their questions were answered.

FORMAL ASSESSMENT OPTIONS IN *The Language of Literature*

Selection Quiz, page 38, Unit One Resource Book

Selection Test, pages 19–20, Formal Assessment Book

Students Acquiring English/ESL

1. Students might benefit from reading along with the recording of "Dial Versus Digital" provided in *The Language of Literature* Audio Library. 🎧

2. Make sure students understand these terms:

on the way out, page 55

mark off, page 55

and so on, page 57

even so, page 58

Additional Challenge

1. Support an Opinion Ask students whether they think, based on the author's ideas, a young child should learn to tell time using a dial or a digital watch. Make sure they support their opinions.

✏️ MARK IT UP

2. Evaluate an Argument Have students star Asimov's three main concerns about the switch from dial to digital. Then ask students to choose the concern they find most intriguing and write a paragraph explaining why they agree or disagree with Asimov's viewpoint.

BEFORE READING

Connect to Your Life
Share with students a favorite place and why it is special to you. Then ask students to write about their favorite place on page 62. Have volunteers share what they have written.

Key to the Essay
Explain that although E. B. White's purpose is to describe a favorite place, he also aims to share insights about the cyclical nature of life. Read aloud the **Key to the Essay**.

Build Background
Have students read the Build Background information on page 112 of *The Language of Literature* to learn about E. B. White's writing style and career.

COMPREHENSION FOCUS

KEY POINTS	STRATEGIES FOR SUCCESS
Target Skill: Making Comparisons Because the author compares his experiences in the same setting during two different time periods, the ability to identify similarities and differences is crucial to understanding this selection.	• **MINI-LESSON** You may wish to teach the **Compare and Contrast** lesson on page 96 of this Guide. • After the *Pause & Reflect* on page 66, guide students in comparing the ways in which the lake is the same as and different from the way the author remembers it. • During or after reading, have students complete the **Active Reading SkillBuilder** on page 71.
Sequence In order to understand the essay, students need to distinguish between events that happen to the author in the present and those that happened when he was a child.	Read the first paragraph of the essay aloud and have students identify the time-order phrases "about 1904," "summer after summer," and "a few weeks ago." Remind them to look for time-order words and phrases that can help them distinguish present and past as they continue reading.

ADDITIONAL WORDS TO KNOW

marred
  page 64, line 24

unsubstantial
  page 66, line 110

jollity
  page 67, line 155

accumulated
  page 69, line 210

perpetuating
  page 70, line 258

VOCABULARY FOCUS: Using Familiar Words or Roots

Teacher Modeling Remind students that they can sometimes use familiar words or roots to help figure out the meanings of unfamiliar words. Then use the following modeling suggestion for the word *placidity* (page 64, line 16):

You could say I've never seen the word placidity, *but I have seen the word* placid. *It means "calm" or "quiet." "*Placidity *must be the noun form of* placid. *The author says that he wished for "the placidity of a lake in the woods." This must mean that he longed for the peace and quiet of a lake's surface compared to the wildness of the sea.*

Student Modeling Now have students follow your lead. A volunteer can model how to use familiar words or roots to determine the meaning of *infinitely* (page 64, line 51):

A student might say An infinite number is a number that goes on forever or one that is greater than any number you can name. So "infinitely remote" must mean "as remote as can be," or "extremely hidden away."

MINI-LESSON See page 89 of this Guide for additional work on **Using Familiar Words or Roots.**

DURING READING

SUGGESTED READING OPTIONS

- An oral reading of "Once More to the Lake" is available in *The Language of Literature* Audio Library. 🎧
- Oral Reading (See page 10 of this Guide.)
- Additional options are also described on page 10 of this Guide.

RECIPROCAL TEACHING SUGGESTION: Visualizing

Teacher Modeling *Pause & Reflect, page 64* Model for students how you would form a mental picture of the scene in which the author wakes up in his camp bedroom as a child:

You could say *When the author says that his bedroom smelled "of the lumber it was made of," I can instantly imagine what that lumber smell is like. When he mentions "the wet woods" I can recall the smell of wet, dew-covered leaves and forest soil. Remembering these smells helps me to imagine exactly what the scene is like.*

Student Modeling *Pause & Reflect, page 66* Ask a volunteer to model how he or she would form a mental image of the school of minnows described in lines 105–108. The volunteer might even draw on the board several minnows and their shadows to explain the meaning of the phrase "doubling the attendance."

Encourage students to use the other five reading strategies when appropriate as they proceed through the rest of the selection. (See page 12 of this Guide.)

AFTER READING

RECOMMENDED FOLLOW-UP

- **Thinking Through the Literature**, page 121, *The Language of Literature*
- **Choices & Challenges**, pages 122–123, *The Language of Literature*
- **SkillBuilders**, pages 71–73, *The InterActive Reader*

INFORMAL ASSESSMENT OPTIONS

Retell Write the following phrases on slips of paper. Have students take turns selecting a slip of paper and explaining how the phrase is important in the essay.

- August for one month
- canoeing in the morning
- outboard motors
- inboard motors
- something infinitely precious and worth saving
- the illusion that my son was I and that I was my father

Spot Check Read the notations students wrote in the margins. Pay particular attention to the details they circled that show how E. B. White feels about the lake.

FORMAL ASSESSMENT OPTIONS IN *The Language of Literature*

Selection Quiz, page 44, Unit One Resource Book

Selection Test, pages 21–22, Formal Assessment Book

Students Acquiring English/ESL

1. Students might benefit from reading along with the recording of "Once More to the Lake" provided in *The Language of Literature* Audio Library. 🎧

2. Make sure students understand these terms:

we settled into, page 65

kept cropping up, page 65

yesterday's catch, page 65

leave to its own devices, page 66

souvenir counters, page 67

ten-mile haul, page 67

catching the first view, page 67

Additional Challenge

1. Analyze Point of View Remind students that the author refers to the lake of his childhood as a "holy spot." Ask: *Do you think the author might still use these words to describe the lake after his most recent visit? Why or why not?* Have students write their opinions.

◣MARK IT UP

2. Understand Author's Purpose Ask students to star the one place in the essay where the author refers to the future (the last sentence). Discuss why the author might have ended his essay this way.

BEFORE READING

Connect to Your Life Ask a volunteer to locate Canada and Mexico on a map. On page 75, have students list what they know and would like to know about Canada and Mexico.

Key to the Essays Have a student read aloud the **Key to the Essays**. Ask: *What aspects of Canadian and Mexican culture have influenced our country?* Have students share examples.

Build Background To help students learn more about the United States' relationship with the countries that border it— Canada to the north and Mexico to the south — have students read the Build Background information on page 170 of *The Language of Literature*.

COMPREHENSION FOCUS

KEY POINTS	STRATEGIES FOR SUCCESS
Target Skill: Compare and Contrast To understand the ideas in each essay, students must be able to identify the comparisons and contrasts the authors develop.	• **MINI-LESSON** Before students read, you might teach the **Compare and Contrast** lesson on page 96 of this Guide. • During or after reading, have students fill in the **Active Reading SkillBuilder** on page 86.
Analogies In "Through the One-Way Mirror," the author uses analogies to explain the relationship between Canada and the United States. These analogies may pose problems for students.	Read aloud the first three paragraphs of the essay, lines 1–37. Then point out the author's two analogies. The first one compares the U.S.-Canadian border to a one-way mirror through which Canadians observe Americans. The second compares Canadians and Americans to contrasting neighbors separated by a fence.
Symbolic Description In "The Border: A Glare of Truth," students may need help interpreting the details that describe the significance of the desert.	Read aloud lines 112–146. Then point out that for the author, the desert highlights the contrast between rich and poor. Explain that the phrase "glare of truth," mentioned in the title and in the last sentence of the essay, reflects this contrast.

ADDITIONAL WORDS TO KNOW

perpetual
page 77, line 31

illusion
page 79, line 91

perception
page 82, line 26

resilience
page 84, line 119

VOCABULARY FOCUS: Using Familiar Words or Roots

Teacher Modeling Remind students that they can often figure out the meaning of an unfamiliar word by using a word or word part they know. Model this strategy for the word *linguistically* (page 82, line 17):

You could say *I've never seen this word before, but I have seen the word* linguist. *I know that a linguist is someone who studies language. The suffix* -ical *means "having to do with," and the suffix* -ly *is used to form adverbs. I think that* linguistically *is an adverb. It means "having to do with language."*

Student Modeling Have a student model the same strategy using the word *conceptually* (page 82, line 17):

A student might say *I see the word* concept *inside this longer word. A* concept *is an idea. I see the suffix* -al, *which means "relating to," and the suffix* -ly *that forms adverbs.* Conceptually *is an adverb that must mean "relating to ideas."*

MINI-LESSON See page 89 of this Guide for additional work on on **Using Familiar Words or Roots.**

DURING READING

SUGGESTED READING OPTIONS

- Oral readings of "Through the One-Way Mirror" and "The Border: A Glare of Truth" are available in *The Language of Literature* Audio Library. 🎧
- Shared Reading (See page 10 of this Guide.)
- Additional options are also described on page 10 of this Guide.

RECIPROCAL TEACHING SUGGESTION: Clarifying

Teacher Modeling *Pause & Reflect, page 78* Model the clarifying strategy to help students understand the author's view of Americans.

You could say *In lines 21–24, the author says that Americans don't regard Canadians as foreigners, except when they do something weird like speak French. Why would the author say that it's weird for Canadians to speak French? French is a language spoken by many Canadians. Then I realize that the author is characterizing Americans' limited perceptions of Canadians, not stating her own views.*

Student Modeling *Pause & Reflect, page 85* Have volunteers model the strategy by clarifying what Pat Mora means in lines 140–143: "In a broader sense . . . most of my fellow humans."

> **Encourage students to use the other five reading strategies when appropriate as they proceed through the rest of the selection. (See page 12 of this Guide.)**

AFTER READING

RECOMMENDED FOLLOW-UP

- Thinking Through the Literature, pages 173, 178, *The Language of Literature*
- Choices & Challenges, pages 179–180, *The Language of Literature*
- SkillBuilders, pages 86–88, *The InterActive Reader*

INFORMAL ASSESSMENT OPTIONS

Retell Have students work in pairs to create a cartoon strip featuring Porky Pig (a Canadian) and Mr. Magoo (an American) as characters. The characters should exchange lines revealing Americans' and Canadians' views of each other as expressed in Atwood's essay.

Spot Check Read the notations students wrote in the margins, paying particular attention to their responses to the *Pause & Reflect* questions and the Challenge activity.

FORMAL ASSESSMENT OPTIONS IN *The Language of Literature*

Selection Quiz, page 80, Unit One Resource Book

Selection Test, pages 31–32, Formal Assessment Book

Students Acquiring English/ESL

1. Students might benefit from reading along with the recording of these selections in *The Language of Literature* Audio Library. 🎧

2. Make sure students understand these terms:

"Through the One-Way Mirror":

one-way mirror; doing body language, page 76

water-skiing emporium, page 77

identity crisis; draft dodgers; snooty Brits page 78

Yank telly; Dreaded Menace, page 79

Mr. Magoo eyes, page 80

"The Border":

steady stream of letters; web of caring, page 82

Heartland; margin, page 83

Additional Challenge

1. Compare Tone Have students compare and contrast the tone of the two essays, and then explain why they think each essay has the tone it does.

◢MARK IT UP◣

2. Identify Imagery Ask students to mark examples of vivid imagery in each essay. Then ask: *How do these images help each author to achieve her purpose?*

BEFORE READING

Connect to Your Life Have students recall some childhood memories and complete the concept web on page 90. Pair students and have them share their memories. Then ask volunteers to share their memories with the class.

Key to the Poems Have a student read aloud the **Key to the Poems.** Ask students to recall specific details about one childhood memory. Ask: *What details seemed unimportant at the time? How do you view those details now?*

Build Background To help students learn about D. H. Lawrence and Robert Hayden, have students read the Build Background information on page 228 of *The Language of Literature.*

COMPREHENSION FOCUS

KEY POINTS	STRATEGIES FOR SUCCESS
Target Skill: Making Inferences To understand these poems, students must be able to make logical guesses about the speakers and their situations.	• **MINI-LESSON** Before students read, teach or review the **Making Inferences** lesson on page 102 of this Guide. • Read aloud lines 1–5 of "Piano." Help students figure out where the speaker might be and what he experiences while listening to the woman singing. Then ask: *Who is the child that the speaker sees sitting under the piano?* • During or after reading, have students fill in the **Inference/Judgment Chart** on page 104 of this Guide.
British Spellings Some of the lines in "Piano" contain words with British spellings.	Ask students to rewrite the words *parlour, clamour,* and *glamour* in the margins and to cross out the letter *u* in each word.
Poetic Language Students may need assistance interpreting the last two lines of "Those Winter Sundays."	Point out the footnotes on page 93 that define the words *austere* and *offices.* Then have volunteers put the last two lines in their own words. *(I knew nothing about the lonely tasks my father did out of love for his family.)*

NEW WORDS TO KNOW

clamour
    page 92, line 9

remembrance
    page 92, line 12

indifferently
    page 93, line 10

VOCABULARY FOCUS: Using Letter-Sound Correspondences

Teacher Modeling Remind students that sometimes they can use the sounds letters stand for to decode an unfamiliar word. Model this strategy by writing the word *poised* (page 91, line 4) on the board:

You could say I came across this word, but wasn't sure how to pronounce it. At first I said pō´ īzd. Then I realized that the vowel pair oi can stand for the same vowel sound as in the words oil and boy. I tried blending the consonant sound "p" with the "oi" sound, the "z"sound, and the "d" sound for the ending -ed. I got poised. I've heard that word before, so it must be right. It means "suspended."

Student Modeling Have volunteers model the strategy for the word *hymns* (page 91, line 8):

A student might say I know that when y acts as a vowel, it usually has a long "i" or a long "e" sound. Neither long "i" nor long "e" sounds right in this word. The letter y can also stand for the short "i" sound in words like synonym. I'll try that sound. Yes—this is a word I know: hymns.

MINI-LESSON See page 90 of this Guide for additional work on **Using Letter-Sound Correspondences.**

DURING READING

SUGGESTED READING OPTIONS

- Oral readings of "Piano" and "Those Winter Sundays" are available in *The Language of Literature* Audio Library. 🎧
- Shared Reading (See page 10 of this Guide.)
- Additional options are described on page 10 of this Guide.

RECIPROCAL TEACHING SUGGESTION: Connecting

Teacher Modeling *Pause & Reflect, page 92* Model using the connecting strategy to help students empathize with the speaker in "Piano":

You could say *I have experienced times when a piece of music has stirred a flood of memories. Sometimes the memories bring powerful emotions with them. I think that is what the speaker experiences when he hears the singing. The music brings a rush of sadness because he remembers his mother playing the piano and singing. He realizes that those happy moments are gone forever.*

Student Modeling *Pause & Reflect, page 93* Invite several volunteers to model how to use the connecting strategy to appreciate the speaker's feelings of remorse in "Those Winter Sundays.'

Encourage students to use the other five reading strategies when appropriate as they proceed through the rest of the selection. (See page 12 of this Guide.)

AFTER READING

RECOMMENDED FOLLOW-UP

- **Thinking Through the Literature,** pages 229, 231, *The Language of Literature*
- **Choices & Challenges,** page 232, *The Language of Literature*
- **SkillBuilders,** pages 94–95, *The InterActive Reader*

INFORMAL ASSESSMENT OPTIONS

Retell Have pairs of students role-play the speakers as they share their memories of Sundays long ago and the feelings that linger.

Spot Check Look at the notes students wrote in the margins. Invite them to explain their answers and share any questions they may still have about these poems.

FORMAL ASSESSMENT OPTIONS IN *The Language of Literature*

Selection Test, page 39, Formal Assessment Book

Students Acquiring English/ESL

1. Students might benefit from reading along with the recording of these poems provided in *The Language of Literature* Audio Library. 🎧

2. Make sure students understand these phrases:

"Piano":

vista of years, line 2

in spite of myself, line 5

my manhood is cast/Down in the flood of remembrance, lines 11–12

"Those Winter Sundays":

blueblack cold, line 2

banked fires, line 5

chronic angers, line 9

driven out the cold, line 11

Additional Challenge

1. Connect to Life Ask students to write a paragraph in response to this prompt: *What insights might young people gain about their parents through reading each of these poems?*

✎ MARK IT UP

2. Examine Figurative Language Ask students to mark examples of figurative language, such as metaphors and similes, in the poems. Then have students discuss how each example relates to the theme of the poem.

Connect to Your Life Have students free write on the difference between a house and a home. Discuss their ideas. On page 97, have them write about the special qualities of the place they live.

Key to the Story Have students read the **Key to the Story** silently. Locate the Sierra Nevada Mountains on a map, and then ask students to hypothesize about what the daily life of a prospector was like.

Build Background To help students learn about the California Gold Rush and its aftermath, have them read the Build Background information on page 303 of *The Language of Literature.*

COMPREHENSION FOCUS

KEY POINTS	STRATEGIES FOR SUCCESS
Target Skill: Narrative Elements To understand this story, students must recognize how the frontier setting affects the characters' emotions and actions.	• **MINI-LESSON** Before students read, you might teach the **Narrative Elements** lesson on page 105 of this Guide. • As students read, have them stop after the *Pause & Reflect* on page 99 to read aloud the details they marked about the setting. Ask them to note the contrast between "the rose-covered cottage" and the typical pioneer cabin. • Have students complete the **Active Reading SkillBuilder** on page 108 before or after reading.
Colloquial Dialogue The dialogue in this story contains colloquial language that may pose problems for some students.	With a volunteer, take turns reading the dialogue in lines 134–147. Make sure students understand for whom the owner of the cottage is waiting and why. Encourage them to read other passages of dialogue aloud in pairs.
Surprise Ending Students must keep track of what happens in the story in order to understand the ending.	Remind students to reread difficult passages if they find they are losing track of events.

ADDITIONAL WORDS TO KNOW

humiliation
    page 99, line 32

affectionate
    page 100, line 80

insistent
    page 102, line 151

expectancy
    page 105, line 222

VOCABULARY FOCUS: Using Structural Analysis

Teacher Modeling Remind students that when they come upon a longer word that looks unfamiliar, they can try breaking the word into parts. Model the strategy for the word *unclassifiable* (page 100, line 72):

You could say I see the base word classify, *which means "sort out" or "put in a group." The prefix* un- *means "not." The suffix* -able *means "able to." I can guess that something* unclassifiable *can't be sorted out or put in a group.*

Student Modeling Have a volunteer model the strategy for the word *unaccountable* (page 100, line 61):

A student might say I see the base word account, *which can mean "to explain." The prefix* -un *means "not," and the suffix* -able *means "able to." I think* unaccountable *is an adjective that means "not able to be explained."*

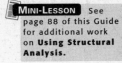
MINI-LESSON See page 88 of this Guide for additional work on **Using Structural Analysis.**

DURING READING

SUGGESTED READING OPTIONS

- An oral reading of "The Californian's Tale" is available in *The Language of Literature* Audio Library. 🎧
- Partner/Cooperative Reading (See page 10 of this Guide.)
- Additional options are also described on page 10 of this Guide.

RECIPROCAL TEACHING SUGGESTION: Connecting

Teacher Modeling *Pause & Reflect, page 99* Model using the connecting strategy to help students identify with the narrator's feelings:

You could say *If I'd been out prospecting alone in the wilderness for as long as the narrator has, I'd be lonely and in need of company, too. I can imagine how delighted he is to find the cozy cottage and to be greeted in such a friendly way by its owner.*

Student Modeling *Pause & Reflect, page 103* Have a student volunteer model the connecting strategy to understand the narrator's conflicting desires. Ask: Does the narrator seem to be attracted to Henry's wife? Why might this make him feel uncomfortable? How would you feel if you were in the narrator's position?

> Encourage students to use the other five reading strategies when appropriate as they proceed through the rest of the selection. (See page 12 of this Guide.)

AFTER READING

RECOMMENDED FOLLOW-UP

- Thinking Through the Literature, page 311, *The Language of Literature*
- Choices & Challenges, pages 312–313, *The Language of Literature*
- SkillBuilders, pages 108–110, *The InterActive Reader*

INFORMAL ASSESSMENT OPTIONS

Retell Have pairs of students role-play a conversation between Tom and Joe as they plan the "party" at Henry's house.

Spot Check Read the notations students wrote in the margins and decide whether or not they reveal a basic understanding of the story.

FORMAL ASSESSMENT OPTIONS IN *The Language of Literature*

Selection Quiz, page 41, Unit Two Resource Book

Selection Test, pages 51–52, Formal Assessment Book

Students Acquiring English/ESL

1. Students might benefit from reading along with the recording of "The Californian's Tale" provided in *The Language of Literature* Audio Library. 🎧

2. Make sure students understand these terms:

surface diggings, page 98

the why and the how, page 101

her people, page 102

broke the old fellow all up, page 104

lost his mind in consequence, page 106

Additional Challenge

1. Write a Sequel Ask students to write a paragraph in response to this prompt: *What happens to the narrator after he discovers the truth about Henry and his wife?*

✏️ MARK IT UP

2. Analyze Mood Have students mark passages that help to create the mood at the beginning, middle, and end of the story. Then discuss how the mood changes, and why.

BEFORE READING

Connect to Your Life

Explain that nature often seems to reflect personal emotions—a rainy day is commonly associated with sad emotions, for example. Ask students to list two more examples on page 112, and then share their ideas with the class.

Key to the Poem Explain that the speaker in the poem describes feelings of lost love. For the **Key to the Poem** on page 112, ask students to record their feelings about lost love in the concept web.

Build Background Have students read the Build Background information on page 351 of *The Language of Literature* to learn more about poetic devices such as metaphors and personification.

NEW WORDS TO KNOW

immense
    page 114, line 13

satisfied
    page 114, line 18

infinite
    page 114, line 26

COMPREHENSION FOCUS

KEY POINTS	STRATEGIES FOR SUCCESS
Target Skill: Making Inferences The poet does not directly state his emotions; students must infer his feelings based on what they know from their own experiences and what the poet says.	• **MINI-LESSON** Before students read this poem, you may wish to teach or review the **Making Inferences** lesson on page 102 of this Guide. • Read lines 1–12 aloud. Then ask: *How do people usually feel after breaking up with a person they love? Based on lines 6, 9, 11, and 12 how would you say the speaker feels?* • Have students use the **Inference/ Judgment Chart** on page 104 of this Guide to keep track of inferences they make as they read the poem, especially from line 27.
Figurative Language The ability to understand and interpret metaphors, similes, and personification is essential to understanding this poem.	Read aloud the first three lines. Help students identify the metaphor in line 2 ("night is shattered") and the personification in line 3 ("blue stars shiver"). Discuss the effect each phrase has on the reader.

VOCABULARY FOCUS: Using Context Clues

Teacher Modeling Remind students that poets often use familiar words in unusual ways. Demonstrate for students how to use context clues to interpret the meanings of *revolves* and *sings* on page 113, line 4:

You could say In line 4, the poet says "The night wind revolves in the sky and sings." Revolves *means "turns in a circle," but wind doesn't usually spin in a circle, and it doesn't sing. I think the poet is using the words* revolves *and* sings *figuratively—he means that the night wind swirls and that he can hear its movement in the trees.*

Student Modeling Now have a student model using context clues to interpret the meaning of *infinite* on page 114, line 26:

A student might say Infinite *means "endless." Eyes can't be endless. What does the poet mean? Earlier in the poem, he says that the woman had "great still eyes." I imagine that her eyes must be large and dark. Infinite eyes must be big, dark eyes that you could gaze into for a long time.*

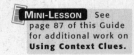 **MINI-LESSON** See page 87 of this Guide for additional work on **Using Context Clues.**

DURING READING

SUGGESTED READING OPTIONS

- An oral reading of "Tonight I Can Write . . ." is available in *The Language of Literature* Audio Library. 🎧
- Shared Reading (See page 10 of this Guide.)
- Additional options are described on page 10 of this Guide.

RECIPROCAL TEACHING SUGGESTION: Visualizing

Teacher Modeling *Pause & Reflect, page 114, line 31*   Model visualizing the setting by interpreting appropriate phrases:

You could say *The poet says that the stars are "blue" and "shivering in the distance," that the wind "revolves in the sky and sings," and that he is remembering times when he was with the woman he loved. I can picture a young man sitting by himself on a beautiful, clear starry night. A cold wind blows and swirls. The man is writing sad poetry.*

Student Modeling *Pause & Reflect, page 114, line 31*   Ask volunteers to model visualizing the young woman's appearance, based on the poet's descriptions of her.

Encourage students to use the other five reading strategies when appropriate as they proceed through the rest of the selection. (See page 12 of this Guide.)

AFTER READING

RECOMMENDED FOLLOW-UP

- Thinking Through the Literature, page 354, *The Language of Literature*
- Choices & Challenges, page 355, *The Language of Literature*
- SkillBuilders, pages 115–116, *The InterActive Reader*

INFORMAL ASSESSMENT OPTIONS

Retell Have students imagine that they are the poet and that 50 years have passed since the writing of the poem. Invite volunteers to describe the night when the poem was written and explain how the poet felt as he wrote it.

Spot Check Read the notations students wrote in the margins, paying particular attention to their responses to the *Pause & Reflect* questions. For students who used the ? notation, ask if and how they cleared up any confusion.

FORMAL ASSESSMENT OPTIONS IN *The Language of Literature*

Selection Test, pages 59–60, Formal Assessment Book

Students Acquiring English/ESL

1. Students might benefit from reading along with the recording of this poem in *The Language of Literature* Audio Library. 🎧

2. Pair students with English-proficient partners who can help them understand the metaphors in the poem. In addition, make sure students understand the following:

lines (of poetry), line 1

the verse falls to the soul, line 14

forgetting is so long, line 28

Additional Challenge

1. Analyze the Theme Ask students what they think the poet means by this line: "Love is so short, forgetting is so long."

2. Write a Poem
Challenge students to write a poem in response to the poet, perhaps offering him advice or chiding him for his lovelorn attitude. Encourage them to mimic the tone or style of "Tonight I Can Write. . ."

✏️ MARK IT UP

3. Interpret Figurative Language Have students circle at least three examples of figurative language in the poem, categorize each example, and write in their own words an interpretation of its meaning.

Connect to Your Life Have students complete the pie chart on page 118. Survey the students about the way the largest percentage of their money would be spent.

Key to the Story Have students complete the **Key to the Story** by listing some important things in life that cannot be bought or sold. Have students prioritize their lists and share their top-list items.

Build Background To help students understand the social and cultural context for the story, have them read the Build Background information on page 386 of *The Language of Literature*.

COMPREHENSION FOCUS

KEY POINTS	STRATEGIES FOR SUCCESS
Target Skill: Cause and Effect The series of conversations that make up this story are linked in a causal chain. Being able to infer the cause-effect relationships that exist between the conversations is crucial to story comprehension.	• **MINI-LESSON** Before students read, teach or review the **Cause and Effect** lesson on page 92 of this Guide. • As students read, have them stop after *Pause & Reflect* on page 124 and tell why Bobby Gillian goes to see Miss Lotta Lauriere. • During or after reading, have students complete the **Active Reading SkillBuilder** on page 128.
Word Choice and Sarcasm In order to understand the characters' attitudes towards one another, students must pay close attention to the author's choice of words as well as his use of sarcasm in various parts of the selection.	Read aloud lines 80–91. Ask: *How does Old Bryson feel about Gillian?* Help them see that Bryson mocks Gillian with his suggestion to make a speech about the difficulties of inheriting money; also point out that he is contemptuous in his suggestion about the sheep ranch.
Plot Twist Because Gillian's actions at the end of the story seem out of character with the way he is portrayed beforehand, students may be confused by the surprise ending.	Encourage students to reread the last two sections of the story and circle clues showing that Gillian is not the selfish, loose-living person others think he is.

ADDITIONAL
WORDS
TO KNOW

disposed
    page 120, line 18
inquiringly
    page 123, line 144
phraseology
    page 126, line 212
unfavorably
    page 126, line 220
mournfully
    page 127, line 243

VOCABULARY FOCUS: Using Structural Analysis

Teacher Modeling Remind students that they can sometimes figure out unfamiliar words by breaking them into parts. Demonstrate this strategy by using the following modeling suggestion for the word *professionally* (page 119, line 14):

You could say In this long word, I see the word profession, *as well as the suffixes* -al *and* -ly. *I know that a profession is a job that requires special study and training, that* -al *means "relating to," and that* -ly *means "in a way that is." By combining the meanings, I know that when Lawyer Tolman speaks in "professionally dry tones," he is speaking seriously and matter-of-factly—in a way that is typical of a lawyer.*

Student Modeling Now ask a volunteer to model how to use structural analysis to determine the meaning of *mournfully* (page 127, line 243):

A student might say The word mournfully *contains the base word* mourn *and the suffixes* -ful *and* -ly. *I know that to* mourn *means "to express sorrow," that* -ful *means "full of," and that* -ly *means "in a specific manner." By putting together the meanings of these parts, I can figure out that the men shake their heads mournfully—in a way that expresses extreme sorrow.*

MINI-LESSON See page 88 of this Guide for additional work on **Using Structural Analysis.**

DURING READING

SUGGESTED READING OPTIONS

- An oral reading of "One Thousand Dollars" is available in *The Language of Literature* Audio Library.
- Partner/Cooperative Reading (See page 10 of this Guide.)
- Additional options are described on page 10 of this Guide.

RECIPROCAL TEACHING SUGGESTION: Predicting

Teacher Modeling *Pause & Reflect, page 122* Model making a prediction about how Gillian will spend his inheritance:

You could say *Although Gillian thanks Old Bryson and says the man has given him an idea for how to spend the money, I don't think Gillian is going to listen to most of Bryson's advice. The two don't seem to like each other very much. Because Gillian leaves suddenly after hearing about Miss Lotta Lauriere, maybe Gillian will buy Miss Lauriere a jewel or some other gift with the money. I'll read on to find out if this is what happens.*

Student Modeling *Pause & Reflect, page 124* After students have finished reading about Gillian's visit with Miss Hayden, have several of them model making predictions about what might happen when Gillian returns to the lawyer's office.

Encourage students to use the other five reading strategies when appropriate as they proceed through the rest of the selection. (See page 12 of this Guide.)

AFTER READING

RECOMMENDED FOLLOW-UP

- Thinking Through the Literature, page 394, *The Language of Literature*
- Choices & Challenges, pages 395–396, *The Language of Literature*
- SkillBuilders, pages 128–130, *The InterActive Reader*

INFORMAL ASSESSMENT OPTIONS

Retell Have students form small groups and assign the roles of all the important story characters except Gillian. Then read this prompt aloud: *You have all learned the truth about Gillian's action. Compare what you thought he did (or would do) with his inheritance with what he really did, and tell what you learned about him.*

Spot Check Read the notations students wrote in the margins, paying particular attention to their responses to the *Pause & Reflect* questions and to the predictions they made. For students who used the **?** notation, ask if and how they were able to clear up their confusion.

FORMAL ASSESSMENT OPTIONS IN *The Language of Literature*

Selection Quiz, page 9, Unit Three Resource Book

Selection Test, pages 63–64, Formal Assessment Book

Students Acquiring English/ESL

1. Students might benefit from reading along with the recording of "One Thousand Dollars" provided in *The Language of Literature* Audio Library.

2. Make sure students understand these terms:

his whole cargo of doubloons, page 120

fairy godmother, page 121

a ward of, page 121

off my hands, page 121

itemizing, page 122

putting up the cap, page 123

black sheep, page 125

his air of/in the air, page 125

Additional Challenge

1. Analyze Plot Ask: *At what point did you figure out that young Gillian would end up giving all his money to Miss Hayden? What details helped you know this?*

◣ MARK IT UP

2. Create a Character Sketch Ask students to underline words and phrases in the story that reveal young Gillian's character. Have them use these details to write a brief character sketch.

BEFORE READING

Connect to Your Life Have students choose a "dream career" and complete the chart on page 132. Discuss their choices, noting the benefits and drawbacks common to many careers.

Key to the Autobiography Explain that the story is about a fifteen-year-old African-American girl. Read aloud the **Key to the Autobiography**. Ask: *What aspects of the setting might influence events in the story?*

Build Background To help students understand the historical context of this excerpt, have them read the Build Background information on page 411 of *The Language of Literature*.

COMPREHENSION FOCUS

KEY POINTS	STRATEGIES FOR SUCCESS
Target Skill: Synthesizing In order to deepen students' understanding and appreciation of the author's accomplishment, readers will need to synthesize information.	• **MINI-LESSON** Before students read, you might wish to teach the **Synthesizing** lesson on page 109 of this Guide. • Have students use the **Synthesis Diagram** on page 110 of this Guide to record the following: what they know about job discrimination and racism in the 1940s; what they learn about it from the Preview on page 132; and what the author shares about it in the selection.
Shifts in Perspective In this selection, the perspective shifts back and forth from Marguerite as a teenager to the adult author's interpretation of events. Students need to be able to distinguish between the attitude of a young person and the insight that the adult author adds in her narration.	Read aloud the first two paragraphs of the selection. Point out that phrases such as "My room had all the cheeriness of a dungeon . . ." and "Mother wouldn't be difficult to convince . . ." are told from the perspective of the teenaged Marguerite, while the sentence "My intellectual pride . . ." sounds more like the insight of the adult author as she analyzes this event from the past. Encourage students to find other examples of the author's adult perspective as she recounts this time in her life.

ADDITIONAL WORDS TO KNOW

indignation
    page 134, line 42

resistance
    page 135, line 61

meditation
    page 136, line 111

exhaust
    page 137, line 149

references
    page 138, line 169

VOCABULARY FOCUS: Using Context Clues

Teacher Modeling Remind students that they can often use context clues to figure out the meanings of unfamiliar words. Demonstrate by using the following modeling suggestion for *restricting* (page 134, line 35):

You could say I'm not sure what restricting means. Angelou's mother has just told her that African Americans are not accepted for jobs on streetcars. Then Angelou talks about her determination to break the tradition. From these clues I can infer that restricting traditions are ones that are "holding back" or "limiting" someone's progress.

Student Modeling Now ask a volunteer to model using context clues to figure out the meaning of *energetically* (page 136, line 117):

A student might say The phrases "my mind shouted" and "made my veins stand out," along with the capital letters used in the next paragraph, lead me to think that energetically must mean "with great force or energy."

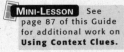 **MINI-LESSON** See page 87 of this Guide for additional work on **Using Context Clues.**

DURING READING

SUGGESTED READING OPTIONS

- An oral reading of "Getting a Job" is available in *The Language of Literature* Audio Library. 🎧
- Independent Reading (See page 10 of this Guide.)
- Additional options are described on page 10 of this Guide.

RECIPROCAL TEACHING SUGGESTION: Visualizing

Teacher Modeling *Pause & Reflect, page 136* Model for students how you would form a mental picture of the Market Street Railway Company office.

You could say *When I read the author's description of the reception room, in my mind I see a dimly-lit room with dusty, padded, slightly worn, dark-colored, moldy-smelling furniture. The floors are swept but are not shiny. The whole room looks old and rundown.*

Student Modeling *Pause & Reflect, page 139* After students have finished reading the selection, have a volunteer explain the scene he or she visualized while reading Angelou's description of riding the streetcars through the streets of San Francisco.

Encourage students to use the other five reading strategies when appropriate as they proceed through the rest of the selection. (See page 12 of this Guide.)

AFTER READING

RECOMMENDED FOLLOW-UP

- **Thinking Through the Literature,** page 417, *The Language of Literature*
- **Choices & Challenges,** page 418, *The Language of Literature*
- **SkillBuilders,** pages 140–142, *The InterActive Reader*

INFORMAL ASSESSMENT OPTIONS

Retell Have students retell the account from the point of view of Maya Angelou's mother.

Spot Check Read the notations students wrote in the margins, paying particular attention to students' thoughts about Angelou, her mother, and the secretary. For students who used the ? notation, ask if and how they were able to clear up any confusion.

FORMAL ASSESSMENT OPTIONS IN *The Language of Literature*

Selection Quiz, page 20, Unit Three Resource Book

Selection Test, pages 67–68, Formal Assessment Book

Students Acquiring English/ESL

1. Students might benefit from reading along with the recording of "Getting a Job" provided in *The Language of Literature* Audio Library. 🎧

2. Make sure students understand these phrases:

caught my fancy, page 134

poor-mouth-looking concern, page 135

hard eyes of white contempt, page 136

dished out as the occasion demanded, page 137

Additional Challenge

1. Evaluate an Idea Remind students that Angelou's mother thought, "in the struggle [of life] lies the joy." Discuss whether this was true for Angelou in her struggles to get a job. Then ask: *Do you agree with the mother's philosophy? Why or why not?* Encourage students to respond in writing.

△MARK IT UP

2. Identify Figurative Language Ask students to circle examples of figurative language in the story. Have volunteers share their favorite images, explaining what each one means.

BEFORE READING

Connect to Your Life Ask students to identify an older person they have learned from and then describe that person on page 144. Ask a few students to share their descriptions.

Key to the Memoir Ask a student to read aloud the **Key to the Memoir**. Ask students to discuss any family traditions they plan to continue in their own lives and why. Have students describe their views on page 144.

Build Background To help students learn about the setting described in this memoir, have them read the Build Background information on page 455 of *The Language of Literature*.

COMPREHENSION FOCUS

KEY POINTS	STRATEGIES FOR SUCCESS
Target Skill: Main Ideas and Details To understand this memoir, students must identify the author's main ideas and the sentences that provide details about those main ideas.	• **MINI-LESSON** Before students read, you might teach the **Main Ideas and Details** lesson on page 100 of this Guide. • Read aloud the second paragraph of the memoir, lines 8–23, on pages 145–146. Point out that the main idea is that the author "learned a wise path of life" from old people. Help students identify the details that describe what the old people shared with him. • During or after reading, have students use the **Main Idea Web** on page 101 of this Guide to help them identify other main ideas and their supporting details.
Memoir Anecdotes Students must understand the points Anaya makes through the use of anecdotes, or brief stories.	Read aloud lines 36–40 on page 146. Help students see that the point of the story is conveyed by the grandfather's words; they teach the importance of self-knowledge.

NEW WORDS TO KNOW

nurturing
   page 145, line 15

sensitivity
   page 145, line 15

participant
   page 146, line 48

transformation
   page 146, line 57

VOCABULARY FOCUS: Using Familiar Words or Roots

Teacher Modeling Remind students that they can use familiar words or roots to figure out the meanings of new words. Use the following modeling suggestion for the word *cultural* (page 145, line 5):

You could say *The word* cultural *looks similar to the word* culture. *I know* culture *refers to the "customs and arts of a people." Since* cultural *is an adjective, it must describe something that comes from or belongs to a particular group of people.*

Student Modeling Ask a volunteer to model how to use familiar words or roots to determine the meaning of *descendant* (page 146, line 26):

A student might say *In the word* descendant, *I see the base word* descend, *which means to go or come down from someone or something. Since the author uses this word to describe his grandfather, I think a* descendant *is someone who comes from a certain set of ancestors.*

MINI-LESSON See page 89 of this Guide for additional work on **Using Familiar Words or Roots.**

DURING READING

SUGGESTED READING OPTIONS

- An oral reading of "A Celebration of Grandfathers" is available in *The Language of Literature* Audio Library. 🎧
- Partner/Cooperative Reading (See page 10 of this Guide.)
- Additional options are also described on page 10 of this Guide.

RECIPROCAL TEACHING SUGGESTION: Evaluating

Teacher Modeling *Pause & Reflect, page 147* Model how to use the evaluating strategy to form opinions about the author's views:

You could say *In lines 12–23, Anaya says that the men and women of his grandfather's generation "had something important to share with the young." As evidence, he describes some of the lessons they passed on, such as the importance of nurturing the earth and helping each other through hard times. I agree with the author that these are valuable lessons to learn.*

Student Modeling *Pause & Reflect, page 148* Have several students model how to use the evaluating strategy to form opinions about statements the author makes in lines 75–82. These statements concern the importance of maintaining ties to old people and of empathizing with them.

> Encourage students to use the other five reading strategies when appropriate as they proceed through the rest of the selection. (See page 12 of this Guide.)

AFTER READING

RECOMMENDED FOLLOW-UP

- **Thinking Through the Literature,** page 460, *The Language of Literature*
- **Choices & Challenges,** page 461, *The Language of Literature*
- **SkillBuilders,** pages 150–151, *The InterActive Reader*

INFORMAL ASSESSMENT OPTIONS

Retell Divide the class into pairs. Have one student in each pair summarize what Anaya learned from his grandfather as a boy visiting the farm. The other student should summarize the insights Anaya gained watching his grandfather in his final years.

Spot Check Read the notations students wrote in the margins, paying particular attention to their responses to the *Pause & Reflect* questions. Ask students who used the **?** notation if they were able to clear up any confusion, and if so, how.

FORMAL ASSESSMENT OPTIONS IN *The Language of Literature*

Selection Quiz, page 42, Unit Three Resource Book

Selection Test, pages 75–76, Formal Assessment Book

Students Acquiring English/ESL

1. Students might benefit from reading along with the recording of "A Celebration of Grandfathers" provided in *The Language of Literature* Audio Library. 🎧

2. Students may also benefit from a class discussion of how the author's use of Spanish words and colloquial phrases reflects the values of his culture.

Additional Challenge

1. Compare Attitudes Ask: *How does Anaya's attitude toward the elderly compare with the attitude toward the elderly in your community?* Then have students explain their views using details from the memoir and from their own experiences.

◁ MARK IT UP

2. Explore Theme Have students mark passages in the essay that suggest Anaya's grandfather's philosophy toward life and death. Then ask: *Would this philosophy work today?*

BEFORE READING

Connect to Your Life In the chart on page 153, have students briefly describe their home culture: traditional foods, customs, treasures or family heirlooms, and language. Ask students to share their responses in small groups.

Key to the Story Ask students to identify elements of the mainstream culture. Ask: *Does this culture conflict with aspects of your home culture?* Read aloud the **Key to the Story.**

Build Background To help students understand the historical context for this story, have them read the Build Background information on page 503 of *The Language of Literature.*

COMPREHENSION FOCUS

KEY POINTS	STRATEGIES FOR SUCCESS
Target Skill: Making Inferences Students must be able to make inferences about the characters and their feelings in order to understand the story.	• **MINI-LESSON** Before students read, you might teach or review the **Making Inferences** lesson on page 102 of this Guide. • As students read, have them stop after the *Pause & Reflect* on page 155 and discuss what they can infer about the narrator at this point in their reading. • During or after reading, have students apply the **Inference/Judgment Chart** on page 104 of this Guide to this selection.
Foil Characters Students may need help identifying and understanding the contrasts between Maggie and her foil, Dee.	Read aloud lines 71–83 on page 156. Help students notice how Mama contrasts Maggie and Dee. While Mama held Maggie, who was badly burned, the uninjured Dee stood apart, inwardly pleased that the house she hated had burned to cinders.
Figurative Language The narrator's use of figurative language may pose problems for some students.	Have a volunteer read lines 157–160 on page 158 and then ask students to identify the comparisons that describe Dee's hair. Tell students that when they come upon figurative language, they should always try to identify the two things being compared.

ADDITIONAL WORDS TO KNOW

hesitation
page 155, line 57

determined
page 157, line 96

cowering
page 159, line 174

priceless
page 162, line 316

heritage
page 163, line 352

VOCABULARY FOCUS: Using Context Clues

Teacher Modeling Remind students that they can often use context clues to figure out the meanings of words. Demonstrate how to use this strategy to determine the meaning of the word *homely* (page 154, line 13):

You could say *I'm not sure what* homely *means, but I can look for context clues in the surrounding words and sentences. The phrase "ashamed of the burn scars down her arms and legs" helps me figure out that* homely *must mean "not good-looking."*

Student Modeling Ask a volunteer to model using context clues to determine the meaning of *envy* (page 154, line 15):

A student might say *The sentence "She thinks her sister has held life always in the palm of one hand" is a clue that* envy *means "jealousy or dislike" felt toward someone for having what you want.*

MINI-LESSON See page 87 of this Guide for additional work on **Using Context Clues.**

DURING READING

SUGGESTED READING OPTIONS

- An oral reading of "Everyday Use" is available in *The Language of Literature* Audio Library. 🎧
- Shared Reading (See page 10 of this Guide.)
- Additional options are also described on page 10 of this Guide.

RECIPROCAL TEACHING SUGGESTION: Predicting

Teacher Modeling *Pause & Reflect, page 155* Model how to use story information and your own knowledge to make a prediction:

You could say *I know from my own experience that differences between family members can sometimes lead to conflicts. The narrator describes her daughter Dee as being more strong-willed than either Maggie or herself. I predict that Dee's strong will will create a problem for Mama and Maggie.*

Student Modeling *Pause & Reflect, page 161* Have volunteers model how to use story details and prior knowledge to predict how the narrator will respond to Dee's request for the quilts.

> Encourage students to use the other five reading strategies when appropriate as they proceed through the rest of the selection. (See page 12 of this Guide.)

AFTER READING

RECOMMENDED FOLLOW-UP

- Thinking Through the Literature, page 513, *The Language of Literature*
- Choices & Challenges, pages 514–515, *The Language of Literature*
- SkillBuilders, pages 164–166, *The InterActive Reader*

INFORMAL ASSESSMENT OPTIONS

Retell Divide the class into two groups. Have students in Group 1 each prepare a retelling of the story from Maggie's perspective. Have students in Group 2 each prepare a retelling from Dee's point of view. Offer these prompts:

- *How did you feel toward your sister and mother as a young child?*
- *How do you feel about them now?*
- *How do you feel about the events that occur in the story?*

Spot Check Read the notations students wrote in the margins, paying particular attention to their responses to the *Pause & Reflect* questions and the *Challenge* activity. Ask students who used the ? notation whether they were able to figure out answers to their questions, and if so, how.

FORMAL ASSESSMENT OPTIONS IN *The Language of Literature*

Selection Quiz, page 63, Unit Three Resource Book

Selection Test, pages 83–84, Formal Assessment Book

Students Acquiring English/ESL

1. Students might benefit from reading along with the recording of "Everyday Use" provided in *The Language of Literature* Audio Library. 🎧

2. Make sure students understand that a quilt is a type of cover or blanket whose top usually consists of pieces of cloth sewn together in a design. "Lone Star" and "Walk Around the Mountain" are the names of two such designs.

Additional Challenge

1. Explore Irony Ask: *What examples of irony do you see in this story? Why do you think the author uses this technique?* Have students respond by writing a brief paragraph.

✏️ MARK IT UP

2. Examine the Title Ask: *What are some possible meanings of the title of the story? What theme, or message, does the title suggest?* Have students mark details in the story that support their answers.

BEFORE READING

Connect to Your Life Ask students to imagine what aspects of their everyday life might be affected during a war. Have them write their ideas on page 168 and then share their responses with the class.

Key to the Story Ask students to consider how soldiers might be affected by their engagement in warfare over an extended period of time. Have students silently read the **Key to the Story**.

Build Background To help students learn about the Franco-Prussian War, have them read the Build Background information on page 546 of *The Language of Literature*.

COMPREHENSION FOCUS

KEY POINTS	STRATEGIES FOR SUCCESS
Target Skill: Narrative Elements To make sense of this story, students must understand how the time and place of the story plays a crucial role in what happens and why.	• MINI-LESSON Before students read, you might teach or review the **Narrative Elements** lesson on page 105 of this Guide. • As students read, have them stop after the *Pause & Reflect* on page 172 and discuss the how the setting of the story creates a problem for the main characters. Make sure students understand the impact of the war upon the lives of Parisians. • During or after reading, have students fill out for this story the **Story Map** on page 106 of this Guide.
Author's Ambiguity Students may find it difficult to understand why the two friends remain silent when the Prussian officer demands the password.	Point out that the author never explicitly states that the two friends were given a password that would enable them to re-enter French territory. The Prussian officer merely assumes that they must have one. Ask students to speculate as to why the two friends say nothing to try to save themselves in this life-or-death situation.

ADDITIONAL WORDS TO KNOW

leisure
> page 169, line 13

mutual
> page 170, line 44

frontline
> page 172, line 89

eccentric
> page 172, line 100

deprived
> page 174, line 164

VOCABULARY FOCUS: Using Context Clues

Teacher Modeling Point out to students that they can use context clues to figure out the meanings of unfamiliar words. Demonstrate how to use this process to determine the meaning of the word *famine* (page 169, line 2):

You could say *I'm not sure what* famine *means. I can try looking for context clues in the surrounding sentences. The phrase "people were eating anything they could get their hands on" tell me that* famine *must mean "a widespread lack of food."*

Student Modeling Have students follow your lead. Ask a volunteer to model how to use context clues to figure out the meaning of *dejectedly* (page 169, line 10):

A student might say *The sentence "Paris was under siege . . . at its last gasp" and the phrase "with an empty stomach" suggest that conditions are desperate. A person living under these conditions would probably feel unhappy and walk in a discouraged way. I think that* dejectedly *means "in low spirits."*

> MINI-LESSON See page 87 of this Guide for additional work on **Using Context Clues.**

DURING READING

SUGGESTED READING OPTIONS

- An oral reading of "Two Friends" is available in *The Language of Literature* Audio Library. 🎧
- Cooperative/Partner Reading (See page 10 of this Guide.)
- Additional options are described on page 10 of this Guide.

RECIPROCAL TEACHING SUGGESTION: Visualizing

Teacher Modeling *Pause & Reflect, page 172* Model visualizing the passage that describes the autumn sunsets that stir the two main friends while fishing together before the war:

You could say *When I read lines 27–29 and 46–51, I picture the two men fishing. I see them sitting next to each other on a rock, with their pant cuffs rolled up and their bare feet dangling over the water. As their floats bob peacefully on the surface of the water, the late afternoon sun begins to color everything in shades of red and gold. The two men contemplate the scene contentedly as golden light warms their faces.*

Student Modeling *Pause & Reflect, page 175* Now have students model visualizing Mont Valérien as cannon fire erupts from it.

> Encourage students to use the other five reading strategies when appropriate as they proceed through the rest of the selection. (See page 12 of this Guide.)

AFTER READING

RECOMMENDED FOLLOW-UP

- **Thinking Through the Literature,** page 556, *The Language of Literature*
- **Choices & Challenges,** pages 557–558, *The Language of Literature*
- **SkillBuilders,** pages 179–180, *The InterActive Reader*

INFORMAL ASSESSMENT OPTIONS

Retell Explain to students the purpose of a eulogy. Then have students prepare a eulogy for the two friends that gives the following information:

- what they most enjoyed doing
- how they met each other
- how they died

Spot Check Read any notations students wrote in the margins, paying special attention to the conclusions they drew. Ask students to describe any points in the story that surprised or confused them, and to explain why.

FORMAL ASSESSMENT OPTIONS IN *The Language of Literature*

Selection Quiz, page 9, Unit Four Resource Book

Selection Test, pages 101–102, Formal Assessment Book

Students Acquiring English/ESL

1. Students might benefit from reading along with the recording of "Two Friends" provided in *The Language of Literature* Audio Library. 🎧

2. This story includes some expressions that will present problems for some students. Make sure students understand these terms:

by trade, page 169

stopped short, page 169

set off, page 170

rod in hand, page 170

on the fringe of, page 172

password, page 176

Additional Challenge

1. Examine Author's Perspective Guy de Maupassant wrote that "life is merciless . . . full of inexplicable, illogical, and contradictory catastrophes." Have students discuss to what extent the story "Two Friends" reflects this idea.

✎ MARK IT UP

2. Evaluate Characters Ask: *Are the two friends victims of fate, or do they play a part in bringing about their own downfall?* Have students mark passages in the story to support their views.

BEFORE READING

Connect to Your Life Have students complete the concept web on page 183. Discuss students' responses, and create a list of words that students associate with the word *fear* on the blackboard. Ask: *What fears have you struggled to overcome?*

Key to the Story Ask a student volunteer to read aloud the **Key to the Story.** Have students compare the agony of suspense—one's inner fears about some future punishment—with real physical punishment.

Build Background To help students understand the setting of this story and learn more about the Spanish Inquisition, have them read the Build Background information on page of *The Language of Literature.*

ADDITIONAL WORDS TO KNOW

delirious
 page 186, line 24

oppressed
 page 190, line 80

tumultuous
 page 190, line 91

impeded
 page 192, line 141

COMPREHENSION FOCUS

KEY POINTS	STRATEGIES FOR SUCCESS
Target Skill: Narrative Elements Since this entire story takes place in the mind of the narrator, students may find it difficult to understand what is happening in the story.	• **MINI-LESSON** Before students read, you may want to teach or review the **Narrative Elements** lesson on page 105 of this Guide. • Tell students to stop at various points to summarize the plot and to describe the narrator's mental and emotional state. • After reading, have students complete the **Story Map** on page 106 of this Guide by applying it to this story.
Style and Diction Poe's formal style and antiquated diction will pose a challenge for students.	• Read aloud the first few sentences of the story and model how to paraphrase them. Suggest that students use this strategy when they come upon difficult passages. • Make sure students use the Guide for Reading to help them with the definitions of difficult words and phrases.

VOCABULARY FOCUS: Using Familiar Words or Roots

Teacher Modeling Remind students that they can sometimes use familiar words or roots to figure out the meanings of words. Then use the following modeling suggestion for the word *indeterminate* (page 186, line 10):

You could say *I'm unfamiliar with the word* indeterminate, *but I do know the word* determine, *which can mean "to figure out." The prefix* in- *often means "not" or "the opposite of." The suffix* -ate *often means "able to be." So in this phrase,* indeterminate *must mean "impossible to figure out." In other words, the voices merged so that the narrator could not tell one from another.*

Student Modeling Ask a volunteer to model using familiar word roots to determine the meaning of *wearisomeness* (page 190, line 86):

A student might say Weary *means "tired." The ending* -some *appears in words such as* troublesome. *Something that is troublesome makes people feel troubled. So, something that is wearisome makes people feel weary, or tired. I think* wearisomeness *is a noun. It means "a situation that causes people to feel tired."*

MINI-LESSON See page 89 of this Guide for additional work on **Using Familiar Words or Roots.**

DURING READING

SUGGESTED READING OPTIONS

- An oral reading of "The Pit and the Pendulum" is available in *The Language of Literature* Audio Library. 🎧
- Shared Reading (See page 10 of this Guide.)
- Additional options are described on page 10 of this Guide.

RECIPROCAL TEACHING SUGGESTION: Questioning

Teacher Modeling *Pause & Reflect, page 190* Model using the questioning strategy to help students understand the narrator's state of mind:

You could say *Since the narrator is the sole character in the story and much of what he says has to do with what is going on in his mind, I know I need to try to understand his state of mind at important points in the story. As I read lines 26–34, I ask myself why the narrator sees the candles first as angels and then as specters. I think he is so frightened and tired that he starts hallucinating. Maybe he sees the candles as angels because he needs to find some hope in his desperate situation. Then he realizes that everyone around him is his enemy, so his mind sees the candles as specters.*

Student Modeling *Pause & Reflect, page 194* Have a volunteer model how to use the questioning strategy to determine the narrator's state of mind when he begins to cross the middle of the dungeon in lines 136–146.

> **Encourage students to use the other five reading strategies when appropriate as they proceed through the rest of the selection. (See page 12 of this Guide.)**

AFTER READING

RECOMMENDED FOLLOW-UP

- **Thinking Through the Literature**, page 575, *The Language of Literature*
- **Choices & Challenges**, pages 576–577, *The Language of Literature*
- **SkillBuilders**, pages 220–222, *The InterActive Reader*

INFORMAL ASSESSMENT OPTIONS

Retell Ask volunteers to describe in detail or draw diagrams of the dungeon and the deadly pendulum.

Spot Check Read students' answers to the *Pause & Reflect* questions and the notations they wrote in the margins. Ask students who used the ! notation what surprised or interested them, and why.

FORMAL ASSESSMENT OPTIONS IN *The Language of Literature*

Selection Quiz, page 15, Unit Four Resource Book
Selection Test, pages 103–104, Formal Assessment Book

Students Acquiring English/ESL

1. Students might benefit from reading along with the recording of "The Pit and the Pendulum" provided in *The Language of Literature* Audio Library. 🎧

2. Pair students with native speakers of English. Have them work together to read aloud and paraphrase key passages in the story.

Additional Challenge

1. Examine Point of View Ask: *What advantage do you see in Poe's using the first-person point of view in this story? What details would be different if the story were told from the perspective of one of the torturers?*

✏️ MARK IT UP

2. Analyze Imagery Ask students to choose a paragraph in the story that is especially rich in sensory detail. Have them mark words or phrases that appeal to the senses of sight, hearing, smell, and touch.

BEFORE READING

Connect to Your Life In the chart on page 224, have students describe how they first learned about the Holocaust and how they felt about what they learned. Ask students to share their responses with the class.

Key to the Memoir Ask students to read the **Key to the Memoir** silently. Ask: *What might be Wiesel's motivation for wanting to write about his concentration-camp experience?*

Build Background Have students read the information on page 593, which describes the circumstances that led to World War II and Hitler's campaign to exterminate Jews. Also have students read the author information on page 601 of *The Language of Literature.*

COMPREHENSION FOCUS

KEY POINTS	STRATEGIES FOR SUCCESS
Target Skill: Making Judgments The ability to make judgments about moral issues will help students understand the horror Wiesel and his fellow prisoners felt at being imprisoned in a concentration camp.	• **MINI-LESSON** Before students read, you might teach the **Making Judgments** lesson on page 103 of this Guide. • Read aloud lines 17–31 and lines 50–60. Discuss the moral implications of the prison conditions and of the "selection process." Ask: *How would you judge the Nazis for the way they treated their prisoners?* • Encourage students to record judgments they make in this selection on the **Inference/Judgment Chart** on page 104 of this Guide.
Character Relationships Students may be confused by the role the Kapos play in this account.	Discuss the political structure of the concentration camp, using footnotes 6, 11, and 12 as needed. Make sure students understand that the Kapos were Jewish prisoners who were put in charge of their block by the Nazis. Stress that Kapos were responsible to the Nazis for the actions of their block.

ADDITIONAL
WORDS
TO KNOW

anguish
   page 225, line 8

merciless
   page 226, line 30

reassure
   page 230, line 159

decisive
   page 230, line 181

inheritance
   page 231, line 190

VOCABULARY FOCUS: Using Context Clues

Teacher Modeling Remind students that many words have multiple meanings and that they can often use context clues to help them determine which meaning of a word is being used. Then use the following modeling suggestion for the word *veterans* (page 226 line 22):

You could say Veterans *can mean "people who have fought in and survived a war." It can also mean "people who have gained knowledge through much experience." The prisoners are comparing their experiences in prison camps they have lived in over the years. So in this selection,* veterans *are probably long-time prisoners who have seen and experienced a great deal.*

Student Modeling Have a volunteer model using context clues to figure out the meaning of *dumb* (page 226, line 38):

A student might say The word dumb *can mean "not smart." It can also mean "incapable of using speech" or "temporarily speechless, as with shock or fear." The fact that the old men are deathly afraid of being selected for the crematory makes me think that in this case,* dumb *describes men that are too frightened to speak.*

MINI-LESSON See page 87 of this Guide for additional work on **Using Context Clues.**

DURING READING

SUGGESTED READING OPTIONS

- An oral reading of this excerpt from *Night* is available in *The Language of Literature* Audio Library. 🎧
- Independent Reading (See page 10 of this Guide.)
- Additional options are described on page 10 of this Guide.

RECIPROCAL TEACHING SUGGESTION: Connecting

Teacher Modeling *Pause & Reflect, page 227*   Model the connecting strategy. An example follows:

You could say   *I know how nervous I am whenever I'm being judged by others. Still, my own experiences of being selected for something based on my ability are nothing compared to what these prisoners endured—I can imagine how terrified they must have felt when they heard that a selection would take place, knowing it would determine whether they would live or die.*

Student Modeling *Pause & Reflect, page 231*   Have several students model the strategy by telling how they would feel if they were in the narrator's position and had just learned that their father had been told to stay for a second selection instead of going out to work.

> **Encourage students to use the other five reading strategies when appropriate as they proceed through the rest of the selection. (See page 12 of this Guide.)**

AFTER READING

RECOMMENDED FOLLOW-UP

- Thinking Through the Literature, page 600, *The Language of Literature*
- Choices & Challenges, page 601, *The Language of Literature*
- SkillBuilders, pages 233–235, *The InterActive Reader*

INFORMAL ASSESSMENT OPTIONS

Retell   Have pairs of students prepare and then deliver an oral summary of the selection. You might offer these prompts:

- *Describe life in the concentration camps. What did prisoners do there?*
- *What was the "selection" process? What did prisoners do to try to avoid being selected?*
- *What happened to Elie Wiesel and his father in this excerpt?*

Spot Check   Read the notations students wrote in the margins, paying particular attention to their responses to the *Pause & Reflect* questions and the *Challenge* activity.

FORMAL ASSESSMENT OPTIONS IN *The Language of Literature*

Selection Quiz, page 23, Unit Four Resource Book

Selection Test, pages 107–108, Formal Assessment Book

Students Acquiring English/ESL

1. Students might benefit from reading along with the recorded excerpt of Night provided in *The Language of Literature* Audio Library. 🎧

2. Make sure students understand these terms:

last judgment, page 227

took stock of them, page 228

head was spinning, page 228

half a ration, page 229

crucible of death, page 230

Additional Challenge

1. Make Judgments   Ask students what they think of the way the Kapo for Wiesel's block behaves. Then ask students to underline details in the account that they used to make their judgment.

✏ MARK IT UP

2. Identify Irony   Point out to students that Elie Wiesel uses irony on several occasions in this excerpt (such as referring to the camp as a paradise) to underscore the cruelty of the camps. Have students mark examples of irony.

BEFORE READING

Connect to Your Life In the concept web on page 237, ask students to list the words they associate with the concept of war. Have students sort their ideas into categories and then share them with the class.

Key to the Poems Read aloud the **Key to the Poems,** and then ask students to predict how Whitman and E. E. Cummings might have viewed war based upon their wartime roles.

Build Background To help students understand how the poets' own experiences with war affected their lives and work, have students read the Build Background information on page 645 of *The Language of Literature.*

COMPREHENSION FOCUS

KEY POINTS

Target Skill: Making Inferences
Because neither speaker directly states his opinions or feelings about his wartime experiences, it is essential that students make inferences about each speaker's point of view based on the details in each poem.

Poetic Language The poetic use of language in "The Artilleryman's Vision" may cause confusion for some students.

Unusual Punctuation Students might have problems reading "look at this)" because the lack of punctuation and the unusual line breaks do not reflect the pauses in natural speech.

STRATEGIES FOR SUCCESS

- **MINI-LESSON** Before students read, teach or review the **Making Inferences** lesson on page 102 of this Guide.

- Discuss with students how each speaker seems to feel about his war experiences. Help students see that in the first poem, the speaker recalls feelings of energy, pride, and courage while in the midst of battle—feelings not expressed by the speaker in "look at this)."

- Have students fill out the **Inference/Judgment Chart** on page 104 of this Guide for both poems.

Help students paraphrase phrases such as *fantasy unreal* (line 5), *rise in detail before me again* (line 10), and *heed not* (line 22).

Read "look at this)" aloud, pausing not at the line breaks but at the places where a person would naturally pause when speaking. Then have students reread the poem silently and think about what is happening in the scene and how the speaker feels.

NEW WORDS TO KNOW

artilleryman
page 238, title

vacant
page 238, line 2

regiment
page 239, line 14

hither; thither
page 240, line 21

patter
page 240, line 24

VOCABULARY FOCUS: Using Familiar Words or Roots

Teacher Modeling Remind students that when they come to an unfamiliar word, they should think about whether the word resembles other words they know. Model the strategy using the word *tumultuous* (page 239, line 9):

You could say *I don't know this word, but I see a word I do know inside it—tumult. It means "violent action or disorder." Maybe this longer word is related to tumult. This part of the poem describes a raging battle. Tumultuous must describe the violence, disorder, and deafening noise of the battle.*

Student Modeling Ask a volunteer to model using familiar words or roots to determine the meaning of *hastening* (page 240, line 21):

A student might say *Inside this longer word, I see a word I know—haste. It means "rapidity of action." To make haste means "hurry." Hastening might mean "speeding up." This meaning makes sense in the sentence.*

MINI-LESSON See page 89 of this Guide for additional work on **Using Familiar Words or Roots.**

DURING READING

SUGGESTED READING OPTIONS

- Oral readings of "The Artilleryman's Vision" and "look at this)" are available in *The Language of Literature* Audio Library. 🎧
- Shared Reading (See page 10 of this Guide.)
- Additional options are described on page 10 of this Guide.

RECIPROCAL TEACHING SUGGESTION: Clarifying

Teacher Modeling *Pause & Reflect, page 240* If students are unclear about what is happening in the speaker's dream in Whitman's poem, read aloud lines 10–13. Then model using the clarifying strategy to clear up confusion:

You could say *I thought the speaker would remember only the awful parts of war and that all the experiences he would describe would be negative, painful ones. Why does he say that one soldier looked eagerly off to note the effect of the cannon he had fired, as if he hoped it would do great damage? The soldiers must have felt a great deal of pride and satisfaction in their actions. Thinking carefully about what the poet says helps me understand what the battle and the soldiers were really like.*

Student Modeling *Pause & Reflect, page 241* Have several students model the clarifying strategy by describing questions or confusions they had while reading "look at this)" and telling how they might have cleared up their confusion.

Encourage students to use the other five reading strategies when appropriate as they proceed through the rest of the selection. (See page 12 of this Guide.)

AFTER READING

RECOMMENDED FOLLOW-UP

- Thinking Through the Literature, page 649, *The Language of Literature*
- Choices & Challenges, pages 650–651, *The Language of Literature*
- SkillBuilders, pages 242–243, *The InterActive Reader*

INFORMAL ASSESSMENT OPTIONS

Retell Have pairs of students work together to paraphrase each poem and then present retellings of the poems in their own words.

Spot Check Review the notations students wrote in the margins, paying particular attention to their responses to the *Pause & Reflect* questions and the *Challenge* activity.

FORMAL ASSESSMENT OPTION IN *The Language of Literature*

Selection Test, pages 115–116, Formal Assessment Book

Students Acquiring English/ESL

1. Students might benefit from reading along with the recordings of "The Artilleryman's Vision" and "look at this)" provided in *The Language of Literature* Audio Library. 🎧

2. Make sure students understand these phrases:

"The Artilleryman's Vision":

men in their pieces,
 page 239, line 11

a fuse of the right time,
 page 239, line 12

a devilish exultation,
 page 240, line 20

I heed not, page 240, line 22

"look at this)":

. . . we was/buddies,
 page 241, lines 9–10

poor cuss, page 241, line 14

pine box, page 241, line 20

Additional Challenge

1. Synthesize Meaning
Ask: *How has reading these two poems influenced your impressions of those who fight in wars? Explain.*

MARK IT UP

2. Examine Tone Ask: *Given the tone of each poem, do you think either of the speakers would reenlist? Circle details from each poem that helped you reach your conclusions.*

The Tragedy of Julius Caesar, Act One
by William Shakespeare   PAGE 244

BEFORE READING

Connect to Your Life Ask students to share the knowledge they have gained about what makes a friendship successful or difficult to maintain. Then have them complete the chart on page 245.

Key to the Play Explain that the characters use various persuasion strategies in the play. Have students list types of persuasion strategies in the concept web under the **Key to the Play**.

Build Background To help students understand the historical context of the events in the play, have them read the Build Background information on page 689 of *The Language of Literature*.

COMPREHENSION FOCUS

KEY POINTS	STRATEGIES FOR SUCCESS
Target Skill: Synthesizing To understand the dialogue in this play, students must relate it to the dramatic context and interpret difficult language and unusual word order. The ability to synthesize information is crucial to this process.	• **MINI-LESSON** Before students read, you might wish to teach the **Synthesizing** lesson on page 109 of this Guide. • Read aloud the Preview on page 245 and the Preview and Focus on page 248. Show students how to use the information in these sources to piece together the dramatic context as Flavius begins speaking. • Read aloud lines 1–16 on page 248. As you do, show students how to use the Guide for Reading, beginning on page 249, for help in interpreting difficult words and challenging passages. • Have students use the **Synthesis Diagram** on page 110 of this Guide to demonstrate how synthesizing various pieces of information given in the text can increase their understanding of the play.
Form and Language The poetic language and unusual word order in Shakespearean drama might cause some readers to lose focus and become discouraged.	Suggest that students read the lines aloud quietly, paying attention to the sense of what they say. When they come to a part they don't understand, they should either reread it or read on to see what happens next. Remind them that the Guide for Reading will help them clarify content as well.

NEW WORDS TO KNOW

conquest
   page 250, line 34

livelong
   page 250, line 43

hinder
   page 256, line 30

deceived
   page 256, line 37

virtue
   page 260, line 90

VOCABULARY FOCUS: Using Letter-Sound Correspondences

Teacher Modeling Remind students that they can use the sounds letters stand for to help them figure out unfamiliar words. Write the word *naughty* (page 248, line 16) on the board, and then use the following modeling suggestion:

You could say When I came to this word, I wasn't sure how to pronounce it. At first I said năf´tē, which didn't make sense. Then I remembered that sometimes the letter combination augh *stands for the "ô" sound, as in* taught *and* caught. *So I tried pronouncing the word again—*nô´tē. *This means "behaving in a bad way."*

Student Modeling Now ask a volunteer to model how to use the letter sounds to decode the word *ancestor* (page 262, line 112):

A student might say At first I pronounced this word as ăn´kĕs´tər. This didn't sound right. Then I remembered that the letter c followed by an e makes the "s" sound. So I tried pronouncing the word ăn´sĕs´tər. I recognize that word.

MINI-LESSON See page 90 of this Guide for additional work on **Using Letter-Sound Correspondences**.

DURING READING

SUGGESTED READING OPTIONS

- An oral reading of Act One of *Julius Caesar* is available in *The Language of Literature* Audio Library. 🎧
- Oral Reading (See page 10 of this Guide.)
- Additional options are described on page 10 of this Guide.

RECIPROCAL TEACHING SUGGESTION: Questioning

Teacher Modeling *Pause & Reflect, page 262*   Model using the questioning strategy to help students understand Brutus' values:

You could say   *In lines 85–87 on page 260, Brutus tells Cassius that he is willing to die for the good of Rome. I wonder why he would say such a thing. Then I realize that Brutus values honor above all else, even more than his own life. His love of honor makes him willing to sacrifice his life for his country.*

Student Modeling *Pause & Reflect, page 286*   Have several students apply the questioning strategy to understand why Cassius and Casca want Brutus to join the conspiracy.

> Encourage students to use the other five reading strategies when appropriate as they proceed through the rest of the selection. (See page 12 of this Guide.)

AFTER READING

RECOMMENDED FOLLOW-UP

- Thinking Through the Literature, page 713, *The Language of Literature*
- SkillBuilders, pages 288–289, *The InterActive Reader*

INFORMAL ASSESSMENT OPTIONS

Retell   Have students work in small groups to give oral summaries of the three scenes in Act One of *Julius Caesar*. Offer these prompts:

- *In Scene 1, whom do Flavius and Marullus meet on the street? What is discussed?*
- *In Scene 2, what does the Soothsayer tell Caesar? What does Cassius want Brutus to do? How does he respond?*
- *In Scene 3, what does Cassius do to try to trick Brutus into joining the conspiracy?*

Spot Check   Read the notations students wrote in the margins, paying particular attention to their responses to the *Pause & Reflect* questions and to any predictions they made. For students who used the **?** notation, ask if and how they were able to clear up their confusion.

FORMAL ASSESSMENT OPTIONS IN *The Language of Literature*

Selection Quiz, page 64, Unit Four Resource Book

Selection Test, pages 123–124, Formal Assessment Book

Students Acquiring English/ESL

1. Students might benefit from reading along with the recording of this excerpt of *Julius Caesar* provided in *The Language of Literature* Audio Library. 🎧

2. Have students work in pairs with native speakers to read aloud several passages from this play.

Additional Challenge

1. Examine Plot   Have students write a paragraph to explain why they think Shakespeare includes the Soothsayer and a violent storm in this play.

2. Evaluate the Conspiracy Ask: *What, in your view, might prevent the conspirators' plans from succeeding? Explain.*

✏️ MARK IT UP

3. Discuss Friendship Have students discuss the relationship between Cassius and Brutus. Ask: *Do you think Cassius is a good friend to Brutus? Is Brutus a good friend to Cassius?* Tell students to mark passages in the play to support their views.

Connect to Your Life Ask students to identify the people, places, or values they are most loyal to and then rank them according to depth of loyalty. Then have students fill in the bar graph on page 291.

Key to the Story Have a student read the **Key to the Story** aloud. Have students write responses to the question: *What do you think about the practice of taxidermy?* Have students share responses and allow peers to pose questions.

Build Background To help students understand the significance of the setting and the appearance and traits of the creature on which the story focuses, have students read the Build Background information on page 822 of *The Language of Literature*.

ADDITIONAL WORDS TO KNOW

consolation
　　page 293, line 24

aggressive
　　page 294, line 88

demure
　　page 297, line 176

stately
　　page 300, line 270

rebukes
　　page 303, line 405

COMPREHENSION FOCUS

KEY POINTS	STRATEGIES FOR SUCCESS
Target Skill: Predicting Through Story Clues Early in the story, details provide clues to Sylvia's feelings about her world, to the threat posed by the stranger, and to Sylvia's conflicting loyalties. Students must make inferences based on these clues in order to predict how Sylvia will resolve her conflict.	• **MINI-LESSON** Before students read "A White Heron," you may want to teach the **Predicting** lesson on page 111 of this Guide. • Read aloud and discuss lines 43–56, 75–82, and 83–92, and 114–118. Help students infer why Sylvia instinctively perceives the stranger as a threat. Ask students to predict how her beliefs may influence her later actions. • After the *Pause & Reflect* on page 297, have students work in pairs to begin filling in the **Predicting Chart** on page 112 of this Guide and to continue using it throughout the selection.
Antiquated Language/Dialect This story is written in a somewhat formal, old-fashioned style. Readers may be unfamiliar with some of the sentence constructions, idioms, and dialect used by the author.	• Read aloud lines 126–134. Point out that footnotes explain the meanings of "pa'tridges" and "squer'ls." • Suggest that students work in pairs to read difficult passages aloud and then paraphrase them in modern, informal language.

VOCABULARY FOCUS: Using Context Clues

Teacher Modeling Remind students that they can often use context clues to help them figure out a word or phrase and its meaning. Then use the following modeling suggestion for the word *spent* (page 293, line 20):

You could say I'm not sure I understand the meaning of spent in the phrase "her childish patience was quite spent." The paragraph above describes how irritating it is for Sylvia when the cow hides from her. So, in this case, spent must mean "exhausted" or "used up." It makes sense that Sylvia's patience was all used up after chasing the stubborn cow.

Student Modeling Now have students follow your lead. Ask a volunteer to model using context clues to determine the meaning of *loitered* (page 293, line 43):

A student might say The story says the grandmother "suspected that Sylvia loitered occasionally on her own account" because "there never was such a child for straying about out-of-doors . . ." From the context, I can tell that loitered means "lingered and strayed about."

MINI-LESSON See page 87 of this Guide for additional work on **Using Context Clues.**

DURING READING

SUGGESTED READING OPTIONS

- An oral reading of "A White Heron" is available in *The Language of Literature* Audio Library. 🎧
- Partner/Cooperative Reading (See page 10 of this Guide.)
- Additional options are described on page 10 of this Guide.

RECIPROCAL TEACHING SUGGESTION: Visualizing

Teacher Modeling *Pause & Reflect, page 297* Model visualizing the scene in which Sylvia first meets the tall young man:

You could say *When Sylvia first hears the young man's whistle, the narration briefly switches to present tense ("Suddenly this little woods-girl is horror-stricken . . .") This gets my attention. The narrator goes on to say that Sylvia stepped into the bushes, trembled, and would not look directly at the stranger. Her head is hanging low. I imagine her expression and movements and then realize how intensely shy she is.*

Student Modeling *Pause & Reflect, page 302* Ask a volunteer to describe how she or he would visualize Sylvia's climb up the old pine tree. If necessary, call attention to phrases such as "monstrous ladder," "great enterprise," and "great mainmast" to show how intimidating a task it is to climb this giant tree with its "angry talons," "great stem," and "ponderous frame."

> Encourage students to use the other five reading strategies when appropriate as they proceed through the rest of the selection. (See page 12 of this Guide.)

AFTER READING

RECOMMENDED FOLLOW-UP

- **Thinking Through the Literature**, page 833, *The Language of Literature*
- **Choices & Challenges**, pages 834–835, *The Language of Literature*
- **SkillBuilders**, pages 305–307, *The InterActive Reader*

INFORMAL ASSESSMENT OPTIONS

Retell Have students play the role of the ornithologist as he tells some friends about his bird-collecting trip. Offer the following prompts:

- *What did you think of Sylvia when you first met her?*
- *What made you think that Sylvia knew where the white heron was?*

Spot Check Read students' answers to the *Pause & Reflect* questions and the notations they wrote in the margins. Ask students who used the ? notation whether their questions were answered, and, if so, how.

FORMAL ASSESSMENT OPTIONS IN *The Language of Literature*

Selection Quiz, page 9, Unit Five Resource Book

Selection Test, pages 135–136, Formal Assessment Book

Students Acquiring English/ESL

1. Students might benefit from reading along with the recording of "A White Heron" provided in *The Language of Literature* Audio Library. 🎧

2. Make sure students understand these expressions:

striking deep into the woods, page 292

on her own account, page 293

hung her head, page 295

I must be off, page 295

a desert islander, page 299

the sharp report of his gun, page 304

Additional Challenge

1. Interpret a Quote Have students write a brief essay in which they interpret the following quote from Shakespeare's *Hamlet* and apply its meaning to "A White Heron": "This above all: to thine own self be true."

⟍MARK IT UP

2. Explore Character's Motivations Ask students to circle descriptive details in the text that reveal Sylvia's "existence heart to heart with nature." Then have them speculate on why Sylvia's feelings towards animals are different from those of her grandmother and the young ornithologist.

BEFORE READING

Connect to Your Life Have students recall something they loved to do when very young. Ask students to compare their earlier feelings toward the activity with their present feelings and jot down their ideas in the Connect to Your Life activity on page 309.

Key to the Poem Ask students to define *simple joys* and provide some examples. Next have them read the **Key to the Poem** and complete the concept web.

Build Background To help students learn about the birch trees of New England, the subject of this poem, have students read the Build Background information on page 838 of *The Language of Literature*.

COMPREHENSION FOCUS

KEY POINTS	STRATEGIES FOR SUCCESS
Target Skill: Cause and Effect Students must be able to identify cause and effect relationships in order to understand the speaker's explanations for bent birches.	• **MINI-LESSON** Before students read, you might teach or review the **Cause and Effect** lesson on page 92 of this Guide. • As students read, have them stop after the *Pause & Reflect* on page 311 and discuss how an ice-storm affects birch trees. • After reading, have students apply the **Cause and Effect Chart** on page 93 of this Guide to the poem.
Descriptive Details Students may get bogged down by the number of descriptive details in lines 1–40.	Point out that the details in lines 1–20 primarily describe the birch trees after an ice-storm and those in lines 21–40 describe an imagined boy climbing a birch tree.
The Speaker's Perspective Students may have difficulty understanding why swinging from birches is so meaningful to the speaker.	Read aloud lines 41–59. Discuss with students why an adult might want to relive—even if only in the imagination—a childhood activity. Call students' attention to the sentence in lines 48–49. Ask how swinging from birches would fulfill the speaker's wish.

NEW WORDS TO KNOW

withered
   page 311, line 14

subdued
   page 312, line 28

VOCABULARY FOCUS: Using Context Clues

Teacher Modeling Remind students that often they can use context clues to figure out the meanings of words. Demonstrate using this process to determine the meaning of the word *heaps* (page 311, line 12):

You could say I can look for context clues in surrounding lines to clarify the meaning of the word heaps. The phrase "avalanching on the snow-crust" suggests an enormous number of ice pellets, so many that it looks like a glass "dome" has shattered, leaving countless bits of glass on the snow. Heaps *must be a noun that means "large piles."*

Student Modeling Have a student model using context clues to determine the meaning of *poise* (line 35):

A student might say The phrases "not launching out too soon" and "climbing carefully" are clues that the word poise has something to do with keeping your balance. I'd say poise is a noun that means "balance or self-control."

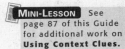 **MINI-LESSON** See page 87 of this Guide for additional work on **Using Context Clues.**

DURING READING

SUGGESTED READING OPTIONS

- An oral reading of "Birches" is available in *The Language of Literature* Audio Library. 🎧
- Partner/Cooperative Reading (See page 10 of this Guide.)
- Additional options are described on page 10 of this Guide.

RECIPROCAL TEACHING SUGGESTION: Visualizing

Teacher Modeling *Pause & Reflect, page 311* Model how to use the visualizing strategy to help students picture the birch trees laden with ice:

You could say *When I read lines 10–13, I can picture the branches of the birch trees glazed with ice and glistening in the morning sun. When the wind blows, I imagine the ice crackling and breaking apart into pieces. I picture tiny pieces of ice littering the snow-covered ground like bits of broken glass.*

Student Modeling *Pause & Reflect, page 312* Have volunteers model the visualizing strategy to form pictures of the boy swinging on the birch trees in lines 32–40.

> Encourage students to use the other five reading strategies when appropriate as they proceed through the rest of the selection. (See page 12 of this Guide.)

AFTER READING

RECOMMENDED FOLLOW-UP

- Thinking Through the Literature, page 841, *The Language of Literature*
- Choices & Challenges, page 842, *The Language of Literature*
- SkillBuilders, pages 314–315, *The InterActive Reader*

INFORMAL ASSESSMENT OPTIONS

Retell Ask students to select their favorite passages from the poem and to read them aloud. Have them tell why they like these particular lines and why they are important to the poem.

Spot Check Read the responses students wrote to the *Pause & Reflect* questions. For students who used the ? notation, ask if and how they cleared up any confusion.

FORMAL ASSESSMENT OPTION IN *The Language of Literature*

Selection Test, pages 137–138, Formal Assessment Book

Students Acquiring English/ESL

1. Students might benefit from reading along with the recording of "Birches" provided in *The Language of Literature* Audio Library. 🎧

2. Make sure students understand these phrases:

never right themselves, page 311, line 16

when Truth broke in, page 311, line 21

same pains you use, page 312, line 37

Additional Challenge

1. Explain an Image Have students write a paragraph to explain how climbing a birch tree is like carefully filling a cup "Up to the brim, and even above the brim."

MARK IT UP

2. Compare and Contrast Ask: *How do the feelings evoked by the images of the ice-storm in lines 10–20 compare with the feelings evoked by the image of the boy's effect on the trees in lines 28–35?* Have students mark details in the poem to support their response.

BEFORE READING

Connect to Your Life Ask students to interpret the statement: *She lives according to her principles.* Have students complete the chart on page 317 and discuss the principles they added.

Key to the Play Explain that the Greek play *Antigone* is about a woman of strong principles. Read aloud the description of Greek Classical drama in **Key to the Play.**

Build Background To help students understand the Greek legend on which *Antigone* is based, have them read the Build Background information on page 1018 of *The Language of Literature.*

COMPREHENSION FOCUS

KEY POINTS	STRATEGIES FOR SUCCESS

Target Skill: Sequence To understand this play, students must keep track of the order of events. For example, students must realize that in the Parados, the Chorus describes events that took place before the beginning of the play.

- **MINI-LESSON** Before students read, you may wish to teach or review the **Sequence** lesson on page 107 of this Guide.
- As students read, have them stop after the *Pause & Reflect* on page 328 and list in order the events in the Prologue and the Parados.
- After reading, have students complete the **Sequence/Flow Chart** on page 108 of this Guide as it applies to the play.

Play Format The dialogue and stage directions in this play may pose problems for some students.

Point out that the stage directions help directors and actors perform the play and readers imagine what is happening on stage. Then read aloud lines 1–84 of the Prologue, and stop frequently to have volunteers summarize the dialogue.

The Central Conflict Students must be able to identify the principles that generate the conflict in this play.

Have students read aloud and discuss the boxed passages on pages 322 and 330. If necessary, point out that Antigone values love of family, but Creon values duty to country.

ADDITIONAL WORDS TO KNOW

traitor
    page 320, line 27

meddling
    page 322, line 52

complexities
    page 330, line 4

summoned
    page 330, line 6

scheming
    page 336, line 115

VOCABULARY FOCUS: Using Structural Analysis

Teacher Modeling Remind students that they can often figure out the meaning of a new word by identifying its parts. Use the following modeling suggestion for the word *intolerable* (page 336, line 107):

You could say I'm not sure what the word intolerable means. I see the prefix in-, which often means "not." I see a base word that looks like tolerate, which can mean "to accept." I also see the suffix -able, which means "capable of." I would guess that intolerable is an adjective that means "not able to be accepted."

Student Modeling Now have students follow your lead. Ask a volunteer to model how to use structural analysis to figure out the meaning of *misfortune* (page 338, line 131):

A student might say I see the prefix mis-, which means "bad or wrong." I also see the word fortune, which means "chance or luck." So, I think misfortune is a noun that means "bad luck or trouble."

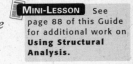 **MINI-LESSON** See page 88 of this Guide for additional work on **Using Structural Analysis.**

DURING READING

SUGGESTED READING OPTIONS

- An oral reading of *Antigone* is available in *The Language of Literature* Audio Library. 🎧
- Oral Reading (See page 10 of this Guide.)
- Additional options are described on page 10 of this Guide.

RECIPROCAL TEACHING SUGGESTION: Clarifying

Teacher Modeling *Pause & Reflect, page 326* Model using the clarifying strategy to help students identify important differences between Antigone and Ismene:

You could say *At first I thought Ismene's fear of being stoned was the reason that she refused to help Antigone bury their brother. As I read further, however, I learned that Ismene values laws made for the public good more than she values family loyalty, which is the most important concern for Antigone. That is a big difference between the two sisters.*

Student Modeling *Pause & Reflect, page 338* Have volunteers explain how to use the clarifying strategy to understand Creon's reaction to the news of Polyneices' burial.

> **Encourage students to use the other five reading strategies when appropriate as they proceed through the rest of the selection. (See page 12 of this Guide.)**

AFTER READING

RECOMMENDED FOLLOW-UP

After reading the rest of the play, use the following:
- **Thinking Through the Literature,** page 1061, *The Language of Literature*
- **Choices & Challenges,** pages 1062–1063, *The Language of Literature*
- **SkillBuilders,** pages 342–344, *The InterActive Reader*

INFORMAL ASSESSMENT OPTIONS

Retell Have students work in small groups to give oral summaries of the play so far. Offer these prompts:
- *What does Antigone ask Ismene to do? How does Ismene react?*
- *Describe what happens when Polyneices attacks Thebes.*
- *What does Creon intend to do to Polyneices' corpse? How does Creon react to the news of Polyneices' burial?*

Spot Check Read the notes students wrote in the margins. For students who used the ? notation, ask if and how they were able to clear up their confusion.

FORMAL ASSESSMENT OPTION IN *The Language of Literature*

Selection Quiz, items 1–5, page 33, Unit Six Resource Book

Students Acquiring English/ESL

1. Students might benefit from reading along with the recording of *Antigone* provided in *The Language of Literature* Audio Library. 🎧

2. Make sure students understand these terms:

yield to those in authority, page 322

windy phrases, page 326

take leave of war, page 328

Additional Challenge

1. Compare Characters
Ask: *In what way do you think Antigone and Creon are alike? In what ways are they different?* Have students write a paragraph to compare and contrast these characters.

✏️ MARK IT UP

2. Examine the Chorus
Ask: *What effect did the Choragus and the Chorus have on your interpretation of the events so far in this play?* Tell students to mark passages in the play to illustrate their views.

from The Acts of King Arthur and His Noble Knights by John Steinbeck PAGE 345

BEFORE READING

Connect to Your Life Have students use the concept web on page 346 to describe the images that come to mind when they hear the word *knight*. Ask students to share their ideas with a partner.

Key to the Story Ask students to identify popular stories about knights. Ask: *What are some common themes in these stories?* Have them silently read the **Key to the Story.**

Build Background To help students understand why and how John Steinbeck wrote his own retelling of the legend of King Arthur and his knights, have them read the Build Background information on page 1090 of *The Language of Literature.*

COMPREHENSION FOCUS

KEY POINTS	STRATEGIES FOR SUCCESS
Target Skill: Making Inferences This selection focuses on the tense interplay between King Arthur, Queen Guinevere, and Lancelot. The ability to infer these characters' feelings from their words and actions is crucial to students' understanding of the excerpt and to their recognition of the excerpt's dramatic tension.	• **MINI-LESSON** Before students begin reading, you might teach or review the **Making Inferences** lesson on page 102 of this Guide. • After students have read the fourth paragraph on page 349, discuss how Lancelot feels as he listens to others describe his deeds. Remind students to "read between the lines" and combine their own knowledge of human behavior with the words and actions provided in the selection in order to understand Lancelot's state of mind. • As students read the selection, have them complete the **Active Reading SkillBuilder** on page 357.
Specialized Terms In order to comprehend the descriptive passages in the first few sections of the selection, students will need to understand terms having to do with life in a medieval town, castle life, and the business of being a knight.	Encourage students to use the footnotes provided in the selection, which will help them decipher certain unusual terms. If a term does not have a footnote, encourage students to try context clues to figure out a basic meaning. It is important, however, for students to keep reading so the flow of the story is not interrupted because of a single term.

VOCABULARY FOCUS: Using Letter-Sound Correspondences

Teacher Modeling Remind students that they can use the sounds letters stand for to help them read unfamiliar words. Demonstrate this strategy by using the following modeling suggestions for the word *gauntlets* (page 350, line 70):

You could say At first I didn't recognize this word (write gauntlets on the board). Then I remembered that when the letters au come together, they often stand for the "ô" sound you hear in the word haunt. So then I read the word as gônt´lits. That sounded right.

Student Modeling Now have a volunteer model using letter-sound correspondences to figure out how to pronounce *stature* (page 348, line 28):

A student might say I'll try pronouncing the letters s-t-a as they are pronounced in the word stand, and pronouncing the letters t-u-r-e as they are pronounced in the word picture. When I put these parts together, I get the word stature.

MINI-LESSON See page 90 of this Guide for additional work on **Using Letter-Sound Correspondences.**

ADDITIONAL WORDS TO KNOW

elite
    page 348, line 20

fended (off)
    page 348, line 26

exploits
    page 348, line 31

immaculate
    page 349, line 40

attributed
    page 349, line 48

quest
    page 352, line 150

DURING READING

SUGGESTED READING OPTIONS

- An oral reading of this excerpt from *The Acts of King Arthur and His Noble Knights* is available in *The Language of Literature* Audio Library. 🎧

- Oral Reading/Independent Reading (See page 10 of this Guide.)

- Additional options are described on page 10 of this Guide.

RECIPROCAL TEACHING SUGGESTION: Visualizing

Teacher Modeling *Pause & Reflect, page 351* Based on the narrator's description in lines 97–103, model visualizing the servants working in the great hall:

You could say *The phrases "shoulders wide and sloping from burdens," "legs short and thick and crooked," and "frame slowly crushed by weights" helps me picture these short, hunched-over figures carrying heavy trays of food. The word "scuttled like crabs, crooked and nervous" help me imagine the servants moving quickly out of the way once they have set the trays down.*

Student Modeling *Pause & Reflect, page 354* Ask several volunteers to model creating a mental image of the stone stairway that leads up to the king's room (lines 117–123) or of King Arthur's chambers (lines 125–134).

Encourage students to use the other five reading strategies when appropriate as they proceed through the rest of the selection. (See page 12 of this Guide.)

AFTER READING

RECOMMENDED FOLLOW-UP

- **Thinking Through the Literature,** page 1099, *The Language of Literature*
- **Choices & Challenges,** pages 1100–1101, *The Language of Literature*
- **SkillBuilders,** pages 357–359, *The InterActive Reader*

INFORMAL ASSESSMENT OPTIONS

Retell Have students retell what happened in the banquet hall and in the king's room from King Arthur's point of view. Offer the following prompts:

- *How did Lancelot seem to be feeling at the banquet? How could you tell?*

- *What were your thoughts about Guinevere and Lancelot's conversation in your room? How do you think they feel about each other?*

Spot Check Read the notations students wrote in the margins, paying particular attention to any inferences they have made. Ask students to describe any points in the selection that surprised or confused them, and to explain why.

FORMAL ASSESSMENT OPTIONS IN *The Language of Literature*

Selection Quiz, page 49, Unit Six Resource Book

Selection Test, pages 173–174, Formal Assessment Book

Students Acquiring English/ESL

1. Students might benefit from reading along with the recording of this excerpt provided in *The Language of Literature* Audio Library. 🎧

2. Make sure students understand these terms:

overthrown, page 349

her inward eyes confessed, page 350

I will retire, page 352

put a bug in [his] ear, page 353

Additional Challenge

1. Create a Sequel Have students continue the story by writing the dialogue for a scene in which Lancelot and Guinevere next meet.

✏ MARK IT UP

2. Compare and Contrast Ask students to write a brief essay in which they compare and contrast the outward behavior of Lancelot with his inner self. Have them give evidence to support their opinions.

Academic and Informational Reading Lesson Plans

Reading a Magazine Article

Introducing the Concept

Some students may be bewildered by the assortment of headings, text, and visuals in some magazine articles. Tell students that using these strategies will help.

Teaching Tips for the Magazine Article

A **Title and Headings:** Have students identify the title of this article. Also make sure they notice the title in the boxed feature. Tell students that many magazine articles also include subheadings that signal how the article is organized.

B **Different Typeface:** Point out the different typeface of the letter "T" at the beginning of the article. This is meant to draw the reader's attention to the introduction, which presents the main topic. Also point out the large italic typeface of the call-out quotation. The use of this typeface brings attention to a quotation that supports the main idea of the article, and it adds visual interest to the page.

C **Quotation Marks, Italics, and Boldface:** Remind students that boldface type is heavier than regular type and that italic type is slightly slanted. These different styles, as well as the use of quotation marks, draw attention to words.

D **Visuals:** Suggest that students preview the visuals in a magazine article before they begin reading. Have students note how the photographs in the example relate to the title of the article.

E **Special Features:** Let students know that many articles include special features that support the main article. These items may include additional and interesting information that doesn't necessarily support the main idea of the central article but is related to it in some way.

Additional Questions

1. What is "youth sports rage"? (violent or angry behavior by spectators at youth sports)
2. According to Mathelier, what causes some parents to exhibit youth sports rage? (Answers might include: unrealistic ideas about college scholarships and professional careers; some parents live through their children.)
3. What measures have some groups taken to prevent youth sports rage? (Answers will vary but might include one of the following: instituting a Sport Parent Code of Conduct; having "Silent Sundays"; or making one parent in charge of crowd control.)

Additional Tips for Reading a Magazine Article

- **Read items in any order:** Tell students that they can read the items in a magazine article in any order they choose. After they preview the article, students can read the charts, sidebars, or introductory text first—whatever catches their interest.
- **Ignore advertising:** Encourage students to mentally screen out the ads that appear in some articles. Sometimes these ads appear as if they were part of the article. However, in most cases, the ads are only there to entice readers to buy something.
- **Understand slang terms:** Point out that magazines aimed at teenagers often use informal language and popular slang. Students whose first language is not English may have trouble understanding such slang. You might suggest that students jot down any words and terms that they don't understand and ask a friend to translate.

Reading a Textbook

Introducing the Concept

Many students are overwhelmed by the titles, subheadings, and features on a textbook page. They may become discouraged if they have trouble finding their way through these items. Tell students that these skills and strategies will help them learn to read textbooks.

Teaching Tips for the Textbook Page

A **Title and Headings:** Have students identify the title of the lesson and the headings that indicate related subtopics. Point out the different sizes and typefaces of the headings. Students should note that subheadings are usually smaller than the lesson title.

B **Terms:** Encourage students to scan the terms and names before they begin reading the lesson. You might ask students to find both of the terms from the list that can be found on this page.

C **Main Idea:** Tell students that the main idea introduces the topic and tells them what they will learn about in the lesson. The "Why It Matters Now" feature explains the relevance of this lesson for people today.

D **Special Typefaces:** Often in textbooks, vocabulary terms are set in bold, italics, or parentheses. Point out that on this page, a vocabulary term is explained in the side margin.

E **Primary Source and Quotations:** Make sure students understand that a primary source provides firsthand knowledge by an eyewitness or participant about a specific event or period of time. Quotations, like primary sources, are often included in textbooks because they help make a topic come alive.

F **Visuals and Captions:** Tell students that the visual on this page presents a portrait of Napoleon. Explain that Napoleon is also the author of one of the quotations in the side feature on the page.

Additional Questions

1. According to this textbook, what was Napoleon's main characteristic? (He was a military genius.)

2. By 1799, what was Napoleon called? (the general)

3. How did Napoleon's wife help his political career? (She used her connections with wealthy directors to influence them.)

Additional Tips for Reading a Textbook

- **Take notes before reading:** Before students begin reading, have them write down what they know and what they want to learn about the topic.

- **Follow the PACER method:** When students read a lesson in a textbook, encourage them to follow the PACER method: **P**review the entire lesson, use section subheadings to **A**nalyze the purpose of the passage, **C**arefully read the text, **E**valuate the material, and, finally, **R**eview their notes.

- **Use a graphic organizer:** As students read, suggest that they use a graphic organizer to help make sense of the material. For example, they might use a concept web to record a lesson's main ideas and supporting details.

Reading a Graph

Introducing the Concept

Graphs can present numerical information in a way that is quick and easy to grasp. Learning how graphs function can make them easier to understand. Tell students that using these strategies will help them interpret graphs more easily.

Teaching Tips for the Graph

A **Title:** A graph's title usually contains key words or phrases that let the reader know what kind of information the graph shows. Before reading a graph, students should read the title and headings to get a quick overview.

B **Labels:** Tell students that the labels in this line graph show the relationship between the date and the temperature. Labels on the axes of a line graph always imply a relationship between sets of data, so it is important for students to read the headings before trying to understand the graph.

C **Pattern of Information:** Explain to students how to read the line pattern in this graph. Have students see that the temperature peaked on December 4, went down dramatically on December 5, hovered around 40 degrees on December 8, 9, and 10, and so on.

Additional Questions

1. On what date was the daily high temperature the lowest? (December 12)

2. On how many days between December 1 and December 14 did the temperature reach 40 degrees? (7)

Other Types of Charts and Graphs

Reproduce the following charts and graphs to show students the variety of visuals they will come across in their reading. Remind students that, when reading a pie chart, they should remember that each slice of pie represents a percentage. For a flow chart, they should follow the arrows; and for a diagram, they should read the labels carefully.

Pie Chart shows percentages

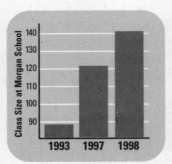

Bar Graph compares numbers

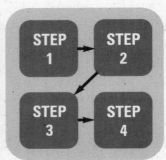

Flow Chart explains the steps of a process

Reading a Map

Introducing the Concept

Some maps show geographical information, such as lakes, oceans, and mountains. Other maps show streets, highways, and landmarks in a particular city. Some maps illustrate historical events, such as the losses or victories of a battle. The map on this page shows the population distribution of Australia. You might want to show students examples of the different types of maps (see list below) and then explain to them that most maps share similar features.

Teaching Tips for the Map

A **Title:** Map titles help the reader understand the type of information represented on the map. Some titles include dates reflecting a time period; others include names of geographic regions or political or economic activity.

B **Legend or Key:** Most keys and legends include a combination of arrows, symbols, colors, letters, numbers, and lines to represent items on the map. The legend on this map shows symbols that indicate population size.

C **Geographic Labels:** Tell students to watch for different type styles on geographic labels. On complicated political maps, for example, recognizing the type style (italic, all capital letters, boldface) and size will help students distinguish capital cities, state names, highways, routes, and so on. As an example, point out the difference in type style and size between the country name *Australia* and the city name *Sydney*.

D **Compass Rose:** A compass rose shows which way the directions north (N), south (S), east (E), and west (W) point on the map.

E **Scale:** Maps often include a scale to show what the distances on the map represent in miles or kilometers.

Additional Questions

1. Compare the population distribution of the southeastern and southwestern coasts of Australia. **(There are more populous cities on the southeastern coast.)**
2. Of the five major cities on this map, which is the least populous? **(Adelaide)**
3. What does this symbol stand for? ◯ **(1 to 3 million people)**

Basic Types of Maps

- **Physical maps** show mountains, hills, rivers, lakes, gulfs, oceans, and other physical features of an area.
- **Political maps** show political units, such as countries, states, counties, districts, and towns. Each unit is typically shaded a different color, represented by a symbol, or shown with a different typeface.
- **Historical maps** illustrate things such as economic activity, migrations, battles, and changing national boundaries.

Reading a Diagram

Introducing the Concept

While diagrams can be an important aid in illustrating and understanding written texts, they pose their own set of challenges for readers. After the first glance, many diagrams require close study and interpretation. Explain to students that although diagrams may look easy because of the pictures, they sometimes contain complex information. These strategies should help students understand the information in many different kinds of diagrams.

Teaching Tips for the Diagram

A **Title:** A diagram's title is not necessarily at the top. Remind students that it might be at the bottom or on the side, and that some diagrams don't even have titles.

B **Images:** Explain to students that the images in this diagram are visual explanations of the numbered captions. Students should glance at the images, read the text, and then study the images more closely. It is this second look at the images that will really help them understand the concept of the states of water.

C **Captions and Labels:** Remind students that they should not overlook the captions because they contain key concepts illustrated in the diagram. Underscore for students the importance of reading each label and determining what each one refers to. Also point out to students that arrows and other special markers often illustrate the diagram's most important concept. For example, in this diagram, the arrows show the effects of heat on the states of water.

Additional Questions

1. What happens when ice absorbs heat? (**It turns to liquid water and then to water vapor.**)

2. In what forms would you find liquid water? (**clouds, rain, dew**)

3. Why does the diagram show two arrows between each state of water? (**The arrows show what happens when heat is absorbed and when heat is released. These processes can go both ways between the states of water.**)

Main Idea and Supporting Details

Introducing the Concept

Students may have trouble identifying the main idea in a paragraph. They may not be able to distinguish the main point of a paragraph from the details that support it. Tell students that these strategies can help.

Teaching Tips for Main Idea and Supporting Details

- **Main Idea:** Tell students that the main idea of a paragraph is presented in a general statement. Specific details in the other sentences in the paragraph support or help to prove this general statement.
- **Summary:** Encourage students to summarize the paragraph by restating the main idea as a headline or title.
- **Supporting Details:** Introduce different types of supporting details, such as sensory details, specific examples, facts and statistics, reasons, quotations, and anecdotes.

Additional Questions

1. What types of details are used to support the main idea of the first paragraph? (facts)
2. How might you restate the main idea of the second paragraph as a headline? (Elizabeth I Made Major Changes in England)

Additional Tips

Tell students that not all main ideas are stated in the first sentence. Some main ideas appear in the middle of the paragraph; some are stated in the last sentence. Sometimes, especially in narrative or descriptive writing, a main idea is implied rather than stated. When the main idea is implied, students must figure out the major point that ties all the sentences together. In the following paragraph, for example, all the sentences are tied together by the following main idea: James is resentful of the way his sister is treated.

"It's not fair!" James shouted. "Lily always gets away with everything! Why doesn't *she* get grounded when she stays out past curfew? Why doesn't *she* get her allowance docked when she refuses to do her chores? I *never* get a break!"

Problem and Solution

Introducing the Concept

Familiarity with common text structures, such as problem and solution, can improve students' comprehension and mental organization of what they read. Explain to students that a text describing a problem and solution can often be broken down into recognizable parts.

Teaching Tips for the Problem and Solution Text

- **Statement of Problem:** Point out to students that the statement of the problem appears in the first paragraph.

- **Explanation of Problem:** Explain to students that a writer will often include an explanation that gives details about the problem. Explain that writers often write persuasively in order to convince a reader that the problem is important. Here, the writer points out how noise pollution is both annoying and dangerous.

- **Proposed Solution:** Remind students that although the proposed solution is stated clearly in the third paragraph, it may be phrased as a question in other cases.

- **Support for Proposal:** Tell students that writers will also often use persuasive language in the details that support a proposal.

- **Evaluating the Solution:** Encourage students to form their own opinions about every proposed solution they read, whether in their schoolwork or independent reading.

Additional Example

The following paragraph contains another problem and proposed solution. Share it with students. Ask them to identify its different elements and evaluate the proposed solution.

No Peanuts at Franklin High!

Every day, students at Franklin High School go to the cafeteria and grab a bite to eat. There are usually healthy and great-tasting meals, such as roasted chicken, pizza, or even the classic peanut butter and jelly sandwich. It seems like our lunch options are harmless enough, right? Wrong! To students with severe peanut allergies, the cafeteria can be a dangerous place.

Approximately 3 million people in this country have peanut allergies. Some people can even die if they breathe in the same room that peanuts are in. Our school needs to be a "peanut-free zone" so that it will be safe for all students.

The cafeteria can provide alternate sandwich options, such as various lunch meats or cream cheese and jelly. Information packets can be sent to parents so that they will know what foods they can and cannot send in with their children. Students, parents, and teachers should all be educated about the seriousness of this allergy, which is rarely outgrown, and the products that need to be banned from the school.

So here's a comment from the peanut gallery: Let's make Franklin High a safer place for all students. One important way to do this is to prohibit peanut products in the school building.

Answers

Statement of problem: "To students with severe peanut allergies, the cafeteria can be a dangerous place."
Explanation of problem: first and second paragraphs
Proposed solution: last paragraph
Support for proposal: third paragraph

Sequence

Introducing the Concept

Ask students to give examples of when they need to use correct sequence in their reading, writing, and speaking. Answers may include writing a report (introduction, body, and conclusion), following instructions in a manual, telling a story, and explaining how to copy files onto a CD. Explain that many reading assignments contain clues that help readers determine the sequence of events. When students recognize sequence, they understand material better and take clearer notes.

Teaching Tips for Sequence

- **Main Steps or Events:** Students may want to number or write down the main steps, events, or stages as they read. For complicated or especially important sequences, advise students to create flow charts or time lines, such as this one.
- **Time Words and Phrases:** Have students suggest other words or phrases that can signal time, such as *last week, shortly, in ten minutes, concurrently*, and *the day before*.
- **Order Words and Phrases:** Ask students to think of more words and phrases that signal order, such as *first, next,* and *finally*.

Additional Questions

1. What period of time does the article cover? (1769 to 1821)
2. What is the first event mentioned in the article? (the birth of Napoleon)
3. What is the last event mentioned in the article? (the death of Napoleon)
4. What event occurred the month after the Russian czar and Prussian king invaded Paris? (Napoleon gave up the throne and was exiled.)

Additional Tips for Recognizing Sequence

- **Sequence Outside the Classroom:** Challenge students to think of written materials outside the classroom that use sequence. Answers may include recipes, directions to a friend's home, posted instructions at campgrounds or other public places, the rules of most board games, and some magazine articles.
- **Sequence in the Content Areas:** Explain that understanding sequence is especially important when reading science and social studies materials. Encourage students to look for dates, times, and numbered steps when reading social studies and science books.
- **Events Out of Sequence:** When students notice that a writer has presented events out of sequence, they may wish to write down the events in their actual order to make sure they understand the material.
- **Numbered or Lettered Items:** Encourage students to look for numbered or lettered items as well as signal words. In some cases, bulleted lists are used to indicate sequence.

Cause and Effect

Introducing the Concept

Writing organized by causes and effects shows that one event took place as a result of another. However, be sure to tell students that events that follow one another in a sequence do not necessarily have a cause-and-effect relationship. Students can use these strategies to determine whether events have a cause-and-effect relationship.

Teaching Tips for Cause and Effect

- **Effects:** Suggest that students look for effects in a piece of writing by posing a question based on the title of the piece. In this example, the title poses the question for the reader: "Why Are Wood Storks Leaving Florida?"
- **Causes:** Tell students that they can also look for causes by posing a question, such as: "What causes wood storks to leave their homes?"
- **Signal Words:** Point out that when cause-and-effect writing does not contain signal words, students can use the "because test" to determine if two events have a cause-and-effect relationship. Have students link the events with the word *because*. If the sentence still makes sense, the relationship is causal.

Additional Questions

1. What signal words occur in the second paragraph? *(as a result)*

2. When high water levels cause fish and other food sources to spread out, what effect does that have on wood storks? **(They must fly long distances to find food.)**

Additional Tips

Point out to students that not all events are linked by a series of causes and effects. Sometimes a single cause can have more than one effect. Also, several causes can result in a single effect. You might use the following chart to demonstrate a single cause with multiple effects.

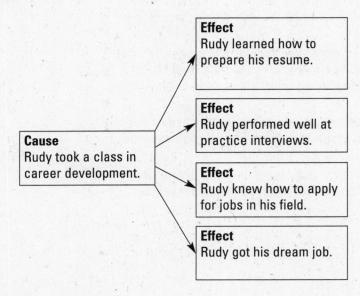

Cause
Rudy took a class in career development.

Effect
Rudy learned how to prepare his resume.

Effect
Rudy performed well at practice interviews.

Effect
Rudy knew how to apply for jobs in his field.

Effect
Rudy got his dream job.

Comparison and Contrast

Introducing the Concept

Explain that although comparisons and contrasts can appear in all types of writing, they are especially common in the following types of materials:

- social studies texts (for example, comparing the governments of different countries)
- science texts (for example, contrasting the properties of hydrogen and helium)
- charts, graphs, and tables in texts, newspapers, and magazines
- reviews of films, television programs, CDs, and Web sites

Teaching Tips for Comparison and Contrast

- **Direct statements:** Ask students to find a direct statement of similarity in the article ("Both the Pyramid of the Sun…and the Great Pyramid…measure nearly the same at their base") and a direct statement of difference ("Egyptian pyramids are taller, however"). Point out that in each case, the author alerts the reader to a similarity or difference that will be discussed. The writer then gives details about the similarity or difference so that the reader will understand the comparison or contrast.
- **Comparison Signal Words:** Give students examples of other comparison signal words and phrases, such as *additionally, neither, on the one hand, as well as,* and *likewise.*
- **Contrast Signal Words:** Mention some other words and phrases that signal a contrast, such as *yet, instead, on the other hand,* and *unlike.*

Additional Questions

1. What things are being compared and contrasted in this article? (**pyramids in Egypt and the Americas**)
2. Name three differences between Egyptian and American pyramids. (**Answers might include: Egyptian pyramids are taller; Pyramids in the Americas have receding steps; and Egyptian pyramids were built to be royal burial chambers, as opposed to those in the Americas, which were built as temple sites for sacrifices.**)
3. Does the article conclude with a comparison or a contrast? What is it? (**a comparison; the pyramids in Egypt and the Americas were both outstanding accomplishments**)

Additional Tips for Recognizing Comparisons and Contrasts

- **Lack of Signal Words:** Point out to students that sometimes a comparison or contrast can be made without using signal words. For example, the author of this article might have written: "The Great Pyramid of Egypt reaches a height of 481 feet. The tallest pyramid in the Americas is 216 feet high." Warn students to be alert for comparisons and contrasts like this that do not use signal words.
- **Multiple Items:** If students are reading a text that compares more than two people or things, suggest that they make a chart with side-by-side columns instead of a Venn diagram. A chart can help students clarify, order, and remember the multiple elements.

Argument

Introducing the Concept

Remind students that an argument is a form of persuasive writing. An effective argument states an opinion clearly and supports that opinion with various kinds of evidence ranging from facts to personal examples to expert opinions. Students need to identify the opinion in an argument and determine if the supporting details are reasonable and accurate.

Teaching Tips for the Argument

- **Signal Words:** Tell students that not all arguments will contain signal words, but looking for such words can help them determine the writer's position or opinion. Some additional examples include *accept, think, agree, propose, reject,* and *oppose.*

- **Support:** A well-supported argument will use a combination of facts, statistics, examples, observations, narratives, or expert opinions. In the example, the writer gives both sides of an issue (whether part-time jobs are helpful or hurtful to students) and presents personal observations, facts and statistics, and examples.

- **Errors in Reasoning:** Have students evaluate the argument by asking them to look closely at the evidence the writer provides to back up the conclusion. Ask: *Does the argument make sense? Is it reasonable and clearly supported with evidence?* Then have students look for errors in reasoning in the argument. In the example, the argument is supported clearly with reasons that make sense and logically support the writer's opinion.

Additional Questions

1. What is the writer's argument? (that students shouldn't work more than 20 hours a week)

2. Do you agree or disagree with the writer? Give reasons to back up your opinion. (Answers will vary. Students who agree may feel that part-time jobs interfere too much with school. Students who disagree with the writer may feel that students can get the most out of their work experience only if they work at least 20 hours a week.)

Avoiding Errors in Reasoning

Fallacious reasoning can weaken an argument and show that the writer has not given careful thought to the points he or she wants to make. Read the following examples aloud or write them on the board, and then ask students to volunteer additional examples for each error in reasoning.

- **Overgeneralizations** are statements that are too broad to be valid. *(Everyone likes the new gym equipment.)* Using words such as *some, many, few, almost,* and *sometimes* can help one avoid overgeneralizations. Caution students that although they may agree with an overgeneralization, agreeing with the statement does not make it true.

- **Circular reasoning** repeats a statement in different words rather than giving reasons to support it. *(The haunted house is scary because it makes people frightened.)*

- **Either/or statements** suggest that there are only two choices available in a situation. *(Either practice your piano lessons every day or be a terrible musician.)* Remind students that there might be other possibilities to consider in either/or statements.

Social Studies

Introducing the Concept

Explain that when students understand the special features of a social studies page, it becomes easier to find, understand, and remember key information.

Teaching Tips for the Social Studies Page

A **Titles and Headings:** Encourage students to pay attention to titles, headlines, and subheads as they preview the chapter as well as during reading. Headings can provide an outline of the lesson.

B **Vocabulary Terms:** Tell students that after reading, they should be able to define these boldfaced, italicized, or underlined terms in their own words.

C **Organizational Patterns:** Have students note the "Setting the Stage" heading, which presents the background for this lesson. Then point out the heading "Indo-Europeans Migrate." Mention that this tells the reader what the main idea of the passage is. Each subheading under this heading should offer details that support the main idea. This part of the chapter is organized by a main idea and supporting details. Other sections or chapters may use organizational patterns such as sequence, cause and effect, or comparison and contrast.

D **Visuals:** Visuals in a social studies text add information to supplement the text or summarize important concepts in an easy-to-understand manner. In the example, the table "Language Family Resemblances" shows how specific words among Indo-European languages are similar and supplements the main text with additional information.

E **Study Tips:** Many social studies books include tips and questions intended to help students assess their understanding as well as their thinking and map-reading skills. Study questions and tips are also found in some science and math textbooks.

Additional Tips for Reading in Social Studies

• **Read and review objectives:** Many textbooks include objectives or goals for each lesson. Students can check their understanding by making sure they can answer what the objective or goal asks of them.

• **Find relationships to prior reading:** Encourage students to think about how the material relates to subjects they already know or have covered before. For instance, what do they know about the migrations of other groups of people? How does their native language relate to that of the original Indo-Europeans?

• **Overcome a lack of prior knowledge:** Students will have no prior knowledge of many historical events. Suggest that students create word webs, charts, cause-and-effect charts, Venn diagrams, and other graphic organizers as they read. Knowing how facts are related makes them easier for the students to remember.

• **Use textbook aids:** Remind students to use the aids in their social studies textbook:
  —sections on how to read maps, charts, and time lines
  —tips on interpreting political cartoons
  —explanations on recognizing text structures such as sequence or comparison and contrast
  —a glossary with definitions of key or difficult words and concepts
  —a Spanish-language glossary

Science

Introducing the Concept

Many textbooks present special reading challenges for students. Science textbooks, for example, use highly specialized vocabulary and difficult, often unfamiliar concepts. They sometimes rely heavily on diagrams and illustrations. Let students know that these strategies will help them develop the special skills required for reading a science page.

Teaching Tips for the Science Page

A **Titles and Headings:** Point out to students the headings "Ocean Life" and "Marine Plant Life." The first heading appears to be a lesson title because it is in larger type than "Marine Plant Life," and it is placed at the top of the page. "Marine Plant Life," therefore, is a subhead within the lesson—it is one topic within the larger topic of ocean life.

B **Key Ideas or Objectives:** Remind students to always read the key ideas or objectives before they read the section. These will alert students to the main points covered in the material and help set a purpose for reading.

C **Boldfaced and Italicized Terms:** Point out that key vocabulary and other terms are often highlighted in the text in boldface or italic type. Tell students that after reading, they should be able to define these boldfaced or italicized terms in their own words.

D **Pictures, Diagrams, and Captions:** Let students know that figures, diagrams, and illustrations are critical to their understanding of the text. Point out that the photograph in the example provides an illustration of one of the examples described in the text. Draw students' attention to the caption.

E **Scientific Concepts:** Point out to students that although they may have no prior knowledge of the scientific concepts in a lesson, the text features and illustrations can be very useful. Ask students how the photograph helps them understand the concept of diversity in the ocean.

Additional Tips for Reading in Science

- **Keep track of references to diagrams or illustrations.** Some pages will contain several diagrams, photographs, tables, or illustrations. Readers should keep track of the figure numbers when going back and forth between the text and the pictures to avoid confusion.

- **Don't assume knowledge of familiar vocabulary terms; be sure to read definitions carefully.** Some science terms are familiar, everyday words that have a more specific meaning in science. (For example, the word *heat* is generally used to describe a feeling of warmth. In science, however, *heat* refers to a form of energy associated with the motion of atoms or molecules.) When readers encounter familiar words among science vocabulary terms, they should take care to read each term's definition and not assume that they already know what the words mean.

- **Be alert to surprising information or information that contradicts prior knowledge.** Readers may find that what they read in a science lesson contradicts what they think they know about the concept. (For example, the fact that falling objects accelerate at the same rate, no matter what their mass, is often surprising to people.) Readers should be alert to startling information or corrections of their prior knowledge, and be ready to consciously revise their understanding of the material.

Mathematics

Introducing the Concept

Although student textbooks are the primary reading material for many students—especially in math and science—they pose some special challenges for readers. In addition to scanning titles and headings, students must make sense of very specific vocabulary and symbols. Let them know that reading a math page takes some special skills, and share these helpful strategies with them.

Teaching Tips for the Math Page

A **Titles and Subheads:** Point out to students the title "The Distributive Property" and the subhead "Using the Distributive Property." The part of the lesson under the first subhead gives a tool for using the distributive property to solve multiplication problems more easily. The section under "Using an Area Model" then provides a sample problem, and the section under "Solution" gives a step-by-step method to solve it. The title and subheads outline the structure of the lesson.

B **Objectives:** Have students rewrite the lesson objectives in the form of questions. For example, "How can I use the distributive property?" and "How can I simplify expressions by combining like terms?" Seeing these goals as questions may help them see the point of the lesson.

C **Explanations:** Remind students that some explanations of mathematical concepts are complex and abstract, and they require extra concentration.

D **Special Features:** Boxed or highlighted text can contain special tips, strategies, or short summaries of important concepts. They are designed to make the material easier to understand and remember or to make the problems easier to solve.

E **Worked-Out Solutions to Problems:** Walk students through each step of the sample problem, making sure that they understand how the problem works and how the answer has been found. Underscore the idea that sample problems are the key to solving other problems in the lesson.

Additional Tips for Reading in Mathematics

- **Reread previous material:** When the text refers to material you have read earlier, be sure to reread the previous material.
- **Watch for special vocabulary:** Keep in mind that some everyday words have different meanings in mathematics. For example, the words *product, base,* and *power* have special meanings in mathematics.
- **Read directions carefully:** Carefully read directions for each exercise or problem set. In some cases, the directions may not ask you to solve a problem, but to answer questions about it.
- **Watch for boldfaced words:** Look out for boldfaced vocabulary words; be sure that you understand what each term means.
- **Read math in special ways:** Math is not always read from left to right. For example, fractions are read from top to bottom.
- **Watch for special words and symbols:** Read every word and symbol carefully to avoid mistaking words such as *hundred* for *hundredth* or 2.5 for .25.

Reading an Application

Introducing the Concept

People generally think of applications as something to fill out rather than something to read. But an application must be read carefully in order to be filled out correctly. Remind students that many applications have numerous features in common, and a few strategies can help them read the applications accurately.

Teaching Tips for the Application

A **Scan from the Top:** Encourage students to always scan something all the way through before reading it. This will give them a general idea of the application as a whole and will help them put the different sections in context once they begin to read closely.

B **Special Instructions:** Caution students not to skip over the fine print on applications; it may contain important instructions or other information.

C **Requests for Materials:** Remind students that although it's easy to overlook requests for supplementary materials, the application will not be considered complete without those materials. These may include a resume, permission from a guardian, copies of a license, proof of citizenship, or tax information.

D **Optional or Blank Sections:** Point out to students that many applications have sections that the applicant can decide whether or not to fill in. Some sections are only meant to be filled in by the people receiving the application. These are often labeled "For office use only." This section frequently appears at the bottom of the application; students should take care to notice this designation and avoid writing in these sections.

E **Difficult Words or Abbreviations:** Tell students that certain abbreviations are standard on applications, such as *NA* (not applicable), *ph.* (phone), *H. phone* (home phone), *W. phone* (work phone), or *SSN* (Social Security Number).

More Practice with Applications

Here is another form that students might read and fill out. Reproduce it for your students and ask them the following questions.

APPLICATION FOR MINISTORAGE

At Al's Ministorage, you can rent various sizes of storage compartments, depending on your storage needs. Fill out the following information completely.

NAME _____ ADDRESS _____ CITY _____ STATE _____ ZIP _____

PHONE _____ Number of boxes you wish to store _____

SIGNATURE _____ DATE _____

FOR OFFICE USE ONLY

Units _____ ID _____ Warehouse No. _____

Additional Questions

1. What is the purpose of this form? (to request storage space)

2. What information does the application ask for? (your name, address, and phone number; how much you want to store and for how long)

3. Circle the part of the form that you are not supposed to fill out. (Students should circle the section marked "For Office Use Only.")

Reading a Public Notice

Introducing the Concept

Explain that public notices can appear on billboards, flyers, and even the Internet. The sample notice alerts people of temporary road closures and detours, but the tips given for reading it can be applied to all kinds of notices.

Teaching Tips for the Public Notice

A **Title:** Point out that the title of the sample public notice, like most titles, appears at the top of the page.

B **Credit:** The sample tells you that the notice was created by the City of Sunnyvale Department of Public Works.

C **Audience and Relevance:** Encourage students to think about whether the notice applies to them or to anyone they know. Students can then concentrate on relevant messages or filter out irrelevant ones.

D **Instructions:** The instructions in this notice give the times and places that certain roads will be closed.

E **Getting More Information:** The notice includes contact information for the department, as well as a URL for a Web site with more information about the road closure locations.

Additional Questions

1. For how long will Mary Avenue and Sunnyvale Avenue be closed? (up to four days)

2. Why are Mary Avenue and Sunnyvale Avenue being temporarily closed? (for roadway improvement)

3. If you normally take Sunnyvale Avenue to get to school, what will you do to get to school on April 13? (take a detour; check the maps at the listed Web site)

Other Types of Public Notices

Other public notices that students should watch for include:

- **rules and warnings for public areas,** such as parks, pools, and community centers;
- **health and safety information,** such as road signs;
- **announcements** of community events, classes, meetings, and elections; and
- **instructions from the federal, state, or local government** describing how to register to vote, obtain a driver's license, or participate in a census.

Mention that some of these notices will use symbols or incomplete sentences, but students can examine them using many of the same techniques they used in studying the sample notice.

Reading a Web Page

Introducing the Concept

Explain that reading a Web page is different from reading a book or newspaper. In general, a Web page has smaller "chunks" of text, which can be read in any order. A Web page also provides ways to interact with the people who created or maintain the site.

Teaching Tips for the Web Page

A **Web Address:** Tell students that a Web address can give clues about the site. For instance, *http://www.pbs.org* contains the extension *.org,* which indicates a not-for-profit company or organization. Other extensions include *.gov* (government), *.edu* (educational), *.com* (commercial/business), and *.mil* (military). Remind students that they can add a URL to their browser's list of bookmarks or favorites if they want to visit the site in the future.

B **Menu Bars:** This site has a menu, or list of links within the same site, in a bar at the top of the page. Also, the browser has menu buttons at the top so that users can navigate back and forth from page to page. Have students use the Back button in the browser or the Home button if they feel they have wandered into pages that are irrelevant to the information they are seeking.

C **Links:** Links let users jump from page to page on one site or to a different site altogether. Remind students that the person who posted the main page does not always review the links for accuracy and timeliness.

D **Search Feature:** Point out the search feature in the sample page. Many sites include such features so that users can quickly find specific information within a very large site.

Glossary of Web-Related Terms

bookmark: a saved link to a Web page. If you bookmark a site, you can call it up again without having to type in the Web address.

browser: a computer program that lets you look at and interact with material on the World Wide Web. Some commonly used browsers are Netscape Navigator and Internet Explorer.

download: to copy a file from another computer. Text files, video clips, audio clips, and image files can all be downloaded from Web sites to your computer.

http: Hypertext Transfer Protocol, the computer rules for exchanging information on the Web. Web addresses include the *http* coding, a colon, and two slashes (http://).

netiquette: etiquette on the Internet. One rule of netiquette is that users should not send or post rude, abusive e-mails or comments, sometimes called "flames."

spam: unsolicited or bulk e-mail. Such mailings often offer products for sale or ask users to visit the sender's Web site.

URL: Uniform Resource Locator, or Web address, such as *http://www.mcdougallittell.com.*

Reading Technical Directions

Introducing the Concept

Examples of technical directions can be found with products such as cameras, CD players, calculators, DVD players, computers, and VCRs. Reading such directions can be challenging because of difficult vocabulary and complex instructions; however, most directions can be broken into easily recognizable parts.

Teaching Tips for the Graphing Calculator Instructions

A **Title and Headings:** Some technical directions will separate sections by using headings. Most headings will indicate the type of procedure involved in each section. For instance, the example has a heading "Zooming on the Graph," which deals solely with how to magnify a specific part of a graph.

B **Diagrams and Images:** Most sets of technical directions include some type of diagram or illustration. In the example, the instructions include illustrations of the calculator's screen as it would look to someone trying to zoom in on a graph. Tell students that it is important to study images such as these carefully and to compare them to the actual item.

C **Written Directions:** Encourage students to read the directions from the beginning to the end at least once because it provides an overall picture of what they must do.

D **Letters or Numbers:** Directions will usually provide letters or numbers to show the order in which the steps should occur. If no numbers or letters are given, tell students they may find it helpful to insert numbers themselves.

E **Warnings or Notes:** Warnings or notes are very important because they often refer the reader to another page for more information, or they may tell the reader to take certain safety precautions before attempting a step.

Additional Practice Using Technical Directions

Reproduce the directions below for your students and ask them the questions that follow.

Copying (Dubbing) Your Videotapes

1. Make sure that you make the appropriate connections between the playback unit and the recording unit.
2. Insert pre-recorded tape into the playback unit. Insert blank tape with record tab into the recording unit.
3. Press *Play*, then *Pause* when you get to the starting point on the playback unit. Press *Record*, then *Pause* on the recording unit.
4. Simultaneously press *Play* on the playback unit and *Pause* on the recording unit.
5. Simultaneously press *Stop* on both units to stop dubbing.

Warning: Unauthorized dubbing of copyrighted materials may be copyright infringement.

Questions

1. What items do you need to copy a tape? (a blank tape, a pre-recorded tape, and two VCRs with the appropriate connections)
2. Which step involves pushing buttons on both VCRs at the same time? (4 and 5)
3. What does the warning tell you? (Make sure that you only dub materials that are legal to copy.)

Product Information: Safety Guidelines

Introducing the Concept

Safety guidelines appear on many home appliances, fixtures, and electronic devices. You might tell students that smart consumers make a habit of locating and carefully reading this information before using a new item to minimize the risks of injury.

Teaching Tips for the Safety Guidelines

A **Title:** Tell students that most household appliances, fixtures, and electronic devices come with a manual that includes safety information regarding their proper use.

B **Recommendations:** Explain to students that safety guidelines usually give recommendations for the proper use for an item. Failure to follow these recommendations may result in injury or even death.

C **Hazards:** Point out that safety guidelines often tell consumers what might happen if an item is used improperly.

D **Reporting Information:** Explain to students that this section provides users with information about how to contact the U.S. Consumer Product Safety Commission (CPSC) to report dangerous items or injuries caused by an item. The CPSC uses this information to update safety information for consumers as well as to investigate potentially dangerous products.

Additional Questions

1. Why should a parent install a fence or barrier around a pool? **(to prevent accidental drownings or injuries)**

2. What precaution should be taken if a wall of the house serves as a side of the barrier? **(alarms should be installed on house doors)**

Other Types of Product Information

Students encounter many different types of product information in their daily lives. For example:

- **Labels on food products** provide consumers with nutritional information. This information lists the ingredients, amount of fat, carbohydrates, and other nutrients in a single serving of a particular food.

- **Medicine labels** tell how to take these products safely and effectively.

- **Product warranties** spell out the guarantees and other consumer protections on a product. A warranty may include covered services or parts, conditions under which the warranty will be effective, and service contact information.

- **Clothing labels** provide cleaning instructions for the item. Failure to read and follow these instructions carefully can result in discolored, shrunken clothing.

Reading a Museum Schedule

Introducing the Concept

Students may have difficulty reading a museum schedule because of the confusing lists of exhibits, dates, and times. Tell students that using these strategies will help them read most museum schedules.

Teaching Tips for the Museum Schedule

A **Title:** Remind students to make sure that they are reading the correct schedule.

B **Date or Day Labels:** Tell students that many museums have different opening and closing times and are closed at least one day a week. Museums may publish different schedules for weekdays, weekends, and holidays.

C **Expressions of Time:** Before they consult a museum schedule, students should know what exhibits they would like to see. They can then check the schedule to see what days and times the exhibits that interest them are open, and they can plan their visit accordingly.

D **Labels:** Point out the labels identifying the events on the schedule. Each event has its own place in the museum and often has its own time schedule.

E **Exceptions:** Point out that museums often change their schedules depending on the expected numbers of visitors. Summer hours might be extended, for example.

Additional Questions

1. At what times on Friday and Saturday evenings can you view an IMAX movie? (5:45, 6:45, 7:45, and 8:45)

2. Where would you go to participate in a tour of the Butterfly Habitat Garden? (Madison Dr. and 9th St.)

3. When could you visit the O. Orkin Insect Zoo? (any time during the museum's regular hours)

Other Types of Schedules

Students encounter many different kinds of schedules in their daily lives. For example:

• Bus, train, and airport schedules

• Class schedules for schools, parks, and sports centers

• Rehearsal and practice schedules for extracurricular activities

• TV scheduling and movie listings

Vocabulary
Mini-Lessons

1 Explain to students that sometimes they can figure out the meaning of an unfamiliar word or term by thinking about the context, or the surrounding words of the sentence or passage.

2 Write the following paragraph on the board and read it aloud:

> LaVonne stood back and admired her painting. She had used dark shades of blue for the ocean, grayish tones of blue for the cliffs, and pale shades of blue for the sky. *Monochromatic* paintings are difficult to produce, but the results of using a single color to represent a scene can be spectacular.

3 Then model how to use context to figure out the meaning of *monochromatic*:

MODEL

I'm not sure what monochromatic *means. I can look for context clues in the sentence this word is in and in the surrounding sentences. The phrases "dark shades of blue," "grayish tones of blue," "pale shades of blue," and "a single color" help me figure out that something* monochromatic *has only one color.*

4 Now write the following paragraph on the board and read it aloud. Have a volunteer underline the context clues that could be used to help determine the meaning of the word *phlox*.

> "How do I choose from among so many beautiful flowers?" Rhea wondered. She admired the roses, the tulips, and the lilies. Then she spotted the *phlox*. Their red, white, and purple blossoms and intense fragrance convinced Rhea. "A bunch of those, please," she told the clerk, pointing to the fluffy, brilliant blooms.

5 Point out to students that in the example above, a type of clue known as **details from general context** helped them figure out the meaning of *phlox*. Encourage students to use this strategy throughout the year, along with other common types of context clues:

Definition and Restatement

Becky's older friend had **counseled** her, advising her on which classes to take her sophomore year.

(The word *advise* is a synonym that restates the meaning of the word *counsel*.)

Example

I looked through nature magazines to find photos of various **marsupials,** including kangaroos, wombats, and opossums.

(*Kangaroos* and *wombats* are examples of marsupials.)

Comparison and Contrast

Unlike **deciduous** trees, evergreens do not lose their leaves at the end of a growing season.

(The contrast with evergreens helps define deciduous trees as "trees that shed their foliage at the end of the growing season.")

1 Explain to students that sometimes they can figure out the meaning of an unfamiliar word by thinking about the meanings of the word parts it contains.

2 Write the word *inconsequential* on the board and read it aloud. Model how to use the base word and affixes to figure out the meaning of the word.

MODEL

I'm not sure what inconsequential *means. I can try breaking the word into parts. I see the prefix* in-, *which usually means "not." I see that the main part of the word looks like a word I know,* consequence, *which means "something that happens as a result of something else." I also see the suffix* -ial, *which usually means "in a way that is." So* inconsequential *must refer to something that has little or no effect on anything else.*

3 Share with students the following list of commonly-used prefixes and suffixes.

Prefixes
ab- (away from, off)
ad- (to)
de- (undo, off)
dis- (opposite)
ex- (out)
in- (with, not)
mis- (wrongly, bad)
pre- (before)
pro- (ahead of)
re- (back, again)
retro- (backward)
sub- (under)
trans- (across)
un- (not)

Suffixes
-al (of)
-ate (to cause to become)
-er (more)
-est (most)
-ify (make)
-ize (to cause to become)
-less (without)
-let (little)
-ly (having the quality of)
-ment (state, quality, act)
-ness (state, quality)
-ory (place where)
-tion or -ion (state of act of being)

4 As the year progresses, you may wish to review this strategy. The following list provides additional words for you and your students to model.

Have volunteers draw vertical lines between the word parts, and ask them to explain how to use those parts to figure out the meaning of each word.

inalienable	nonconformist
disassemble	mismanagement
preapproval	disillusioned
substandard	reconstruction
retroactively	inappropriateness

1 Explain to students that sometimes they can figure out the meaning of an unfamiliar word by thinking about its relationship to words they know that look similar or that share a common root. You may want to explain that a **root** is a word part that must be combined with other word parts, such as prefixes or suffixes, in order to form a word.

2 Write the word *cohabit* on the board and read it aloud. Model how to use similar words to figure out its meaning.

MODEL

I've never seen the word cohabit *before, but I have seen the word* habitat. *I know that a habitat is an environment a person or animal lives in. I know the word part* co- *often means "together," as in the word* coexist. *I think* cohabit *means "live together in a place."*

3 Now write the following chart on the board:

Root	Meaning
spec	"see"
photo	"light"
aud	"hear"
therm	"heat"

4 Have volunteers use the information in the chart as they try to define the words below. Make sure they explain the process they used to figure out the meaning of each word.

spectacles	audience
inspect	auditorium
spectator	audible
photograph	thermometer
telephoto	thermal
photosynthesis	thermos

5 As the year progresses, you may wish to review this strategy. The following chart provides you with additional words, roots, and meanings.

Root	Meaning	Examples
mon	"advise; warn"	admonish, monitor, admonition
mut	"change; interchange"	commute, mutation, immutable
soph	"wise"	sophisticated, philosopher
hydro	"water"	hydrant, dehydrated, hydroelectric

1 Explain to students that sometimes they can figure out an unfamiliar word by using what they know about the sounds that letters stand for. Point out that sometimes certain letters or letter patterns can stand for several sounds and that if one sound they try does not result in a familiar word, they should try another sound.

2 Then model the process:

MODEL

When I was reading, I came to this word (write philosophy *on the board) but wasn't sure how to pronounce it. At first I said "fī′lō-sō′fē," but that didn't make sense. Then I remembered that the letter "i" often has the short sound when it appears between consonants, as does the letter "o." I tried pronouncing it "fĭ lŏ′-sə′fē." That sounds right.*

3 Now write the following words on the board:

concede	receptive
infamous	financier
circuitous	

Have volunteers read each word aloud, explaining how one might use familiar letter patterns and the sounds that letters stand for to decode it.

4 As the year progresses, you may wish to review this strategy. The following list provides you with additional words to model or have students model:

torrential	symmetrical
controversial	impartiality
meandering	enviable
bicuspid	specialize
epidemic	orchestral

Comprehension
Mini-Lessons

with Graphic Organizers

1 Read this sentence aloud:

> Marnie put on her jacket after the wind grew stronger.

Ask students which event caused the other event to happen (*The wind growing stronger caused Marnie to put on her jacket*). Introduce the concept of cause and effect by writing the following points on the board and reading them aloud to students:

- A **cause** is an action or event that makes something else happen.

- An **effect** is what happens because of a certain action or event.

- Sometimes writers use signal words or phrases such as *because, since,* and *as a result* to indicate causes and their effects. Other times, readers must figure out causes and effects on their own.

2 For reference, write on the board the signal words and phrases listed above. Then duplicate the following passage and read it aloud:

> Marnie cheered when Pam stole the soccer ball from the other team. Marnie didn't really enjoy sports, but seeing her friend play well made her excited. Suddenly, another player on Pam's team twisted her ankle and had to be helped from the field. Since the team only had eleven players, it looked as if they'd have to play short-

handed. Then Pam suggested that Marnie play. At first, Marnie resisted. "No way!" she yelled. When she saw how disappointed her friend looked, however, Marnie decided to give it a try. She had so much fun playing that after the game she asked Pam if she could join the team.

3 Duplicate and distribute the Cause-and-Effect Chart on page 93. Work with students to fill in the first cause-effect relationship. Then have students complete the chart and share what they listed. Possible responses are shown below.

4 Point out to students that a single cause can result in more than one effect, as in the case of the first cause listed in the chart below. Also note that several causes can lead to a single effect. (Charts for a single cause with multiple effects and multiple causes with a single effect are available on page 94 of this Guide.)

5 Explain to students that sometimes a series of events are linked in a cause-and-effect chain in which one event causes another, which—in turn—causes another, and so on. (A Cause-and-Effect Chain is available on page 95 of this Guide.)

6 Make additional copies of the charts found on pages 93–95 and have them available for students to use at appropriate times during the year.

Cause	→	Effect(s)
Pam steals the ball from the other team.	→	Marnie cheers.
Marnie sees Pam play well.	→	Marnie becomes excited about the game.
One of Pam's team members twists her ankle.	→	The player is helped off the field. Pam asks Marnie if she will play.
Marnie sees how disappointed Pam is after Marnie refuses to play.	→	Marnie decides to play.
Marnie has fun playing.	→	She asks Pam if she can join the team.

Cause-and-Effect Chart

Name _____ Date _____

Cause	→	Effect(s)

Name _____ Date _____

Single Cause with Multiple Effects

Multiple Causes with Single Effect

Name _____ Date _____

Cause-and-Effect Chain

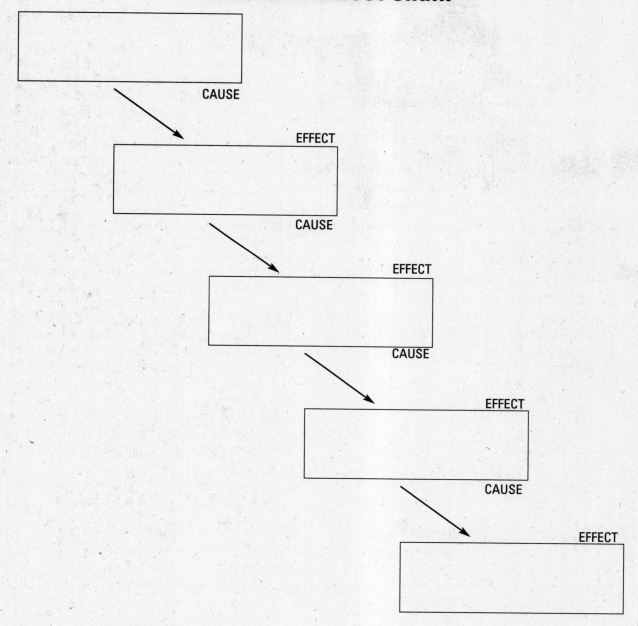

1 Read this paragraph aloud:

Lena and Anna love to ride bicycles long distances. The sisters have just bought new bikes with money they saved from their jobs. Lena enjoys riding her mountain bike on dirt trails near their home. Anna likes to take her road bike for long rides on winding country roads.

Ask students how Lena and Anna are alike. (*They both love to ride bicycles long distances. Both bought bikes with money earned on jobs.*) Have them tell how the sisters are different. (*Lena rides a mountain bike on dirt trails. Anna prefers to use a road bike on winding country roads.*) Introduce the concept of compare and contrast by writing the following points on the board and reading them aloud to students:

- **Comparing** means to think about the ways in which two people or two things are alike.

- Writers sometimes make comparisons by using words or phrases such as *both, same, like, also, similarly,* and *too.*

- **Contrasting** means to think about the ways in which two people or two things are different.

- Writers sometimes make contrasts by using words or phrases such as *but, although, instead, yet, even though, however,* and *on the other hand.*

2 For reference, write on the board the words and phrases listed above. Explain, however, that sometimes there are no signal words given; then readers need to infer what is being compared or contrasted from the details provided. Then duplicate the following paragraph and read it aloud:

All bicycles have a frame, handlebars, wheels, and pedals. However, each type of bike has features that make it different from other types. Mountain bikes are designed for riding on rough terrain, such as rocky trails and dirt roads. They have flat handlebars, sturdy frames, and wide, knobby tires. Some mountain bikes even have front and rear suspension systems to minimize the impact of bumps. Road bikes, on the other hand, are designed for riding on smooth pavement. They typically have curved handlebars, light frames, and thin tires.

3 Duplicate and distribute the Venn diagram on page 97. Have students fill in the diagram, using information in the paragraph along with what they already know to compare and contrast cherries and apples.

4 Have volunteers share the information in their diagrams by first describing the similarities between the two types of fruit and then describing the differences. Possible responses are shown below

5 Make additional copies of the Venn diagram and have them available for students to use at appropriate times during the year.

Mountain Bikes
for riding on rocky trails and dirt roads
flat handlebars
sturdy frames
wide, knobby tires
some have suspension system

Both
have frames
have handlebars
have wheels and pedals

Road Bikes
for riding on smooth pavement
curved handlebars
light frames
thin tires

Venn Diagram

Name _____ Date _____

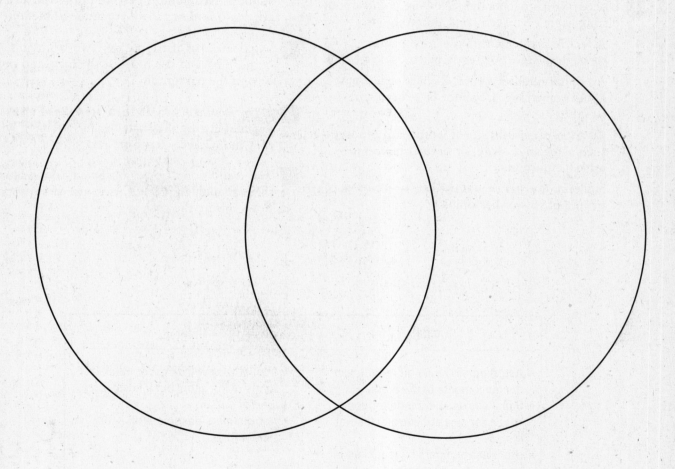

1 Read this paragraph aloud:

> **Astronomy is the study of the objects that make up the universe. I think it is the most interesting field of science. It is also one of the oldest sciences.**

Ask students to identify the writer's opinion about astronomy (*It is the most interesting field of science*). Have students tell one fact the writer states about astronomy (*It is one of the oldest sciences*).

2 Discuss with students the following points about distinguishing between facts and opinions:

- A **fact** is a statement that can be proven through observation, experience, and research.

- An **opinion** tells a writer's beliefs or feelings about something. It cannot be proven true or false.

- A writer often uses signal words and phrases such as *believe, think,* or *in my opinion* to indicate an opinion.

- Sometimes a writer will use one or more facts to support his or her opinion.

3 For reference, write on the board the signal words and phrases listed in the third bulleted item. Then duplicate the following paragraph and read it aloud:

> **Astronomers study more than just the movement of the stars. Some monitor deep space for signs of extraterrestrial life. This is undeniably a worth pursuit, though I doubt they will discover other forms of life soon. Other astronomers have looked for signs of life on planets in our solar system. Mars has been the focus of several recent studies. Astronomers deserve praise for their efforts to find out if we are alone in the universe.**

4 Duplicate and distribute the Two-Column Chart on page 99 and use it to list the facts and opinions in the paragraph.

5 Have volunteers share their completed charts, explaining why they listed each statement where they did. Correct responses are shown below.

6 Make additional copies of the chart and have them available for students to use at appropriate times during the year.

Fact	Opinion
• Astronomers study more than just the movements of the stars. • Some astronomers monitor deep space for signs of extraterrestrial life. • Other astronomers have looked for signs of life on planets in our solar system. • Mars has been the focus of several recent studies.	• I doubt they will discover other forms of life soon, but it is still a worthy pursuit. • Astronomers deserve praise for their efforts.

Two-Column Chart

Name _____ Date _____

1 Read this paragraph aloud:

Ice climbers use a variety of specialized equipment. Even the most skilled climbers rely on axes, hammers, ice screws, and ropes to help them ascend icy surfaces. Crampons, sets of sharp spikes that clamp onto hiking boots, make it possible to gain a foothold on nearly any frozen surface—even the vertical ice of a frozen waterfall.

2 Ask students what this paragraph's most important point is (*Ice climbers use a variety of specialized equipment*).

3 Discuss the following points about main ideas and details:

- A **main idea** is the central or most important point a writer tries to make in a paragraph or passage.
- **Supporting details** provide information about the main idea.
- Sometimes the main idea will appear as a sentence in a paragraph or passage. Other times readers must figure out the main idea by thinking about the details.

4 Duplicate or write the following paragraph on the board and read it aloud:

In the early days of ice climbing, climbers ascended frozen slopes by hacking out steps and handholds with a woodchopper's ax. This practice was both physically grueling and extremely dangerous, and it had its limitations. Even the most skillful climbers never attempted to climb vertical ice. Then, in 1966, a climber named Yvon Chouinard designed an ice ax that had a curve on its pick. This innovation allowed climbers to drive their axes more deeply into the ice, giving them a more solid hold. Other innovations in gear, including sophisticated ice screws, hooks, helmets, and climbing ropes, have made ice climbing both safer and more popular. Today, the most daring and elite group of ice climbers tackle vertical ice slopes and even frozen waterfalls.

5 Duplicate and distribute the Two-Column Chart on page 99. Have students work in pairs to fill in the chart with the main ideas and details of both paragraphs. Possible responses are shown below. A Main Idea Web is also available on page 101 of this Guide.

6 Make additional copies of the charts on pages 99 and 101 and have them available for students to use at appropriate times during the year.

Main Idea	Details
More sophisticated ice climbing gear has helped advance the sport of ice climbing.	• The curved ice pick designed in 1966 allows climbers to get a better hold on ice. • Ice screws, hooks, helmets, and climbing ropes have made ice climbing safer and more popular. • Ice climbers can tackle vertical slopes and frozen waterfalls with the help of their sophisticated gear.

Main Idea Web

Name _____ Date _____

Detail:

Detail:

Main Idea:

Detail:

Detail:

1 Read this paragraph aloud:

Noelle had just moved the last of her luggage out to the front porch when she heard the horn of the airport shuttle. She slipped on her knapsack, checked to see that she had her tickets and other necessary papers, and then locked the door behind her.

Ask students whether the writer tells where Noelle is going. (*No.*) Have them explain where they think she is going. (*Possible responses: She is going to the airport. She is going somewhere by airplane.*)

2 Discuss with students the following points about making inferences:

- It is not possible for writers to include every detail about what is happening in a work of literature.

- Often, writers purposely choose to hint at details rather state them; this can add meaning and suspense for the reader.

- Readers must know how to make inferences. **Inferences** are logical guesses based on clues in the text and on your own knowledge and common sense.

3 Duplicate the following passage and read it aloud:

The shuttle dropped Noelle off at the international terminal. While checking her bags, she showed the airline agent her heavily-used passport. Once aboard the jet, Noelle thought about how this trip would be different from her usual travels; this time she had no need for a laptop computer and had no appointment book to study. She opened her knapsack and took out a piece of paper. On it was the name and address of the resort where she would be staying. She smiled as she sank back into her seat.

4 Duplicate and distribute the Inference/Judgment Chart on page 104. Work with students to fill in the first row. Then have them add to the chart any other inferences they make about the story. Sample responses are shown below.

5 Make additional copies of the chart and have them available for students to use at appropriate times during the year.

Selection Information	+	What I Know	=	My Inference
Noelle is dropped off at the international terminal.	+	Flights to foreign countries often leave from the international terminal.	=	Noelle is traveling to a foreign country.
Noelle has used her passport a lot.	+	Passports get used when people visit foreign countries.	=	Noelle has made many visits to foreign countries.
Noelle doesn't need a laptop computer or appointment book.	+	People sometimes bring laptop computers and appointment books on business trips.	=	Noelle is not going on a business trip.
Noelle smiles after looking at the name and address of the resort where she would be staying.	+	People go to resorts for vacations.	=	Noelle is going on a vacation.

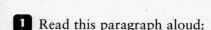

1 Read this paragraph aloud:

Lisa had lost track of the time. She was about to play another video game when she suddenly remembered to look at her watch. It was 2:45. "Oh, no! My job interview is at 3:00!" she exclaimed. She ran out of the arcade and looked for a taxi.

Ask students: *Do you think Lisa is a responsible person? Explain your answer. (Possible response: No. If she were a responsible person, she would have made sure she had enough time to get to the interview.)*

2 Point out to students that in answering the question above, they made a judgment. Discuss with students the following points about making judgments:

- When you **make judgments,** you make decisions about what is accurate or inaccurate, true or false, valid or invalid, right or wrong—according to certain standards or criteria.

- In order to make judgments, you use clues from the selection along with your own opinions and information you already know.

- You can make judgments about story characters in fiction and about a writer's opinions in nonfiction.

3 Write the following passage on the board and read it aloud:

While scanning the street for a taxi, Lisa saw a man who had obviously been waiting for a taxi for quite a while. He, too, seemed in a hurry. When a taxi finally pulled up, they both ran toward it. Lisa was closer and got in first. The man pleaded, "Please, I'll miss my train." Lisa shook her head. "Too bad. I'm in a hurry, too." She closed the door and gave directions to the driver.

The driver, however, had an idea. "Sir, this woman's stop is on the way to the train station. I can drop her off first and then take you there. That is, if *she* doesn't mind." The driver looked directly at Lisa, awaiting her response. Suddenly, Lisa felt ashamed about the way she'd been acting. She apologized to the man and told him he could share her taxi.

4 Duplicate and distribute the Inference/Judgment Chart on page 104. Work with students to fill in the first row. Then have them add to the chart any other judgments they make about the characters. Ask volunteers to explain the judgments they made. Sample responses are shown below.

5 Make additional copies of the chart and have them available for students to use at appropriate times during the year.

Selection Information	+	What I Know	=	My Inference
Lisa takes the cab even though the man had been waiting longer.	+	People should wait their turn.	=	Lisa is wrong to take the cab.
The man says he'll miss his train. Lisa said, "Too bad."	+	People should be polite to others and helpful when possible.	=	Lisa is being thoughtless and rude.
The cab driver finds a way to solve the problem.	+	People who help strangers are kind and thoughtful.	=	The driver is smart and thoughtful.
Lisa feels ashamed, apologizes, and lets the man share the taxi.	+	Decent people are willing to admit their mistakes and try to make up for them.	=	Lisa is a decent person who is just in a hurry.

Inference / Judgment Chart

Name _____ Date _____

Selection Information	+	My Opinion/ What I Know	=	My Inference/ My Judgment
	+		=	
	+		=	
	+		=	
	+		=	

1 Read this paragraph aloud:

> The wind howled as the storm moved closer to the house. "It's getting worse," I said in a voice loud enough to be heard above the rattling windows. Suddenly, lightning flashed and the lights went out. A loud thud sounded at the door. "Who is it?" yelled my cousin Richie. No one answered. Richie and I stared at each other, speechless.

Ask students where and when this story takes place (*in a house on a stormy night*). Have them tell who the story is about (*the narrator and the narrator's cousin Richie*). Ask students what the story problem is (*The characters don't know who is at their door*).

2 Discuss with students the following elements of a narrative:

- The **setting** is when and where a story takes place.

- **Characters** are the people in a story. The main character is the person who the story is mostly about.

- Sometimes characters can be animals or imaginary creatures.

- The **plot** is the series of events that happen in a story. Most stories have a problem, or **conflict,** that the main character must try to resolve. The **resolution** is the solution to the problem.

3 Continue the story above by duplicating the following passage and reading it aloud:

> I peeked out the front window but saw no one. As I turned to tell Richie that there was nothing there, we heard a scraping sound at the door. This time I asked, "Who is it?" Again, there was no answer. Then Richie went to the door and yelled, "What's going on here?" As he turned the knob, the door flew open. When we saw the huge fallen pine branch resting in the doorway, we both breathed a sigh of relief.

4 Duplicate and distribute the Story Map on page 106. Work with students to fill in the setting and characters. Then have them complete the plot portion of the map. Possible responses are below.

5 Make additional copies of the story map and have them available for students to use at appropriate times during the year.

Setting: a house on a stormy night	**Characters:** the narrator and the narrator's cousin Richie

Plot

Problem: The characters don't know who is banging on their door.

Events:
1 The narrator looks out the front window but doesn't see anyone.
2 The characters hear a scraping sound at the door.
3 The narrator asks, "Who is it?" but again, no one answers.
4 Cousin Richie decides to open the door.

Resolution: The characters discover that a fallen tree branch has caused the sounds.

Story Map

Name _____ Date _____

Setting:

Characters:

Plot

Conflict:

Events:

1

2

3

4

Resolution:

1 Read this paragraph aloud:

> Jorge entered his last name, "Vargas," in the Internet search window. He pressed the "Enter" key. Moments later, links to twenty-five websites appeared on the screen.

Ask students what happened first, next, and last (*First, Jorge entered his name in the Internet search window. Next, he pressed the "Enter" key. Then links to twenty-five websites appeared on the screen.*)

2 Discuss with students the following points about sequence:

- The **sequence** of events is the order in which things happen.
- Writers sometimes use words such as *first, next, after,* and *then* to indicate the order in which events occur.
- Words, phrases, or dates that tell when something is happening can also help readers figure out the sequence of events.

3 Duplicate the following passage and read it aloud:

> Earlier in the day, Jorge's history teacher had given the class an unusual assignment: Jorge and his classmates were to use the Internet to find out about someone interesting who shares the same last name. Jorge eagerly scanned the various websites that he'd uncovered. One was about an important criminal case now in the courts. Jorge remembered that last week he'd read something about the case in the newspaper. Jorge clicked on the link. On screen appeared an article revealing that the defendant had been found not guilty. The lead defense attorney was named Jorge Vargas!

4 Duplicate and distribute the Sequence/Flow Chart on page 108. Work with students to fill in the first event. Point out that sometimes a story begins in the present and then goes back in time to tell about things that happened beforehand. Then have students complete the chart. Ask for volunteers to share what they filled in. Possible responses are shown in the chart below.

5 Make additional copies of the chart and have them available for students to use at appropriate times during the year.

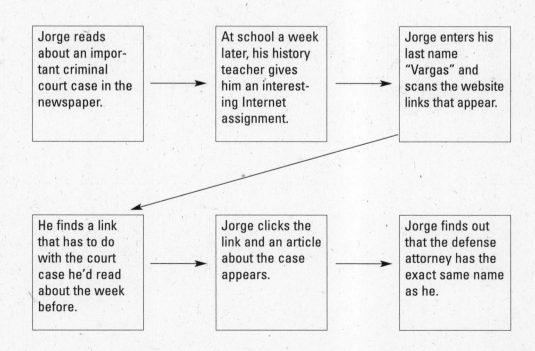

Jorge reads about an important criminal court case in the newspaper.	At school a week later, his history teacher gives him an interesting Internet assignment.	Jorge enters his last name "Vargas" and scans the website links that appear.
He finds a link that has to do with the court case he'd read about the week before.	Jorge clicks the link and an article about the case appears.	Jorge finds out that the defense attorney has the exact same name as he.

Sequence/Flow Chart

Name _____ Date _____

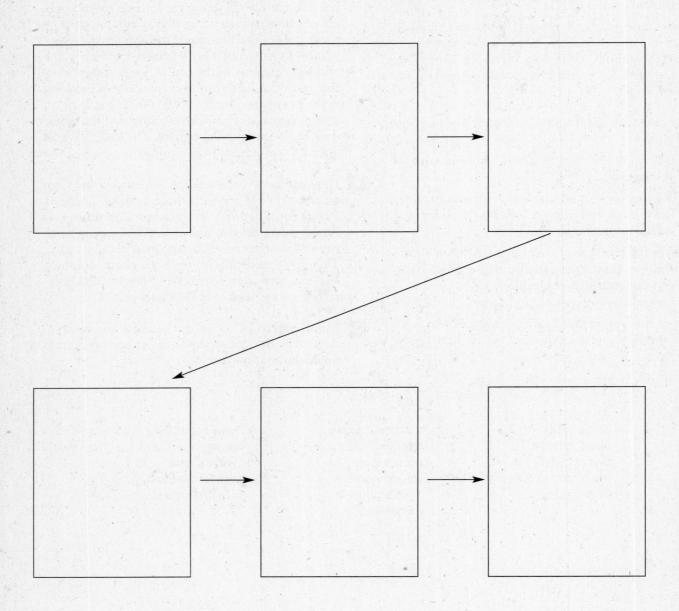

1 Read this paragraph aloud:

Many farmers advocate the use of pesticides as an efficient, effective way of controlling insects, bacteria, and other pests that threaten crops. Many environmentalists, on the other hand, warn that these chemicals can upset the world's natural ecological balance.

Point out to students that the writer of this paragraph probably used several sources of information in order to become familiar with both sides of the issue of pesticides versus the environment. Discuss the fact that when writing a term paper or article, it is usually necessary to take information from several sources and then combine, or synthesize, that information. Also explain that when reading, it is sometimes necessary to synthesize information from different parts of a selection.

2 Discuss with students the following points about synthesizing:

- When you **synthesize** while reading, you combine information from different parts of a selection to deepen your understanding.

- When you come upon new information, you should think about how it relates to information you have already come across or gathered.

3 Duplicate the following quotations and statements, plus a copy of the Synthesis Diagram on page 110. Inform students that these quotations were gathered by a student whose purpose was to determine how noted researcher-author Rachel Carson helped change people's perceptions about the use of pesticides. Ask them to identify the statement that is the best synthesis of the quotations (*the second statement*).

Quotations

If we are going to live so intimately with these chemicals—eating them, drinking them, taking them into the very marrow of our bones—we had better know something about their nature and their power.
—Rachel Carson, *Silent Spring*

In 1962 marine biologist Rachel Carson, with her eloquent book *Silent Spring,* aroused the English-reading world to the destructive effects of man-made pesticides and started a controversy that is still hotly debated.
—Barbara Tufty, *The Women's Book of*

World Records and Achievements
[Carson's] arguments helped lead to restrictions on the use of pesticides in many parts of the world.

Statements

—*The World Book Encyclopedia*
1. Rachel Carson, a marine biologist, wrote an eloquent book called *Silent Spring,* which was read by many people.

2. Rachel Carson's book *Silent Spring* sparked a debate over pesticides that led to the limiting of their use in many places.

3. Rachel Carson was very interested in creatures of the natural world, particularly marine life.

4 Make additional copies of the diagram and have them available for students to use at appropriate times during the year.

Synthesis Diagram

Name _____ Date _____

First Source

Second Source

Third Source

1 Read this paragraph aloud:

Julie worked for hours, carefully addressing each invitation in rich black ink. Satisfied with her work, she left the envelopes to dry. When she returned, little paw prints formed a maze on the once beautiful envelopes. Her cat Slick meowed and rubbed against her leg.

Ask students to make a guess about what happened (*Julie's cat walked across the invitations while the ink was still wet*). Have them guess what will happen next (*Julie will get angry at her cat and have to start over with the invitations*).

- When you **predict**, you try to figure out what will happen next.

- To make a prediction, you must combine selection clues plus your own knowledge and experience to make a reasonable guess.

- Good readers make and revise predictions as they read. Sometimes, they don't even realize they're doing it.

- Sometimes you must first make an inference about what is happening before you make a prediction about will happen next.

2 Duplicate the following passage and tell students that they should listen carefully as you prepare to read it aloud. Explain that by the end of the passage, they should be ready to infer what has happened and to predict what will happen next.

Jon slammed his locker and sauntered down the hall. He had big plans for the weekend, and he couldn't wait to see Jenny. At the end of the corridor he spotted her—smiling and laughing with his ex-friend Mike. Jon stopped abruptly. Then he strode the other way, fists clenching his books so tight that his knuckles turned white. Jon's teammates saluted him as he walked by, but Jon never heard them. He had to get outside.

3 Duplicate and distribute the Predicting Chart on page 112. Have students work in pairs to complete the chart, inferring what has happened and predicting what will happen next. Remind them that the inference and prediction they come up with should be based on clues that the passage provides, plus their own knowledge and experience. Possible responses are shown below.

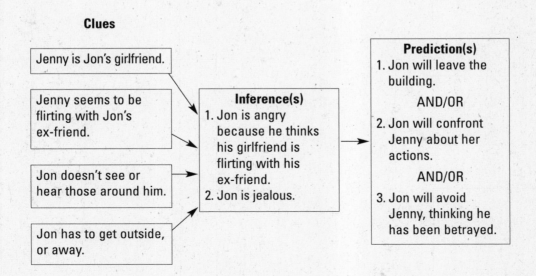

Clues

Jenny is Jon's girlfriend.

Jenny seems to be flirting with Jon's ex-friend.

Jon doesn't see or hear those around him.

Jon has to get outside, or away.

Inference(s)
1. Jon is angry because he thinks his girlfriend is flirting with his ex-friend.
2. Jon is jealous.

Prediction(s)
1. Jon will leave the building.

AND/OR

2. Jon will confront Jenny about her actions.

AND/OR

3. Jon will avoid Jenny, thinking he has been betrayed.

Name _____ Date _____

Clues

Inferences

Prediction(s)

Additional Graphic Organizers

How to Use Additional Graphic Organizers

On the following pages you will find additional graphic organizers that can be used in a number of different situations to help students comprehend and monitor what they read. Consult the chart below to decide how and when to use each graphic organizer.

Graphic Organizer	Purpose	When and How to Use
K-W-L Chart (page 116)	To help students comprehend a nonfiction selection	*Before Reading:* 1. Identify the topic for students. 2. Have students write what they already **know** about it in the *K* column. 3. Have them write what they **want** to find out in the *W* column. *During Reading:* 4. Have students record what they **learn** in the *L* column.
Q & A Notetaking Chart (page 117)	To help student memorize key facts in a nonfiction selection	*During Reading:* 1. Tell students that as they read they should turn each heading or main idea into a question and write it in column 1. *After Reading:* 2. Have students answer the questions they wrote without opening their books. 3. Have students reread the selection to find answers to any questions they could not answer.
Concept Web (page 118)	To guide students to think of related words or concepts	*Before Reading:* Have students form small groups. List key concepts or vocabulary words on the board. Ask students to discuss meanings, fill out a web for each concept or word by writing it in the center of the web, and then write related terms in the ovals around the center.
Reflection Chart (page 119)	To help students stop and think about key points or events	*During Reading:* 1. Ask students to note important or interesting passages in the left column. 2. Have them record in the right column their thoughts about each passage noted.
Event Log (page 120)	To help students keep track of story events	*During Reading:* 1. Have students list each event as they read about it. *After Reading:* 2. Students should use the list to give an oral retelling or summary of the selection.

Graphic Organizer	Purpose	When and How to Use
Story Frames (page 121)	To help students summarize story events	*After Reading:* 1. Ask students to draw sketches of key events in the selection. 2. Have them use the sketches to retell the selection orally.
Plot Diagram (page 122)	To help students classify events as being part of the exposition, rising action, climax, or falling action	*After Reading:* 1. Review the terms *exposition, rising action, climax,* and *falling action* with students. 2. Encourage students to use the diagram to list the events that form each of these plot phases.
Character Profile Chart (page 123)	To help students identify character attributes	*During or After Reading:* Have students write the character's name at the center and then list qualities and behaviors that exemplify these qualities in the surrounding boxes.
New Word Diagram (page 124)	To help students understand new vocabulary they encounter	*During or After Reading:* 1. Have students write a new word in the box at the top of the diagram. 2. Encourage them to think of—or look in the dictionary for—synonyms and antonyms of the word and record them in the appropriate boxes. 3. Ask students to think of real people or characters they've read about who they associate with the concept of the word. They can then add the names to the diagram.
Reading Log (page 125)	To encourage students to keep track of what they read	*After Reading:* Have students record on this form each selection they read during the year. Review the form periodically with students.

K-W-L Chart

Name _____ Date _____

Topic: _____

K What I Know	W What I Want to Find Out	L What I Learn

Q & A Notetaking

Name _____ Date _____

Turn the Heading or Main Idea of Each Passage into a Question	Write a Detailed Answer Here
1.	
2.	
3.	
4.	
5.	
6.	
7.	

Concept Web

Name _____ Date _____

Reflection Chart

Name _____ Date _____

Quotation or Paraphrase from Text (include page number)	Thoughts About It

Event Log

Name _____ Date _____

Event 1
Event 2
Event 3
Event 4
Event 5
Event 6
Event 7
Event 8
Event 9
Event 10

Name _____ Date _____

Plot Diagram

Climax

_____
_____
_____
_____
_____
_____

Rising Action

_____
_____
_____
_____
_____
_____

Falling Action

_____
_____
_____
_____
_____

Exposition

_____
_____
_____
_____
_____
_____

Character Profile Chart

Name _____ Date _____

Quality: _____
Example: _____
_____
_____
_____

Quality: _____
Example: _____
_____
_____
_____

Quality: _____
Example: _____
_____
_____
_____

_____

Character's Name

Quality: _____
Example: _____
_____
_____
_____

Quality: _____
Example: _____
_____
_____
_____

Quality: _____
Example: _____
_____
_____
_____

New Word Diagram

Name _____ Date _____

```
┌─────────────────────────────────────────────────┐
│ Word:                                           │
│                                                 │
│                                                 │
│                                                 │
└─────────────────────────────────────────────────┘
```

```
┌───────────────────────┐          ┌───────────────────────┐
│ Synonyms:             │          │ Antonyms:             │
│                       │          │                       │
│                       │          │                       │
│                       │          │                       │
│                       │          │                       │
│                       │          │                       │
│                       │          │                       │
└───────────────────────┘          └───────────────────────┘
```

```
┌─────────────────────────────────────────────────┐
│ People or Characters I Associate with the Word:  │
│                                                 │
│                                                 │
│                                                 │
└─────────────────────────────────────────────────┘
```

Reading Log

Name _____ Date _____

Selection Title	Type of Literature	Date Finished	Reactions

Answer Key

This key answers all questions asked in the *InterActive Reader Plus*, the *InterActive Reader Plus with Additional Support*, and the *InterActive Reader Plus for English Learners*. Pause & Reflect answers have parenthetical notes *(Plus, AS, or EL)* as necessary to indicate the books to which they apply.

Harrison Bergeron, page 2
Connect to Your Life, page 3
Sample response: I have a great memory. If I couldn't use it, my life would be a lot different and more difficult. I wouldn't do as well in school or remember phone numbers and birthdays as well. My life would be more complicated and because my school work would be harder, I might do as well and so might have a less-interesting job later in life.

Key to the Story, page 3
Sample response: fairness, justice, same, freedom

Reading Check, page 6
The two ballerinas that fell were the only two intelligent enough to have the same sound handicap that George has, so when he hears the "doozy," so do they.

Pause & Reflect, page 7
1. Possible answers include: Everybody is expected to be like everyone else. Government laws force those that are naturally more gifted to wear handicaps. Nobody can share their true feelings.
2. George's handicap makes it hard for him to think about anything for very long. Hazel does not have a good memory. Her mind seems to forget past events and associations.
3. George believes that everyone should be exactly like everyone else and that competition is bad.

Reading Check, page 8
Someone who is probably not very intelligent, or who has a sound handicap, has been assigned to run the equipment. This had led to incompetence.

Pause & Reflect, page 9
1. Seven feet tall; fourteen years old; wearing a multitude of handicaps, including a pair of earphones, thick glasses with wavy lenses, a red rubber ball clown nose, black caps on his teeth, and three hundred pounds of scrap metal. Harrison has escaped from jail and is breaking into the television station.
2. Possible predictions: Harrison will break out of his handicaps and escape. Harrison will take over the television station.

Read Aloud, page 9
Harrison plans to get rid of his handicaps, take over the world, and become Emperor.

Pause & Reflect, page 11
1. Some students may feel sad that Harrison and the ballerina died and that George and Hazel are not even aware of his death. Others may find the absurdity of the situation amusing. Still others may be slightly angered by Harrison's fate and the life his father continues to lead.
2. Students should circle lines 245–246 ("She fired twice . . . hit the floor"). Because Diana Moon Glampers is the Handicapper General and ultimate law enforcer, she cannot allow anyone to break the law in such a blatant way, especially in full view of the people.

3. Harrison's death had almost no impact on his parents. His mother experiences a moment of sadness, but does not know why. His father may never know that his son was killed.

Challenge, page 11
Students should circle the following kinds of sentences: "George was toying . . . his thoughts" (lines 44–52), "Harrison tore . . . five thousand pounds" (lines 192–294), "He flung away . . . god of thunder" (200–201), and "And then neutralizing . . . long time." (240–242). Vonnegut uses humor and exaggeration to show how the good intentions of society can go awry as a result of too much government control.

Active Reading SkillBuilder, page 12
Sample responses are provided.
Clue: "They really weren't very good—no better than anybody else would have been, anyway."
Inference: Everyone in this society was mediocre and bland.
Clue: "And she had to apologize at once for her voice, which was a very unfair voice for a woman to use."
Inference: To excel at anything was shameful and unfair.
Clue: "The music began. It was normal at first—cheap, silly, false."
Inference: All pleasure in life was reduced to the ridiculous.
Clue: "'You can say that again,' said George." (Hazel says her sentence again.)
Inference: There was no higher-level thinking; only literal, flat interpretation.

Literary Analysis SkillBuilder, page 13
To complete the chart on page 13, students might add the following kinds of clues: "George Bergeron correctly identified . . . in his head" (lines 171–176) and "Hazel turned to comment . . . a can of beer" (lines 251–252); "And then, neutralizing . . . hit the floor" (lines 240–246); and "You've been crying . . . Forget sad things" (lines 255–261). These clues would support the following themes: Legislated equality, when taken to extremes, becomes destructive; when government interferes with the family structure, society suffers; forcing sameness can backfire. A second example follows:
Clue: "And it was easy to see that she was the strongest and most graceful of all the dancers, for her handicap bags were as big as those worn by two-hundred-pound men."
Clue: "Even as I stand here—crippled, hobbled, sickened—I am a greater ruler than any man who ever lived! Now watch me become what I can become!"
Clue: "She must have been extraordinarily beautiful, because the mask she wore was hideous."
Theme: Equality in society cannot be measured, or adjusted, by reducing the differences in individuals' talents and skills to the lowest common denominator.

Words to Know SkillBuilder, page 14
A.
1. watchfulness	6. cringe
2. flinch	7. measured
3. fear	8. balance
4. brilliant	9. unclear
5. matching	10. obstacle

B.
1. E	4. C
2. A	5. B
3. D	

C. Accept letters that accurately use at least three Words to Know.

By the Waters of Babylon, page 15
Connect to Your Life, page 16
Sample response: **Rite of Passage:** graduation **Associated words:** pride, completion, on to college, happiness, satisfaction.
Reading Check, page 18
The Dead Places are a dangerous area forbidden to all except priests.
Reader Success Strategy or **Reading Tip,** page 19
Students' time lines should accurately reflect the order of events in the story and be organized around John's journey. A sample response is provided.
Before John's Journey: He has a dream about the Place of the Gods; his father gives him a bow and three arrows; he fasts.
During John's Journey: He travels for eight days; he crosses the river and sings his death song on his way to the Place of the Gods; his raft overturned; he explores the Place of the Gods; wild dogs follow him; he goes into a ruined house; he explores the house and later builds a fire and sleeps; he has a vision of the Place of the Gods and the Great Burning and Destruction; he finds a body of a "dead god"; he returns to his home.
After John's Journey: He is greeted by his father who says he is a priest now; John's people start taking books and other items—not just metal—from the dead places; he says they will build again.
Pause & Reflect, page 19 *(Plus)*
1. It is forbidden to travel east to the Dead Places. It is forbidden to cross the great river. It is forbidden to look upon the Place of the Gods.
2. afraid to go on his journey
3. Possible predictions include: John will disobey the three laws of his people. He will visit the Place of the Gods.
Pause & Reflect, page 19 *(AS, EL)*
1. It is forbidden to travel east to the Dead Places. It is forbidden to cross the great river. It is forbidden to look upon the Place of the Gods.
2. afraid to go on his journey
Reader Success Strategy or **Reading Tip,** page 20
The highlighted term is a phonetic distortion of "Hudson." The river is the Hudson River.
Read Aloud, page 21
It is better to die with honor than to live with the humiliation of being afraid.
Reading Tip, page 21
The setting is New York State along the Hudson River, north of New York City. You might refer students to a map of New York State to help them track John's movements throughout the story.
Reading Check, page 21
John thinks he is about to die, so he sings a song to celebrate his journey and the deeds he has done and the things he has seen. The song prepares him to meet his death.
What Does It Mean?, page 22
Possible response: Earth has fresh and salt water. Salt water probably is more likely to taste bitter to John, so the Bitter Water is probably an ocean or sea—most likely the Atlantic Ocean.
Pause & Reflect, page 22 *(Plus)*
1. Students should circle lines 105–109 ("Then three deer . . . a very great sign."), 111–119 ("My heart was troubled . . . that was my journey"), 126–130 ("Always when I looked . . . in spite of the law").
2. Most students will say that John goes to the forbidden place because he feels that it is his destiny to go there,

because he received several signs that it was the right thing to do, or because the gods are leading him there. Others may say that he goes there to test his metal, to meet and overcome his fears, or to grow in knowledge of the world.
3. Most students will say that the river presented the greatest danger. A few may say that killing the panther was his greatest challenge.
Pause & Reflect, page 22 *(AS, EL)*
1. Students should circle lines 105–109 ("Then three deer . . . a very great sign."), 111–119 ("My heart was troubled . . . that was my journey"), 126–130 ("Always when I looked . . . in spite of the law").
2. Most students will say that the river presented the greatest danger. A few may say that killing the panther was his greatest challenge.
Reading Check, page 23
John sees an island on which there are broken, empty towers, with grass growing in the ruins. There are heaps of broken stone and columns and butterflies and birds flying around. The towers are old skyscrapers.
Read Aloud, page 23
George Washington
Reading Check, page 23
a ruined city
Reading Check, page 24
boxes and jars of preserved food
Read Aloud, page 25
Possible responses: an expressway or a major thoroughfare through the city
Reading Check, page 26
sink, shower, or tub; oven or stove; electric light fixtures
Pause & Reflect, page 26
1. John is in a high-rise apartment building, perhaps in a penthouse suite. Students might star lines 331–332, 336–348, and 351–360.
2. John runs into a tall apartment building and slams the door behind him, locking the dogs out.
3. John sees a sink or other plumbing appliance and a stove.
Reader Success Strategy, page 27
Possible responses: chariots/cars and trucks; night to day/electric lights; great vines of their bridges/suspension cables; fire falling out of the sky/bombs; mist that poisoned/poisonous gas.
Pause & Reflect, page 28
1. Possible summary: Some natural force or some kind of humanmade instrument of destruction, such as a bomb, created the fires, crumbling buildings and roads, toxicity, and fallout that destroyed the Place of the Gods.
2. The Great Burning and the Destruction could have been caused by massive conventional bombing or by some natural cause, such as a meteor shower hitting the earth. Perhaps Benét had a premonition that something like a nuclear bomb would some day exist, or he was referring to incendiary bombs and mustard gas of the type used in World War I.
Reading Check, page 29
That the dead god had died watching the city die, but had not lost his soul.
Read Aloud, page 29
John is experiencing curiosity, sadness, and awe.

Reading Check, page 30
John means, ironically, that his people must learn all that the gods knew to rebuild society to the state in which it was before it was destroyed.

Pause & Reflect, page 30 *(Plus, EL)*
1. John learns that the gods were really just men like him.
2. If you learn about things you are not ready to understand, you may die as a result of inappropriate actions you take that are based on this knowledge.
3. John resolves to teach his people the truth about the "gods."

Pause & Reflect, page 30 *(AS)*
1. John learns that the gods were really just men like him.
2. If you learn about things you are not ready to understand, you may die as a result of inappropriate actions you take that are based on this knowledge.

Challenge, page 30
Some students will say that Benét was concerned by or afraid of the changes brought about by science and technology because he observed people using advances in these fields in irresponsible ways. Perhaps this was his way of warning people to also study the possible consequences of their actions. Students might cite lines 489–494 to support this opinion.

Active Reading SkillBuilder, page 31
Sample responses are provided.
Event: When John boasted or wept without reason he was punished more strictly than his brothers.
Narrator Learns: to be both humble and strong
Event: Liked to hear about the Old Days and the stories of the gods. Asked self many questions that he could not answer, but knows it is good that he wonders.
Narrator Learns: to seek knowledge and to always ask questions and wonder
Event: As a young man, John tells his father that he has had a powerful dream and that it is time he leaves on his journey to manhood. John asks for his father's blessing.
Narrator Learns: that one must become independent in order to mature and grow

Literary Analysis SkillBuilder, page 32
Sample responses are provided.
Exposition: John explains he is the son of a priest. John reveals that he was afraid when he and his father first went to the Dead Places together.
Rising Action: John's father gives him a bow and three arrows and tells him to go on his journey. He reminds John that it is forbidden to travel east, that it is forbidden to cross the river, and that it is forbidden to go to the Place of the Gods.
Climax: When John comes to the Place of the Gods he is afraid and can feel evil spirits about him.
Falling Action: When John sees his father again, John prays and is purified. His father says, "You went away a boy. You come back a man and a priest." John vows to teach his people about the gods.

A Sound of Thunder, page 33

Connect to Your Life, page 34
Sample response: If I could travel in time, I would like to travel to the past, to Roman times. I would choose that era because I love Roman history and I think it would be great to see the emperors, the buildings as they were when they were new, listen to people speak Latin, and see chariot races.

Read Aloud, page 36
Some students may say that the imagery used in this advertisement makes the prospect of time travel very appealing. Others may respond that the air of mystery created in this ad and the repetition of the word death make the idea unappealing or frightening. Accept all responses students can support.

Reader Success Strategy, page 36
The official at the desk tells Eckels that he can only shoot when and what he is told to shoot. If he shoots anything else or shoots when told not to, he will be fined 10,000 dollars and may be punished by the government. Later, Travis tells Eckels that also he must never step off the special path and Travis repeats the instruction not to shoot anything that he does not okay.

Reader Success Strategy, page 37
Sample response:
Eckels: emotional, eager, excited, questioning, weak
Travis: solid, calm, brave, experienced
Both: hunters

Reading Check, page 37
Eckels is traveling back in time to hunt a Tyrannosaurus Rex.

Pause & Reflect, page 38 *(Plus, AS)*
1. Eckels has to be careful to stay on the path and avoid touching the world of the past in any way. He must also be careful to shoot only at certain animals.
2. Some students might like to experience life in the past. Others may believe that interfering with the past will have negative affects. Accept any responses students can support.
3. Most students will predict that Eckels will disobey the rules and step off the path, citing the highlighted lines on page 36 and the discussion on page 37 concerning the proper way to shoot a dinosaur. Accept any predictions that students can support with details from the story.

Pause & Reflect, page 38 *(EL)*
1. Some students might like to experience life in the past. Others may believe that interfering with the past will have negative affects. Accept any responses students can support.
2. Most students will predict that Eckels will disobey the rules and step off the path, citing the highlighted lines on page 36 and the discussion on page 37 concerning the proper way to shoot a dinosaur. Accept any predictions that students can support with details from the story.

Pause & Reflect, page 41 *(Plus, EL)*
1. The future might be changed for the worse.
2. The animal would die two minutes later anyway. Students should circle lines 206–207.
3. Possible responses: safety, staying on the path

Pause & Reflect, page 41 *(AS)*
1. The future might be changed for the worse.
2. Possible responses: safety, staying on the path

Reading Check, page 42
Possible Response: The Tyrannosaurus Rex is huge and frightening, with sharp teeth, claws, and talons.

Pause & Reflect, page 43
1. Travis: in control, self-assured, aggressive, short-tempered, bossy Eckels: scared, unsure of himself

2. Eckels panics when he sees just how big a Tyrannosaurus rex is in real life. Eckels blames his condition on the guide and tries to escape from the situation.

3. Students will most likely circle words like "towered thirty feet above half the trees, "a great evil god," "Each lower leg was a piston," "thick ropes of muscle," "skin like the mail of a terrible warrior," "It ran, its pelvic bones crushing aside trees and bushes." Accept all reasonable responses.

Pause & Reflect, page 45 *(Plus)*

1. Eckels steps off the path as he tries to get away.

2. Most students will predict that Eckels did step on something when he walked off the path and that his actions will change the future in some way. Accept all reasonable predictions about how the world may change.

3. Students should circle lines 378–381 ("'The body has to stay . . . Everything in balance'").

Pause & Reflect, page 45 *(AS, EL)*

1. Eckels steps off the path as he tries to get away.

2. Most students will predict that Eckels did step on something when he walked off the path and that his actions will change the future in some way. Accept all reasonable predictions about how the world may change.

Reading Check, page 46
Travis sees that Eckels' shoes are muddy, meaning he must have stepped off the Path.

Pause & Reflect, page 47 *(Plus, AS)*

1. Eckels has dirt and moss on his shoes. Travis is afraid that the government will revoke the company's license and make them pay a large sum of money as a penalty. Travis also worries that Eckels's actions have somehow altered time. Travis does not want to take the blame.

2. Students should circle 416–418. Travis makes Eckels return to the dinosaur to collect the bullets that killed it because the bullets are not part of the past.

3. Some students will say that Travis made the right decision because Eckels needed to stand up and take responsibility for his actions. Others might argue that Eckels already showed that he could not cope with the situation and that sending him out again will only lead to more trouble.

Pause & Reflect, page 47 *(EL)*

1. Eckels has dirt and moss on his shoes. Travis is afraid that the government will revoke the company's license and make them pay a large sum of money as a penalty. Travis also worries that Eckels's actions have somehow altered time. Travis does not want to take the blame.

2. Some students will say that Travis made the right decision because Eckels needed to stand up and take responsibility for his actions. Others might argue that Eckels already showed that he could not cope with the situation and that sending him out again will only lead to more trouble.

Reading Check, page 48
The spelling on the sign for Time Safari, Inc., has completely changed.

Pause & Reflect, page 49

1. Some students may star lines 480–484 ("TYME SEFARI . . .YU SHOOT ITT."), while others may star lines 499–501 (You know who . . . a man with guts!").

2. Eckels steps on a butterfly and kills it. The absence of the butterfly in the ecosystem affects the life and existence of other creatures and events over time.

3. Travis shoots Eckels because he is angry that the world is altered. He also believes that the election of the dictator Deutscher over the more liberal Keith will be very harmful to his world.

Challenge, page 49
Bradbury views nature with respect and reverence. He realizes the importance of nature in the life of humankind and worries that humans are destroying things in nature that cannot be replaced. Students may cite lines 130–133, 165–170, 495–496, or 504–507.

Active Reading SkillBuilder, page 50
Sample responses are provided.
Text Clues: "We're lucky. If Deutscher had gotten in, we'd have the worst kind of dictatorship." (Lines 47–49)
Predictions: Deutscher will be elected and the country will come under dictatorship.
Text Clues: "We don't want to change the Future. We don't belong here in the Past." (Lines 126–127)
Predictions: By being in the past, where they should never be, they will change the future.
Text Clues: ". . . say we accidentally kill one mouse here. That means all the future families of this one particular mouse are destroyed, right?" (Lines 135–137)
Predictions: Something, perhaps a mouse, will get destroyed, and life as it is now will change.
Text Clues: "The room was there as they had left it. But not the same as they had left it." (Lines 147–148)
Predictions: History will be altered by their actions.

Literary Analysis SkillBuilder, page 51
Sample responses are provided.
Hint: "We're here to give you the severest thrill a real hunter ever asked for." (Lines 64–65)
Outcome: Eckels does receive a severe thrill—death.
Hint: "We don't want to change the Future." (Line 126)
Outcome: The future gets changed.
Hint: "Killing one butterfly couldn't be *that* important! Could it?" (Lines 495–496)
Outcome: Killing one butterfly is extremely important and alters history.
Follow Up: Students may say that foreshadowing adds to the suspense and excitement because it provides the reader with vague clues about what is going to happen. The clues keep the reader engaged and guessing about the outcome of the story.

Words to Know SkillBuilder, page 52
A. 1. sheathed
2. revoke
3. taint
4. expendable
5. annihilate
6. infinitesimally
7. undulate
8. subliminal
9. primeval
10. resilient
B. Accept warning signs that accurately use at least four Words to Know.

Dial Versus Digital, page 53
Connect to Your Life, page 54
Sample response:
Change in Technology: Cell phones became very common.
How It Affected You: Everyone I know has one and so do I; I can talk to my friends all the time, wherever I am. I can also be in touch with my family if there is an emergency.

How It Might Change in the Future: Cell phones might get so tiny that we could wear them, or we might be able to have them surgically implanted.

Reader Success Strategy, page 56

Students' outlines should begin by stating the main idea of the selection, that "there will be a loss in the conversion of dial to digital, and few people seem to be worrying about it." (lines 13–14). Outlines should then include Asimov's arguments and at least one supporting detail for each.

Reading Check, page 56

Asimov suggests using clenched fists as an alternative model and referring to right-hand and left-hand twists.

Pause & Reflect, page 57 *(Plus)*

1. There will be a loss of the concept of clockwise and counterclockwise so the terms *clockwise* and *counterclockwise* will become obsolete. The word *o'clock* will lose its meaning as a visual locator.

2. Students should star the word *negative*.

3. Some students will agree that the clock dial will be on its way out, citing the growing number of digital watches and clocks and the use of digital numbers on computers, VCRs, etc. Others might disagree, responding that "old-fashion" time keeping is still taught in schools and many of the clocks in public buildings still have traditional clock faces.

Pause & Reflect, page 57 *(AS)*

Asimov does not like the switch from dial to digital.

Pause & Reflect, page 57 *(EL)*

Some students will agree that the clock dial will be on its way out, citing the growing number of digital watches and clocks and the use of digital numbers on computers, VCRs, etc. Others might disagree, responding that "old-fashioned" time keeping is still taught in schools and many of the clocks in public buildings still have traditional clock faces.

Pause & Reflect, page 58

1. Digital clocks will change the way children learn and think about time.

2. Some students might say that digital clocks will cause the kinds of problems Asimov mentions in his essay. Others may respond that students will be able to adapt and that teaching only digital time will not be a problem.

3. Students should circle the words "Here is still another point" (line 59) to signal the third effect. The first and second effects are signaled by the words "But if dial clocks disappear, so will the meaning of those words . . ." (lines 22–24) and "Here is another example" (line 41).

Challenge, page 58 *(Plus)*

Students should learn that the atomic clock is the most accurate way of measuring time known to man. Atomic clocks, such as the hydrogen maser, work by the microwave resonance of certain atoms in a magnetic field.

Challenge, page 58 *(AS, EL)*

Students' time lines should include several time-keeping devices developed throughout history, such as water clocks, sand clocks, sun dials, pendulum clocks, and the like. As the same type of device may have appeared at different times in different cultures, you may want to ask students to include a reference to the source that helped them determine where each item should fall on their time lines.

Active Reading SkillBuilder, page 59

Sample responses are provided.

Cause: Digital clocks are replacing dial clocks.

Effect: People won't know the meaning of "clockwise" and "counterclockwise."

Effect: There will be a loss of the ability to locate objects by using the reference points of 1 to 12 o'clock.

Effect: People will no longer see time as a fraction of space, that is, half-past, or a quarter past.

Literary Analysis SkillBuilder, page 60

Sample responses are provided.

- "If you clench your fists with your thumbs pointing at your chest and look at your forefingers, you will see that the forefinger of your right hand curves counterclockwise . . ."
- "If you are hovering around a pole of rotation and the body is rotating counterclockwise, it is the north pole . . ."
- "Suppose you are looking through a microscope at some object on a slide, or through a telescope at some view in the sky."
- "You simply note the position of the hands, and they automatically become a measure of time . . ."

Follow Up: Students' responses will vary, but they might focus on the disappearance of typewriters, stores, or even animals that are currently endangered.

Once More to the Lake, page 61

Connect to Your Life, page 62

A sample response is provided.

- My favorite place is any campsite in the mountains in summer.
- When I'm there, I see how green everything is, how much taller the trees are than at home, and how thick the plants grow along the creek.
- When I'm there, I smell the spicy pine needles, the fresh, cool air, and the campfire.
- When I'm there, I hear the campfire crackle and settle as it burns, the water rushing in the creek, and the wind swirling through the pines.
- When I'm there, I always eat potatoes roasted on the campfire and hot chocolate before bed.
- This place makes me feel happy, rested, and safe.

Reading Check, page 64

It is the lake he and his family used to stay at each summer.

Reader Success Strategy, page 64

Examples of sensory words from the story:

Taste: sweet; blueberry; apple

Touch: cool; thin and clear and unsubstantial; steamed; soggy; icy

Sight: motionless; cottages sprinkled; green; fade-proof

Sound: softly; stillness

Smell: scent; smelled of lumber

Pause & Reflect, page 64 *(Plus)*

1. Possible responses: White was very happy at the lake. Although mishaps occurred, the family always put events in a positive light. It was a time for the family to be together.

2. Students should cross out the word *dangerous*.

3. Some students might predict that the lake will be surrounded by new homes, condos and shops. Others might say that the lake dried up or became overrun by seaweed and the area had become even more wild and rustic.

Pause & Reflect, page 64 *(AS, EL)*

1. Possible responses: White was very happy at the lake. Although mishaps occurred, the family always put events in a positive light. It was a time for the family to be together.

2. Some students might predict that the lake will be surrounded by new homes, condos and shops. Others might say that the lake dried up or became overrun by seaweed and the area had become even more wild and rustic.

Read Aloud, page 65

White is about the same age as his father. White is a father himself. He imagines himself in the role his father had filled so many years ago—performing the same actions, saying the same words, watching over his son.

Reading Check, page 65

The fact that nothing has changed much at the lake makes it seem as though no time has passed.

Pause & Reflect, page 66 *(Plus)*

1. White is pleased and comforted by the fact that little has changed.

2. Students should star lines 77, 87–88, and 112. White is trying to emphasize that everything was as he remembered it from the past.

3. fish, swim

Pause & Reflect, page 66 *(AS)*

1. White is pleased and comforted by the fact that little has changed.

2. Students should star lines 77, 87–88, and 112. White is trying to emphasize that everything was as he remembered it from the past.

Pause & Reflect, page 66 *(EL)*

Students should star lines 77, 87–88, and 112. White is trying to emphasize that everything was as he remembered it from the past.

Reading Check, page 66

fish; swim

Pause & Reflect, page 69 *(Plus)*

1. The middle track on the road to the farmhouse was missing. The sound was different because of the presence of modern outboard motors. There was more Coca-Cola and less of other types of "old-fashioned" soft drinks in the local store.

2. White seems most bothered by the sound of the outboard motors.

3. Summer reminds him of his happy, childhood days.

Pause & Reflect, page 69 *(AS, EL)*

1. The middle track on the road to the farmhouse was missing. The sound was different because of the presence of modern outboard motors. There was more Coca-Cola and less of other types of "old-fashioned" soft drinks in the local store.

2. White seems most bothered by the sound of the outboard motors.

Reading Check, page 69

It reminds him of his happy, childhood days, and he is sharing a special place with his son.

Pause & Reflect, page 70 *(Plus)*

1. The thunderstorm seems to make White feel melancholy and slightly sad. The incident ends with his feeling the "chill of death."

2. He finally realizes that his youth is over and that he is growing old.

3. Accept any reasonable responses.

Pause & Reflect, page 70 *(AS, EL)*

1. The thunderstorm seems to make White feel melancholy and slightly sad. The incident ends with his feeling the "chill of death."

2. Accept any reasonable responses.

Challenge, page 70

Most students will respond that White's style is personal, thoughtful, and sentimental. Students should note White's use of first-person point of view, figurative language, and long sentences in their discussion of his style.

Active Reading SkillBuilder, page 71

Sample responses are provided.

Then:

People and their trunks were taken to the lake in a farm wagon.
There was a small steamboat on the lake.

Now:

People drive their own cars to the lake.
The tarred road comes closer to the lake.
The 15-year-old waitresses are more sophisticated.

Both:

There was a person bathing in the lake with a bar of soap.
People ate dinner at the farmhouse.
The waitresses were still 15-year-old country girls.
There's still an excitement about coming to camp.

Literary Analysis SkillBuilder, page 72

The greater fraction of students' circles should represent personal reflection.

Follow Up: Students may conclude that if the essay included significantly less personal reflection, the literary piece would have less emotional appeal. They may also decide that they would have less of a sense of the character and personality of E. B. White if he had included less personal reflection.

Words to Know SkillBuilder, page 73

A. 1. indelible
2. petulant
3. haunt
4. tentatively
5. languidly

B. 1. languidly
2. indelible
3. petulant
4. tentatively
5. haunt

C. Accept messages that accurately use at least two Words to Know.

Through the One-Way Mirror/The Border: A Glare of Truth, page 74

Connect to Your Life, page 75

A sample response is provided.

Canada: What I know: It's to the north of the US; some Canadians speak French, others English; hockey is the national sport. **What I would like to know:** What are Canadian schools like? How do they feel about Americans? Does everyone need to learn French?

Mexico: What I know: It's to the south of the US; Mexicans speak Spanish and are mostly Catholics; it's hot in Mexico and they have earthquakes; Texas used to be part of Mexico. **What I would like to know:** What do kids there do for fun? Is the geography all desert-like or are there different kinds of environments?

Reading Check, page 77

Atwood says Americans only think about Canadians when there is cold weather or issues with water or a dispute, such as the one over fishing territory.

Pause & Reflect, page 78 *(Plus)*

1. Atwood is using a simile. She is trying to emphasize how much time Canadians spend observing and studying the behavior of Americans. She compares their behavior to that of someone whose face is pressed up against a mirror, trying to get a better view.

2. Students should mark each phrase as follows:
loud and messy—A
clean and tidy—C
tend to worry—C
unaware of being watched—A

Pause & Reflect, page 78 *(AS, EL)*
Students should mark each phrase as follows:
loud and messy—A
clean and tidy—C
tend to worry—C
unaware of being watched—A

Reading Check, page 79
Atwood says that when Washington catches cold, Ottawa sneezes, meaning that the Canadian government reacts to whatever the United States' government is doing or wants.

Reading Check, page 79
Atwood means wanting to conquer and rule an empire. She cites three examples of empires from history—the Roman, British, and French.

Pause & Reflect, page 80 *(Plus, AS)*

1. Students will most likely circle lines 73–77.
2. Canadians and Americans often don't understand one another.
3. Mr. Magoo is a cartoon character who suffers from severe myopia, or nearsightedness. By saying that Americans have Mr. Magoo eyes, Atwood is implying that Americans do not see the rest of the world clearly, as it really is.

Pause & Reflect, page 80 *(EL)*

1. Students will most likely circle lines 73–77.
2. Canadians and Americans often don't understand one another.

Pause & Reflect, page 82

1. Mora's friends said she would "miss the visible evidence of Mexico's proximity" and the "good Mexican food."
2. Mora misses her family and family get-togethers, but she also misses the sound of her native language and being able converse in Spanish.
3. Students will most likely star lines 15–17. Some students may star lines 26–29 or 32–35.

Reading Check, page 83
Mora has adjusted well to her new life in the Midwest, although she still misses aspects of her old life in Mexico and her family ties, and is working to keep her culture alive within herself.

Pause & Reflect, page 84 *(Plus)*

1. Mora misses the rhythms and the sounds of the music she grew up with. She misses the things she associates with the music, such as the dancing, the celebrations, and the warmth of her relationships with family and friends.
2. Some students, like Mora, may name the music of their homeland. Others may name other styles of music or specific songs that cause them to feel strong emotions.
3. Students should circle the following phrases, which appear at the top of page 83: "this furry, scurrying companion," "the silence of the bare tree limbs against an evening sky," "updrafts of snow outside our third-floor window," "the

ivory light of the cherry blossoms." Mora also appreciates living in the "heartland."

Pause & Reflect, page 84 *(AS, EL)*
Mora misses the rhythms and the sounds of the music she grew up with. She misses the things she associates with the music, such as the dancing, the celebrations, and the warmth of her relationships with family and friends.

Pause & Reflect, page 85

1. Students should cross out the last statement, *She fears the truth revealed by the desert.*
2. Some students may star "That desert—its firmness, resilience, and fierceness, . . . shaped us as geography always shapes its inhabitants . . . both inspiring and compelling me . . . thorns" (lines 118–124). Other students may star "The culture of the border illustrates this truth [that the world is saturated with inequality, power, and domination] daily, glaringly . . . music, celebration" (lines 135–140).

Challenge, page 85
Atwood's purpose for writing seems to be to chide Americans for their self-centered, self-important attitudes and to chide Canadians for their inferiority complex. Mora's purpose for writing is to explain the important ways in which the border has influenced her life. Atwood writes from a third-person point of view and uses humor and mild sarcasm to make her point. Mora uses vivid description, first-person point of view, and an emotional tone to explain what living on the border has taught her.

Active Reading SkillBuilder, page 86
Sample responses are provided.

Through the One-Way Mirror
Life in U.S.: Americans don't expand their vision past their own country. (difference)
Life in Canada: Canadians are always peering into America to observe the culture. (difference)
Life in U.S.: Americans are taught about the United States first, then about other places. (difference)
Life in Canada: Canadians are taught about the rest of the world first, then Canada. (difference)
Life in U.S.: Americans watch closely what goes on in Washington, D.C. (similarity)
Life in Canada: Canadians watch closely what goes on in Washington, D.C. (similarity)

The Border: A Glare of Truth
Life in El Paso: land of bare, stark desert (difference)
Life in Ohio: land of snow and of cherry blossoms (difference)
Life in El Paso: shaped by geography (similarity)
Life in Ohio: also shaped by geography (similarity)
Life in El Paso: "saturated with inequality, power, and domination" (difference)
Life in Ohio: insulated, economically privileged life (difference)

Literary Analysis SkillBuilder, page 87
Sample responses are provided.

Atwood's Perceptions
- Americans sometimes regard Canadians as unpatriotic, for Americans don't really see Canadians as foreigners.
- Canadians and Americans are educated in opposite ways from each other—Americans are taught about the United States first, then about the world; Canadians are taught about the world first, then about Canada.

- Americans are myopic—they have "Mr. Magoo eyes, with which they see the rest of the world."

Theme: Americans, who live in a country of major international influence, and Canadians, who live in a neighboring country of lesser international influence, have a friendly but wary relationship.

What Mora Misses
- her family—children, parents, siblings, niece, nephews
- meals seasoned with the family phrase, "Remember the time when . . ."
- the music of mariachi groups

Theme: Richness cannot be measured only in terms of financial privileges.

Words to Know SkillBuilder, page 88

A.
1. uncommon
2. courtesy
3. unwisely
4. distance
5. single-mindedness
6. farsightedness
7. melodious
8. clear
9. misinterpret

B.
1. raucous
2. proximity
3. prevalent
4. analyze
5. versatility
6. astutely

C. Accept anecdotes that accurately use at least four Words to Know.

Piano/Those Winter Sundays, page 89

Connect to Your Life, page 90

Sample response: summers, neighborhood, turtles, ice skating

Pause & Reflect, page 92

1. the speaker
2. Students should circle *happiness* and *singing*.
3. Possible responses: It was a time of happiness and innocence. The speaker could be close to his mother. He remembers how the music made him feel. He was warm and cozy at home, safe from the winter cold.

Reading Check, page 92

The speaker is very sad to the point of crying; he feels a deep loss over his past.

Pause & Reflect, page 93 *(Plus)*

1. Possible response: The speaker remembers his father getting up early to build up the fire and to help him get up and get dressed. He remembers that no one, including himself, ever thanked his father.
2. Possible response: The speaker now appreciates how much trouble his father went to in order to take care of him. He realizes that his father was showing love through these actions. Before he spoke indifferently to his father, but now he feels grateful.

Pause & Reflect, page 93 *(AS, EL)*

Possible response: The speaker now appreciates how much trouble his father went to in order to take care of him. He realizes that his father was showing love through these actions. Before he spoke indifferently to his father, but now he feels grateful.

Challenge, page 93

Possible responses to what the two speakers have in common: They both are now able, as adults, to appreciate something good about their childhoods. They both have feelings of nostalgia for the past. They both see their adult selves as very different from their childhood selves.

Possible responses to what makes them different from each other: In "Piano," the speaker remembers Sundays as an especially happy time; in "Those Winter Sundays," the speaker remembers how Sundays were like weekdays. In "Piano," the speaker's memory of childhood contains only good things; in "Those Winter Sundays," the speaker remembers a mix of good and bad things. The speaker of "Piano" is overcome with emotion; the speaker of "Those Winter Sundays" has a moment of insight. The speaker of "Piano" identifies with his childhood self; the speaker of "Those Winter Sundays" is struck by the limitations of his childhood self.

Active Reading SkillBuilder, page 94

Sample responses are provided.

Piano

(Students may focus on the present, the past, or both.)

Where: a concert or café (present); in the parlor of the speaker's boyhood home (past)

When: at dusk (present); Sunday evening in winter (past)

Who: speaker as adult and female singer (present); speaker as child and mother singing (past)

What the people look like: speaker as adult male, weeping; female singer perhaps wearing an evening gown (present); speaker as small boy; mother has small feet, is smiling, perhaps wearing a Sunday dress

What details in the setting trigger mental pictures: cozy parlour, child sitting under the piano

Images easily visualized: speaker as adult male with a pained expression on his face, weeping; child sitting under the piano, pressing on his mother's "small, poised feet"

Those Winter Sundays

Where: speaker's childhood home

When: Sunday morning in winter

Who: speaker, father

What the people look like: speaker as young boy, has a frightened, then indifferent, expression on his face; father has work-worn hands, is strong and severe looking

What details in the setting trigger mental pictures: blueblack cold of early morning, banked fires blaze

Images easily visualized: father dressing in blueblack cold of early morning, father's cracked hands

Literary Analysis SkillBuilder, page 95

Sample responses are provided.

Piano

"Softly, in the dusk, a woman is singing to me" (line 1)/hearing, sight

"a mother who smiles as she sings" (line 4)/sight, hearing

"hymns in the cozy parlour" (line 8)/hearing, sight, touch

Those Winter Sundays

"blueblack cold" (line 2)/touch, sight

"cracked hands that ached" (line 3)/touch, sight

"I'd wake and hear the cold splintering, breaking" (line 6)/hearing

The Californian's Tale, page 96

Connect to Your Life, page 97

Sample response: I think a home is where the people you love live, like your family. Where I live is special because I really like my bedroom and my parents have a vegetable garden in the backyard and we eat what they grow in the summer. The kitchen is big and we all spend time there together having meals and playing games sometimes.

Reader Success Strategy, page 99
Students' outlines should include the major events in the story.
Pause & Reflect, page 99 *(Plus)*
1. Descriptions of the setting should include the following kinds of words: *magnificent, charming, rustic, picturesque, peaceful, woodsy, pine-scented, solitary, desolate, lonely, cozy cabins.*
2. Possible responses: When the gold rush ended, many settlers and their families left the area for places with more promise. Once the miners left, the towns died out because there were very few ways for the people who stayed to make a living.
3. The narrator is a prospector who is still hoping to strike it rich. He seems to like the solitude of the area. Perhaps, like the men he describes, he, too, left home with dreams of glory and riches and was too embarrassed or humiliated by his failure to return home.

Pause & Reflect, page 99 *(AS, EL)*
1. Descriptions of the setting should include the following kinds of words: *magnificent, charming, rustic, picturesque, peaceful, woodsy, pine-scented, solitary, desolate, lonely, cozy cabins.*
2. Possible responses: When the gold rush ended, many settlers and their families left the area for places with more promise. Once the miners left, the towns died out because there were very few ways for the people who stayed to make a living.

Reading Check, page 100
The narrator is happy to be in the cottage because he has spent the last weeks roughing it in miners' cabins with dirt floors. The cottage is homey, clean and pretty, and beautifully decorated.

Pause & Reflect, page 101 *(Plus)*
1. Henry's cabin was meticulously clean and lovingly decorated with many feminine touches. Details students may circle include: "rag carpets"; "wallpaper and framed lithographs, and brightly colored tidies and lamp mats"; "varnished whatnots, with seashells and books and china vases on them"; "soft Japanese fabrics"; "white counterpane, white pillows, carpeted floor, papered walls, pictures, dressing table . . . dainty toilet things . . . soap in a china dish . . ."
2. his wife
3. They love each other dearly.

Pause & Reflect, page 101 *(AS, EL)*
1. Henry's cabin was meticulously clean and lovingly decorated with many feminine touches. Details students may circle include: "rag carpets"; "wallpaper and framed lithographs, and brightly colored tidies and lamp mats"; "varnished whatnots, with seashells and books and china vases on them"; "soft Japanese fabrics"; "white counterpane, white pillows, carpeted floor, papered walls, pictures, dressing table . . . dainty toilet things . . . soap in a china dish . . ."
2. his wife

Reading Check, page 102
Henry's wife is in the photograph.

Reading Check, page 102
Henry says his wife has gone to visit relatives about forty or fifty miles away.

Pause & Reflect, page 103 *(Plus)*
1. The narrator is infatuated with her.
2. Most students will say that the narrator is a kind, honest, and thoughtful man who wants to be a good guest.
3. He is attracted to Henry's wife and doesn't want to upset himself.

Pause & Reflect, page 103 *(AS, EL)*
1. The narrator is infatuated with her.
2. Most students will say that the narrator is a kind, honest, and thoughtful man who wants to be a good guest.

Reading Check, page 103
Henry's neighbors drop by to inquire about his wife and to ask if there will be a celebration when she returns.

Pause & Reflect, page 104 *(Plus)*
1. Henry's neighbors drop by to inquire about his wife and to ask if there will be a celebration when she returns.
2. The neighbors respect her and seem genuinely fond of her. They seem to miss her.
3. Students will most likely respond that they would be thankful to have such friendly and caring neighbors. A few might say that because Henry's wife is so beautiful and kind and because so many of the men live alone, they would feel suspicious or jealous of the men's affections.

Pause & Reflect, page 104 *(AS, EL)*
1. The neighbors respect her and seem genuinely fond of her. They seem to miss her.
2. Students will most likely respond that they would be thankful to have such friendly and caring neighbors. A few might say that because Henry's wife is so beautiful and kind and because so many of the men live alone, they would feel suspicious or jealous of the men's affections.

Reading Check, page 105
The narrator gets annoyed with Henry and speaks so harshly to him that Henry is hurt.

Reading Check, page 106
Henry is afraid because he is worried about his wife. She was due back at nine o'clock and the clock is about to strike nine and she has not appeared.

Pause & Reflect, page 107
1. Most students will respond that they were surprised by the outcome of the story. Accept any responses students can support with details from the story.
2. Henry's wife was captured by the Indians and was never heard from again (lines 292–295).
3. Henry's friends hold a party to help him get through the anniversary of the day his wife disappeared. Their purpose is to distract Henry by pretending as if the event never occurred.

Challenge, page 107 *(Plus)*
Twain uses precise language with many descriptive details, varied sentence lengths, a first-person point of view, a conversational tone, and realistic dialogue to help the reader visualize the setting and sympathize with the characters. His folksy, personal style of writing and his use of colloquialisms make readers feel as if the narrator is speaking directly to them.

Challenge, page 107 *(AS, EL)*
Sample response: (As Joe) We all take care of Henry. He's a good man and been a good neighbor. Since his wife didn't come home, all them years ago, we just felt like we was obligated to take care of him. So we've gone on pretending she's just gone visiting her people. And then each year on the

date when she was due to come home, we make a point of all being here to spend the evening with Henry and keep him company till the night passes. Just being neighborly and he deserves it; she was a good young woman and it broke his heart when she never came home.

Active Reading SkillBuilder, page 108
Sample responses are provided.

Frontier surroundings
Detail: a lonesome land; no sound but insects
Detail: lovely region, woodsy, balmy, uninhabited
Detail: wide expanse of emerald turf
Detail: pretty little cottage houses, overgrown with roses
Detail: solitary log cabins

Henry's cottage
Detail: cozy little rose-clad cottages, didn't have a deserted look
Detail: garden of flowers, abundant, gay, flourishing
Detail: rag carpet, wallpaper, lithographs, knick-knacks, vases, Japanese fabrics
Detail: bedroom is spotless, clean, dazzling white, full of dainty things

Insight from frontier surroundings
The frontier is a lonely, deserted place, without the comforts of a community. The narrator feels the loneliness keenly; what he sees mirrors how he feels.

Insight from Henry's cottage
Henry's cottage stands out from the other cottages because it is so well maintained, cozy, and attractive. Henry and his wife obviously worked hard to make the house a home, revealing that it was once full of life and full of hope. All the little decorating touches that Henry's wife gave their home also reveal that Henry's wife loved the house and loved Henry. But in reality it is Henry, and not his wife, who for the last 19 years has provided the "woman's touch." The care he takes to keep the house as it once was shows that Henry still cares deeply about the home that he and his wife made together.

Literary Analysis SkillBuilder, page 109
Sample responses are provided.

Setting
Time: toward the end of World War II
Place: an apartment in Germany

Characters
Heinrich, a German citizen
Inge, his Jewish wife

Problem
The larger setting is that of bombed-out Germany, right before its downfall. While out searching for food, Inge has disappeared, and Heinrich is out of his mind with worry. Inge has probably been taken to a concentration camp and killed, but Heinrich believes she will return and tries to keep their apartment as it was when she was there. He is sure that when the war is over, she will return to him.

Events
1. Inge leaves the apartment to search for food.
2. She is captured by the Nazis and taken to a concentration camp.
3. Heinrich keeps the apartment just as it was when Inge left, in the mistaken belief that she will return when the war is over.
4. Heinrich's friends try to keep his hopes alive.

Resolution
Heinrich's friends gather around him on the anniversary of the war's end to help maintain the illusion that Inge will eventually return.

Words to Know SkillBuilder, page 110
A.
  1. sever
  2. predecessor
  3. supplicating
  4. imploring
  5. furtive

B.
  1. balmy
  2. boding
  3. sedate
  4. desolation
  5. grizzled

C. Accept responses that accurately use at least four Words to Know.

Tonight I Can Write . . . , page 111
Connect to Your Life, page 112
A sample response is provided on the student page.

Key to the Poem, page 112
Sample responses: sadness, broken heart, alone, hurt

Reading Check, page 114
The speaker and the woman were in love with each other, but the woman seems to have left him.

Pause & Reflect, page 114 *(Plus)*
1. The speaker and the woman were in love (or at least infatuated) with each other. The woman seems to have left him.
2. Many students will respond that the speaker still loves the woman because he cannot forget her and because he speaks of her in such emotional terms. Others may say that he does not love the woman, but is merely infatuated with her or with the idea of being in love.
3. Most students will conclude that the speaker will forget the woman over time. Others may argue that while he will lose his strong feelings for her, he will never forget her.

Pause & Reflect, page 114 *(AS, EL)*
Many students will respond that the speaker still loves the woman because he cannot forget her and because he speaks of her in such emotional terms. Others may say that he does not love the woman, but is merely infatuated with her or with the idea of being in love.

Challenge, page 114
References to "the immense night," the "night is shattered," and the "blue stars that shiver," reflect the despair, sadness, hurt, and loneliness the speaker feels. The night wind that "revolves in the sky and sings" symbolizes the brokenhearted speaker crying out for the woman he loves.

Active Reading SkillBuilder, page 115
Sample responses are provided.
- "The night is shattered and the blue stars shiver in the distance."/Brokenhearted, upset, hurt; the speaker's whole world is falling apart.
- "The night wind revolves in the sky and sings."/Loneliness; the speaker is as lonely as a wind blowing with nothing to interfere with it.
- "And the verse falls to the soul like dew to the pasture."/Inevitability; when the speaker sits down to write, it is inevitable that he will write about her since she is in his thoughts always.

- "My voice tried to find the wind to touch her hearing."/ Hopelessness; the speaker tried to convince her to remain, but to no avail.

Literary Analysis SkillBuilder, page 116
Sample responses are provided.
- "I loved her, and sometimes she loved me too." (line 6); "She loved me, sometimes I loved her too." (line 9)/The speaker feels regret that sometimes their love ebbed and flowed.
- "Through nights like this one I held her in my arms." (line 7); "Because through nights like this one I held her in my arms." (line 29)/The speaker misses the closeness they used to share.
- "My soul is not satisfied that it has lost her." (line 18); ". . . my soul is not satisfied that it has lost her." (line 30)/ The speaker yearns for her.

Follow Up: Some students might say that Neruda adds new information to repeated lines to emphasize that the speaker is revising his thoughts about his lover as he writes. Others may think that Neruda uses this approach to show the speaker's ambivalent feelings about the loss of his lover.

One Thousand Dollars, page 117
Connect to Your Life, page 118
Students' spending should total $25,000 and the items in the pie chart should total 100 percent.

Key to the Story, page 118
A sample response is provided.

Things That Money Can't Buy: love, happiness, health, friends, nature, good weather

Reading Check, page 120
Gillian has inherited $1,000 and must give the lawyers an account of how he spent it.

Reading Check, page 121
The two men are acquaintances, if not very good friends and belong to the same club. Gillian respects Bryson, if not Bryson's privacy. Bryson takes the time to talk to Gillian, so he must like him on some level.

Reader Success Strategy, page 121
A sample response is provided.

Good Uses: buy a home; send wife to the South to be cured; buy milk for 100 babies; put someone through college; buy a famous painting; live in New Hampshire for two years; rent Madison Square Garden; go off to a sheep ranch in Idaho; give the money to Miss Hayden.

Poor Uses: play faro; buy Lotta a pendant

Pause & Reflect, page 122 (Plus)
1. Possible responses: Gillian has no interest in the money. He thinks the inheritance is funny and treats it as a big joke. He thinks the amount is so small that it is useless. He feels the money is a lot of trouble because he can't think of how to spend it. He's disappointed that the inheritance wasn't more.
2. Students should circle the passage "You are required . . . stipulates that" (lines 16–18). Gillian has to report to the lawyer how he spends the money.
3. Most students will circle funny, spoiled, friendly, and carefree.
4. Students may say that they would spend the money on clothes, electronic equipment, or gifts. Some might say that they would put it in a savings account or invest it.

Pause & Reflect, page 122 (AS, EL)
1. Possible responses: Gillian has no interest in the money. He thinks the inheritance is funny and treats it as a big joke. He thinks the amount is so small that it is useless. He feels the money is a lot of trouble because he can't think of how to spend it. He's disappointed that the inheritance wasn't more.
2. Most students will circle funny, spoiled, friendly, and carefree.

Reading Check, page 123
The blind man shows Gillian a bank deposit book showing that he has $1,785 saved.

Pause & Reflect, page 124 (Plus)
1. One possible response follows:
Gillian doesn't give jewelry to Miss Lauriere because she is spoiled and greedy—when he offers her a thousand-dollar necklace, she mentions one that costs $2,200.
He rides with a cab driver who knows exactly what he would do with a thousand dollars—start his own business.
He meets a blind man who saves all his money and already has more than a thousand dollars.
2. Gillian returns to the lawyers' office to ask if Miss Hayden was left anything by his uncle besides the ring and the $10. Perhaps he is thinking of giving her the money.
3. Some students will predict that Gillian will give the money to Miss Hayden. Others may predict that he will find a reason for not giving her the money either. Still others may predict that he will use the money to gain favor with her.

Pause & Reflect, page 124 (AS, EL)
Gillian returns to the lawyers' office to ask if Miss Hayden was left anything by his uncle besides the ring and the $10. Perhaps he is thinking of giving her the money.

Pause & Reflect, page 125 (Plus)
1. Possible responses: He doesn't want her to be hurt by his uncle's stinginess toward her. He doesn't want her to think he is offering her the money so she will love him.
2. Students should circle lines 181–183 ("Paid by the black sheep . . . dearest woman on earth.") Possible response: that he loves her and thinks very highly of her.
3. Students will probably say that they admire Gillian for his selflessness and generosity. Some may say Gillian is foolish to give up both the money and the opportunity to get credit for a good deed. Accept any reasonable responses.

Pause & Reflect, page 125
Possible responses: He doesn't want her to be hurt by his uncle's stinginess toward her. He doesn't want her to think he is offering her the money so she will love him.

Reading Check, page 126
If Gillian spends the money well, he will inherit the $50,000; if he doesn't spend it well, the money will go to Miss Hayden.

Reading Check, page 126
He did not want the lawyers to know that he had been generous with the money, because if they found out, he, and not Miss Hayden, would inherit the $50,000.

Pause & Reflect, page 127
1. Possible responses: Yes—he had a chance to get the $50,000 and passed it up. No—he doesn't care about money or worry about impressing people.
2. He learns that if he has spent the thousand dollars wisely, he will receive another $50,000, but if not, the extra money will go to Miss Hayden.

3. He takes back the envelope containing the explanation of how he spent the thousand dollars and gives a false explanation—that he lost the money gambling.

Challenge, page 127

Possible passages to star include: lines 4–12 (instead of being glad to receive a thousand dollars, Gillian thinks it is a bother), lines 44–50 (he treats his rich uncle's leaving him only a small part of his fortune as a joke), lines 92–95 (he plans to take Old Bryson's advice to squander the money), line 114 (he changes his mind about spending the money on Miss Lauriere), lines 160–169 (he gives the money to Miss Hayden and makes up a story about where it came from), lines 172–173 (he tells Miss Hayden that he loves her, but isn't upset when she rejects him), lines 221–231 (we learn there is an addition to the will that may give Gillian a larger inheritance), lines 235–242 (Gillian takes back the envelope and makes up a story about losing the money at the races). Students' reasons for being surprised will vary, but should be clearly reasoned, and show that they understood the plot.

Active Reading SkillBuilder, page 128

Sample responses are provided.

Cause: Conversation between Lawyer Tolman and Young Gillian; $1,000 given to Gillian

Conversation: Conversation between Gillian and Old Bryson. Bryson gives advice on how Gillian should spend his money. He suggests that he buy Lotta Lauriere a diamond pendant.

Conversation: Conversation between Gillian and Miss Lauriere; Gillian offers to buy her a pendant, but she scoffs at the paltry sum of money he is willing to spend on her.

Conversation: Conversation between Gillian and Lawyer Tolman; Gillian realizes that he wants to do something useful with the money, asks about Miss Hayden's inheritance, and finds out that she only inherited $10 and a ring.

Conversation: Conversation between Gillian and Miss Hayden; Gillian lies that his uncle had willed her $1,000, gives her his money, and is rejected after admitting that he loves her.

Conversation: Conversation between Gillian and Lawyer Tolman; after finding out that Miss Hayden will inherit $50,000 if Gillian spends his money foolishly, Gillian pretends that he lost his $1,000 on a bet at the races.

Literary Analysis SkillBuilder, page 129

Sample responses are provided.

Rising Action: Conversation between Gillian and Old Bryson, Conversation between Gillian and Miss Lotta Lauriere, Conversation between Gillian and a cabby, Conversation between Gillian and a blind man, Conversation between Gillian and Lawyer Tolman about Miss Hayden's inheritance

Climax: Conversation between Gillian and Miss Hayden

Falling Action: Conversation between Gillian and Lawyer Tolman about the supplement to his uncle's will

Words to Know SkillBuilder, page 130

A.
1. prudent
2. expenditure
3. genially
4. precariousness
5. pendant
6. stipulate
7. venerable
8. acquaint
9. disreputable
10. encumber

B. Accept descriptions that accurately use at least four Words to Know.

Getting a Job, page 131

Connect to Your Life, page 132

A sample response is provided.

My dream career is being a rock star.

Benefits: performing/singing/playing instrument; money; fame; fans

Drawbacks: loss of privacy; crowds; always working; need to keep making hits

Reading Check, page 133

The idea that she should get a job came to her as though she were in a collision.

Pause & Reflect, page 134 *(Plus)*

1. lack of office skills, her age, her race
2. Marguerite is attracted by the dark-blue uniform, the money changer, and the sense of freedom that she believes would come from sailing up and down the hills of San Francisco on a streetcar.
3. Students who choose words like *determined, stubborn, industrious,* or *single-minded* to describe Marguerite may cite lines 5–13 or 41–44. Students who describe her as *self-sufficient* might cite lines 5–6 or 43–45. Students who describe her as *proud* might cite lines 41–42.

Pause & Reflect, page 134 *(AS, EL)*

1. lack of office skills, her age, her race
2. Students who choose words like *determined, stubborn, industrious,* or *single-minded* to describe Marguerite may cite lines 5–13 or 41–44. Students who describe her as *self-sufficient* might cite lines 5–6 or 43–45. Students who describe her as *proud* might cite lines 41–42.

Reader Success Strategy, page 135

A sample response is provided.

- Marguerite decides to get a job.
- She wants to work on streetcars.
- She goes to the company to apply.
- She insists on seeing the personnel manager.
- She is determined to get that job.
- She tries to get help from organizations.
- She keeps going to the streetcar office.
- She lies on her job application.
- She passes all the tests.

Pause & Reflect, page 136

1. Possible responses include: The secretary is prejudiced against people of color. The secretary's boss is prejudiced and has made it clear that people of color are not welcome in the firm.
2. Students should circle the phrase *a victim of an old tragedy.* They will most likely cite lines 107–115.
3. Students will probably reply that they would feel hurt and angry in Marguerite's place. Accept any logical student response.

Reading Check, page 137

They cannot understand why she does not want a job that pays more, when there are lots of those jobs available. They do not understand that her goal is not the money but the job itself, which is forbidden to her.

Reading Check, page 137

Marguerite and her mother are beginning to form a close, supportive, and mutually admiring relationship that will last the rest of their lives.

Reading Check, page 138
Marguerite is forced to lie about her age and work experience on her application. She is too young to work legally, and is making up her age and job history.

Pause & Reflect, page 138 *(Plus)*
1. Possible answers: Marguerite has proven her willingness to work hard and persevere. She has worn down her opponents. Her constant presence has become an embarrassment to the company.
2. Her mother offers emotional support, keeps her body well nourished, and gives her money for carfare.
3. Some students may predict that she will be happy now that she reached her goal. Others may predict that getting the job will lead to other complications that will make her less than satisfied with her position.

Pause & Reflect, page 138 *(AS, EL)*
1. Possible answers: Marguerite has proven her willingness to work hard and persevere. She has worn down her opponents. Her constant presence has become an embarrassment to the company.
2. Some students may predict that she will be happy now that she reached her goal. Others may predict that getting the job will lead to other complications that will make her less than satisfied with her position.

Pause & Reflect, page 139
1. Marguerite is able to open a bank account and buy clothes that will help her fit in with her peers. She also develops an appreciation for and a renewed interest in education. In addition, Marguerite develops a new, more mature outlook on life and a new set of goals.
2. Most students will respond favorably to Marguerite's spirit of perseverance and righteousness. They may say that they admire the way she stood up for her rights. A few may say that they do not admire her because they find her behavior to be self-centered or confrontational.

Challenge, page 139
Possible response: The grim description of the Railway Company office in lines 55–62 reflects the old-fashioned, mean-spirited prejudice of the people who worked there. The feelings the description evokes help the reader understand how difficult it must have been for Marguerite to continue fighting for her rights in the face of daily rejection. The description of Marguerite's streetcar route (lines 187–193) helps the reader understand and appreciate how much Angelou's experiences taught her about the world outside her own neighborhood.

Active Reading SkillBuilder, page 140
Sample responses are provided.
Cause: wanted a job but did not want to do office work; was not old enough to work at defense jobs
Cause: women had replaced men as streetcar conductors
Cause: refused to accept prejudice against African Americans working as streetcar conductors
Effect: gained independence
Effect: became older and wiser
Effect: realized that she and her schoolmates were on very different paths in life

Literary Analysis SkillBuilder, page 141
Sample responses are provided.
Plot: ". . . on a blissful day, I was hired as the first Negro on the San Francisco streetcars . . ."

Character: "On the streetcar, I put my fare into the box and the conductorette looked at me with the usual hard eyes of white contempt. . . . Her Southern nasal accent sliced my meditation and I looked deep into my thoughts."
Setting: "Downtown San Francisco became alien and cold, and the streets I had loved in a personal familiarity were unknown lanes that twisted with malicious intent."
Theme: Angelou comprehends the perversity of life, that in the struggle lies the joy.
Point of View: first-person point of view (One example of Angelou's participation in the narrative occurs with her response to learning that "colored people" cannot work on the streetcars: "From disappointment, I gradually ascended the emotional ladder to haughty indignation, and finally to that state of stubbornness where the mind is locked like the jaws of an enraged bulldog.")

Words to Know SkillBuilder, page 142
A. 1. descend
2. rambling
3. humble
4. awkward
5. purposefully
B. 1. hypocrisy
2. ostensibly
3. comprehend
4. diametrically
5. charade

A Celebration of Grandfathers, page 143
Connect to Your Life, page 144
A sample response is provided.
Name: Grandmother
Relationship to You: Same
Description: My grandmother is one of my favorite people in the world. She is 50 years older than I am but is really cool and fun to be with.
What You Have Learned: I have learned a lot from her. I have learned how to cook, how to sew, and how to put on makeup. I also learned how to do my hair and how to say some things in Spanish.

Key to the Memoir, page 144
A sample response is provided.
My family has a tradition of going camping on Memorial Day Weekend. We do it every year and it is a great family experience. We sleep in tents, cook over a fire, go on long hikes and swim if it is warm enough. When I have children of my own, I want to continue the same tradition with them.

Reader Success Strategy, page 146
Students may highlight phrases such as the following: "'Know where you stand.'" (line 39); ". . . he was a participant with the forces that filled our world" (lines 48–49); "'Death is only this small transformation of life.'" (lines 56–57); "He never raised his whip.'" (line 64); "'*Ten paciencia.*'" (line 85).

Read Aloud, page 146
Anaya's grandfather had a strong belief in God and in the forces of nature. He believed in a power outside himself.

Reading Check, page 146
Anaya remembers his grandfather most for his silence.

Pause & Reflect, page 147 (Plus)
1. Anaya admires his grandfather's physical strength. He admires that his grandfather was strong in his beliefs. He admires that his grandfather knew the value of nurturing and was sensitive to the lives around him. He envies his grandfather's connections to and understanding of the earth.
2. simple, strong, calm, wise
3. Students will most likely say that they would like to have known Anaya's grandfather, citing his innate intelligence, his gentle manner of teaching, and his love for his family. Accept any answers students can support with details from the selection.

Pause & Reflect, page 147 (AS, EL)
1. Anaya admires his grandfather's physical strength. He admires that his grandfather was strong in his beliefs. He admires that his grandfather knew the value of nurturing and was sensitive to the lives around him. He envies his grandfather's connections to and understanding of the earth.
2. Students will most likely say that they would like to have known Anaya's grandfather, citing his innate intelligence, his gentle manner of teaching, and his love for his family. Accept any answers students can support with details from the selection.

Reading Check, page 147
Anaya's grandfather knew that a time was coming when conditions in the United States would make fluency in English a necessity and that Anaya would not be able to live his whole life in one place, like he did in his valley.

Reader Success Strategy, page 148
Possible responses: "Gone were . . . the strength of his young manhood" (lines 102–103); "Gone also was his patience . . ." (lines 103–104); "Small things bothered him" (lines 104–105).

Pause & Reflect, page 148 (Plus)
1. Some students may find the idea of respect for others most important, while others may decide that the grandfather's lessons on religion or being one with nature are the most important lessons the grandfather passed on to his grandchildren. Accept any responses students can justify.
2. Anaya recalls that his grandfather was no longer patient and that he was becoming dependent on others for the first time in his adult life. Anaya also recalls that his grandfather lost the strong, earthy scent he had had as a younger man.
3. to provide a complete and honest portrait of his grandfather

Pause & Reflect, page 148 (AS, EL)
1. Some students may find the idea of respect for others most important, while others may decide that the grandfather's lessons on religion or being one with nature are the most important lessons the grandfather passed on to his grandchildren. Accept any responses students can justify.
2. to provide a complete and honest portrait of his grandfather

Reading Check, page 148
Anaya recalls that his grandfather was no longer patient and that he was becoming dependent on others for the first time in his adult life. Anaya also recalls that his grandfather lost the strong, earthy scent he had had as a younger man.

Pause & Reflect, page 149 (Plus)
1. His grandfather's values may be lost.
2. Possible responses: Both men use their professions to nurture others and help them grow stronger. Anaya uses words to influence the lives and minds of others, while his grandfather uses the lessons he learned as a farmer to nurture his family and community.

Pause & Reflect, page 149 (AS, EL)
Possible responses: Both men use their professions to nurture others and help them grow stronger. Anaya uses words to influence the lives and minds of others, while his grandfather uses the lessons he learned as a farmer to nurture his family and community.

Challenge, page 149
Possible responses: Anaya's ancestors were a close-knit group who cared for and nurtured each other. There is a strong tradition of respect for the elders of the community, who hold an important place in their society. Religion plays an important role in the people's lives. There is also a close connection between the people, the land, and nature. Passages students might find significant include lines 1–7, 8–13, and 13–16.

Active Reading SkillBuilder, page 150
Students may find statements pointing to all of the purposes listed on the chart, but they will likely find more evidence for these purposes: to inform, to persuade, and to express ideas, opinions, and feelings. Sample responses are provided.
Statement: "They had something important to share with the young, and when they spoke, the young listened." (lines 12–13)
Purpose: to express ideas, opinions, and feelings
Statement: "My grandfather was a plain man, a farmer from the valley called Puerto de Luna on the Pecos River." (lines 24–25)
Purpose: to inform
Statement: "Bearded and walrus-mustached, he stood five feet tall, but to me as a child he was a giant." (lines 29–30)
Purpose: to entertain
Statement: "If we don't take the time to watch and feel the years of their final transformation, a part of our own humanity will be lessened." (lines 29–32)
Purpose: to persuade
Statement: "So time brings with its transformation the often painful wearing-down process. Vision blurs, health wanes; even the act of walking carries with it the painful reminder of the autumn of life." (lines 126–129)
Purpose: to analyze

Literary Analysis SkillBuilder, page 151
Sample responses are provided.
Tone: serious, loving, respectful
Anaya's Perspective: He thinks the elderly should be valued and listened to. He thinks they should be treated with respect because they can teach valuable lessons.

Everyday Use, page 152
Connect to Your Life, page 153
Sample responses are provided.
Family Treasures: painting of great-grandmother
Customs: Thanksgiving Day hike
Traditional Foods: corned beef and cabbage
Language: Gaelic

Pause & Reflect, page 155 (Plus)

1. Possible responses: Dee lives a charmed life. Dee is bold, stubborn, and determined to have her way. Dee seems critical and stuck-up.
2. poor, direct and plainspoken, a farmer, big and strong
3. Most students may wonder why Dee is so different from her mother and sister or why Maggie is so nervous about her sister's visit.
4. Most students will predict that the visit will not be a pleasant one because both the narrator and Maggie seem to be uncomfortable around Dee. Some students may also cite the information in the Preview to support their prediction that the visit will not be happy for everyone.

Pause & Reflect, page 155 (AS, EL)

1. Possible responses: Dee lives a charmed life. Dee is bold, stubborn, and determined to have her way. Dee seems critical and stuck-up.
2. Most students may wonder why Dee is so different from her mother and sister or why Maggie is so nervous about her sister's visit.
3. Most students will predict that the visit will not be a pleasant one because both the narrator and Maggie seem to be uncomfortable around Dee. Some students may also cite the information in the Preview to support their prediction that the visit will not be happy for everyone.

Reader Success Strategy or **Reading Tip,** page 156

In their Venn diagrams, students should include details such as Maggie's shyness and lack of education and Dee's confidence and greater experience in the world. Their similarities include that they both want the quilts.

Read Aloud, page 156

Dee uses her readings to effect a change in those around her, to make them conform to her vision of the world. Yet she "shoves" them away as they are about to understand, perhaps, because she needs to feel superior to them.

Reading Check, page 157

The narrator is the mother of two girls; she is big-boned with rough hands from working hard. She has very little education, but she is very smart, witty, and extremely strong.

Pause & Reflect, page 157 (Plus)

1. thin and homely—M
   confident and independent—D
   insecure and shy—M
   scarred from a fire—M
   ambitious and strong-willed—D
2. Dee: thinks Dee is attractive, sophisticated, determined, self-centered, brazen, and without feeling; she loves Dee because Dee is her daughter
   Maggie: compares her to a lamed animal; thinks she is painfully shy and insecure, homely, of low intelligence, and dull; feels sorry for Maggie, but loves her despite her faults
3. Some students will say that they dislike Dee because she is self-centered and selfish, but that they like Maggie because she is the "underdog." Others may respond that they appreciate Dee's drive and sophistication. A few may respond that they feel sorry for Maggie because she has had to endure so many hardships. Accept any response that demonstrates the student's understanding of the characters.

Pause & Reflect, page 157 (AS, EL)

1. Dee: thinks Dee is attractive, sophisticated, determined, self-centered, brazen, and without feeling; she loves Dee because Dee is her daughter
   Maggie: compares her to a lamed animal; thinks she is painfully shy and insecure, homely, of low intelligence, and dull; feels sorry for Maggie, but loves her despite her faults
2. Some students will say that they dislike Dee because she is self-centered and selfish, but that they like Maggie because she is the "underdog". Others may respond that they appreciate Dee's drive and sophistication. A few may respond that they feel sorry for Maggie because she has had to endure so many hardships. Accept any response that demonstrates the student's understanding of the characters.

Reading Check, page 158

Most students will mention that Maggie reacts to Dee's companion as one might to a snake underfoot. Some students will comment on the narrator's negative reaction as well as Maggie's.

Read Aloud, page 159

Responses should reflect the following ideas: While Asalamalakim's attempts at connecting with Maggie seem funny on the surface, it is sad to picture Maggie so uncomfortably shy and withdrawn. Some students may find it difficult to imagine two people having such difficulties connecting. Other students may respond that it is sad to see the young man trying so hard to be something he is not.

Reading Check, page 159

Dee felt her old name was a "white" name, and that white people were oppressing her. She changed her name to Wangero because it was more reflective of her African heritage.

Pause & Reflect, page 160 (Plus)

1. Dee has become so interested in her African heritage that she dresses in African clothing and has even changed her name.
2. Possible responses: Dee believes that pictures of her ramshackle home and poor family will demonstrate to others her connection to her African heritage. She believes that this connection will give her status in her new community. She has a romantic ideal of herself that she is trying to reinforce.
3. Possible responses: The narrator thinks her daughter's desire to change her name is silly, but she is willing to go along with her daughter's wishes. Perhaps she is slightly angered by her daughter's attempts to create a new connection to the past where one already exists. She may also be slightly insulted to think that the name she picked for her daughter, a name passed down from generation to generation by people she loved, was not good enough for Dee.
   Students may cite the following passages: "'You know as well as me . . . War through the branches" (lines 191–200), "'There I was not,' . . . that far back?'" (lines 203–204), and "'I'll get used to it,' I said. "Ream it out again'" (line 215).

Pause & Reflect, page 160 (AS, EL)

1. Dee has become so interested in her African heritage that she dresses in African clothing and has even changed her name.

2. Possible responses: Dee believes that pictures of her ramshackle home and poor family will demonstrate to others her connection to her African heritage. She believes that this connection will give her status in her new community. She has a romantic ideal of herself that she is trying to reinforce.

Pause & Reflect, page 161 *(Plus)*

1. Dee wants the butter churn and dasher and some old handmade quilts. Because she closes her hand over her Grandmother's butter dish, some students may say that she also wants this item. Dee will use the things she takes to decorate her home and to show off her heritage.

2. Dee sees the churn and dash as status symbols. To her, these heirlooms are just objects to decorate her home. She feels no real love for the items or for the people who made them.

The narrator sees the objects as useful items that have connections to the past and to the people she loves.

3. Possible responses: she is in touch with her past; her life is rooted in the land and her family.

Pause & Reflect, page 161 *(AS, EL)*

1. Dee wants the butter churn and dasher and some old handmade quilts. Because she closes her hand over her Grandmother's butter dish, some students may say that she also wants this item. Dee will use the things she takes to decorate her home and to show off her heritage.

2. Dee sees the churn and dash as status symbols. To her, these heirlooms are just objects to decorate her home. She feels no real love for the items or for the people who made them.

The narrator sees the objects as useful items that have connections to the past and to the people she loves.

Reading Check, page 162

When Dee left for college, she turned down her mother's offer of a quilt because she thought they were old-fashioned and out of style. She now sees them as priceless folk objects that she feels entitled to take from the house.

Pause & Reflect, page 163 *(Plus)*

1. The narrator knows that Maggie will truly appreciate and cherish the quilts because they hold meaning for her younger daughter.

2. Possible answers: Maggie gives in because she is used to Dee getting her way; experience has taught Maggie to have low expectations in life for things generally do not go her way. Students will most likely cite lines 328–330 and 335–337.

3. Students may say that although Mama is uneducated and poor, she is a good, hard-working person who loves and understands her daughters. A few may argue that Mama should try to learn more from Dee and work harder to change her life, rather than accept it. Accept all responses students can support with examples.

Pause & Reflect, page 163 *(AS, EL)*

1. The narrator knows that Maggie will truly appreciate and cherish the quilts because they hold meaning for her younger daughter.

2. Possible answers: Maggie gives in because she is used to Dee getting her way; experience has taught Maggie to have low expectations in life for things generally do not go her way. Students will most likely cite lines 328–330 and 335–337.

Challenge, page 163 *(Plus)*

The character of Hakim-a-barber serves both to emphasize the shallowness of Dee's approach to life and to bring some humor to the story. Like Dee, he is trying hard to be something he is not. His superior attitude and condescending behavior reveal that he does not truly understand his heritage or himself.

Challenge, page 163 *(AS, EL)*

Students should circle words and phrases such as the following: "Maggie will be nervous," "burn scars running down her arms and legs" (page 154); "chin on chest, eyes on ground, feet in shuffle," (page 156); "Maggie reads to me," "not bright," (page 157); "Maggie's brain is like an elephant's" (page 161); "never winning anything," "kind of dopey," "just enjoying," (page 163). Most students will probably feel that they have learned that Maggie seems slow and shy, but that is probably because of her burn scars. Inside, she has knowledge and wisdom and is a steady, caring person.

Active Reading SkillBuilder, page 164

Sample responses are provided.

The narrator: daydreams about being on TV with her successful daughter, Dee, but knows it would never happen to her; accustomed to doing "man's" work; decides to give the family's heirloom quilts to Maggie

Dee: attended college, likes nice things, suddenly interested in her African heritage, takes numerous photographs of her mother and sister, wants the quilts to hang them on a wall.

Maggie: ashamed of her scars, envies her sister, walks like a lame dog, knows about and respects her family's history, wants to use the quilts after she is married

Conclusions: The narrator and her daughter are very different from each other. Mama is very realistic. Dee is selfish and sees the family's heirlooms as fashionable, valuable decorations. On the other hand, Maggie is practical and wants to incorporate the quilts into the life of her home because the people in her family who made the quilts intended that they be used.

Literary Analysis SkillBuilder, page 165

Sample responses are provided.

Nature of Conflict: Dee's conflict with her poverty as a child

Resolved? If so, how? Yes. She gets an education, moves away, and surrounds herself with nice things.

Nature of Conflict: The mother's conflict with Dee's new life and attitude

Resolved? If so, how? No.

Nature of Conflict: Maggie's conflict with her physical appearance after she was burned in a fire

Resolved? If so, how? No.

Nature of Conflict: Maggie and Dee's conflict over how to show appreciation of their family heritage

Resolved? If so, how? No.

Words to Know SkillBuilder, page 166

A. 1. side; open
2. think; plan
3. rule; believes
4. secret; spy
5. power; resent

B. Accept descriptive sentences that accurately use at least three Words to Know.

Two Friends, page 167
Connect to Your Life, page 168
Possible response: It would be dangerous to live in a war area. My freedom of movement and ability to go to school or work would be limited. There might not be enough food or fuel.
Reading Check, page 170
Both men are particularly sensitive to the beauties of nature and understand each other's appreciation of it.
Reading Check, page 171
The two friends enjoy fishing very much; it was something they loved doing together.
Pause & Reflect, page 172 *(Plus)*
1. Possible responses: Paris is "under siege" (line 1)—it's being shelled by the Germans; Paris is "in the grip of famine" (lines 1–2)—people have nothing to eat; people are so hungry they are eating sparrows (lines 2–3) and rats (lines 4–5) and "anything they can get their hands on" (lines 6–7).
2. The two men love fishing.
3. Some students may answer yes, because the men love fishing and it would be a good way to escape the hardship of life in Paris. Other students may answer no, because going so close to the battlefront could be dangerous.

Pause & Reflect, page 172 *(AS, EL)*
Some students may answer yes, because the men love fishing and it would be a good way to escape the hardship of life in Paris. Other students may answer no, because going so close to the battlefront could be dangerous.

Pause & Reflect, page 173 *(Plus)*
1. The men are afraid of the Prussians. Possible passages to circle include: lines 116–119 ("The Prussians . . . creeping through them), lines 120–126 ("The Prussians! . . . this unknown, victorious race"), lines 127–128 ("What if we . . . said Morissot nervously"), lines 132–134 ("Even so . . . going any further"), lines 138–144 ("And they scrambled . . . dry rushes"), lines 145–147 (Morrisot pressed . . . completely alone").
2. Possible responses include: They really want to go fishing. They are enjoying their risky adventure. Neither man wants to appear cowardly to the other.
3. Some students will predict that the two men will be caught by the Prussians. Others may predict that they will be left alone because they are only fishing. Still others may predict that they will outsmart the Prussians.

Pause & Reflect, page 173 *(AS, EL)*
1. The men are afraid of the Prussians. Possible passages to circle include: lines 116–119 ("The Prussians . . . creeping through them), lines 120–126 ("The Prussians! . . . this unknown, victorious race"), lines 127–128 ("What if we . . . said Morissot nervously"), lines 132–134 ("Even so . . . going any further"), lines 138–144 ("And they scrambled . . . dry rushes"), lines 145–147 (Morrisot pressed . . . completely alone").
2. Possible responses include: They really want to go fishing. They are enjoying their risky adventure. Neither man wants to appear cowardly to the other.

Reading Check, page 174
cannon fire
Reading Check, page 174
Morissot feels that all governments are pretty much the same—war-mongering. Sauvage feels that a republican government would not be fighting a war.

Pause & Reflect, page 175 *(Plus)*
1. Morrisot loves peace, and the war is destroying the peace.
2. Students should circle the passage "On one point . . . never be free" (lines 201–203).
3. Students will most likely say that the author thinks war is cruel and stupid. Some students may feel that the author believes that war is inevitable and that people should ignore the conflicts and focus on the good things in life, as do the two friends.

Pause & Reflect, page 175 *(AS, EL)*
1. Morrisot loves peace, and the war is destroying the peace.
2. Students will most likely say that the author thinks war is cruel and stupid. Some students may feel that the author believes that war is inevitable and that people should ignore the conflicts and focus on the good things in life, as do the two friends.

Reader Success Strategy or **Reading Tip,** page 175
Possible events students might include on their time lines: they are taken to the island; officer promises they will live if they tell him the password but die if they don't; each refuses to tell the officer the password; officer privately offers each man a chance to tell; Morissot weeps at the sight of the fish; friends say goodbye; the soldiers shoot the two friends; the soldiers throw their bodies into the water; the officer has a soldier cook the fish the two friends caught.
Reading Check, page 176
The officer says that if they tell him the password they can return across the French front line alive.
Reading Check, page 177
The officer means that the two friends will soon be dead and their bodies tossed into the river for the fish to eat.
Pause & Reflect, page 178
1. He wants to know the password the men were going to use when they went back behind the French lines so that he can use it to send someone to spy on or to sabotage the French army.
2. The officer says to each of the friends that if the man will tell him the password, the officer will keep the fact a secret from the other man. The officer will then pretend he has had a change of heart and will let them both go.
3. Possible responses: They don't want to betray their country. They think the officer will have them shot anyway. They want to keep the officer's attention focused on the password so that he won't think to search them for a written pass. Some students may question whether there was a password or only a written pass.

Challenge, page 178
Possible responses: The men are peaceful and harmless. They are helpless victims. They get "caught" by the Prussian officer. They are as unsuspecting as fish—they don't think that they might get "hooked" into the war. They end up at the bottom of the river. They become food for another creature.
References to fish include lines 21–22 ("The minute he reached this land of his dreams he would start to fish"), line 70 (And what about those fishing trips, eh?"), line 87 ("Fishing!"), line 131 ("Oh, we'll just offer them some nice fish to fry!"), line 155 ("It was Monsieur Sauvage who caught the first fish"), line 159 ("This really was a miraculous draft of fishes"), line 160 ("They carefully placed each fish into a fine-meshed net"), line 168 ("They were fishing!"), lines 229–230 ("One of the soldiers placed at the officer's feet the net full of fish"), line 149 ("A ray of sunlight fell on the heap of glittering fish"), line 311 ("Well,

now it's the fishes' turn"), and lines 319–320 ("Fry me these little creatures . . . They'll be delicious!").

Active Reading SkillBuilder, page 179
Sample responses are given.
Initial Prediction: The two men will go fishing.
New Prediction/Adjustment: The two men will drink too much as they go from bar to bar.
New Prediction/Adjustment: The men will get caught by the Prussians.
New Prediction/Adjustment: At least one of the men will be killed.

Literary Analysis SkillBuilder, page 180
Sample responses are given.
Character's Comments About War
Morissot
"They've got to be really stupid . . . to go on killing each other like that!" (page 174)
"And it'll never be any different so long as we have governments!" (page 174)
"Look! Under kings you have war against other countries. Under republican governments you have civil war" (page 174).
"Better to call it death" (page 175).

Sauvage
"They're worse than animals" (page 174).
"Oh, no . . . The Republic would never have declared war" (page 174).
"Such is life" (page 175).

Follow Up: Some students may say that the ironic ending contributes to their understanding of the theme about war by demonstrating the abrupt and destructive nature of war. One minute, a person could be at peace and alive and the next minute that same person could be fighting—or dead.

Words to Know SkillBuilder, page 181
A. 1. rejuvenated
2. fanatical
3. respite
4. atrocity
5. pensive
B. 1. E
2. A
3. B
4. C
5. D
C. Accept responses that accurately use at least two Words to Know.

The Pit and the Pendulum, page 182
Connect to Your Life, page 183
Sample response: snakes, spiders, not afraid of flying anymore, getting an F

Mark It Up, page 187
Possible details to circle: "white—whiter even than the sheet upon which I trace these words" (lines 16–17), "thin even to grotesqueness" (line 18), "the intensity of their expression of firmness" (lines 18–19), "immoveable resolution" (line 19), "stern contempt of human torture" (lines 19–20), "decrees of what to me was Fate" (lines 20–21), "writhe with a deadly locution" (line 22).

Jot It Down, page 189
Students will most likely say he faints because he is terrified by the thought of the torture and death that await him. Some may

mention his lengthy and painful captivity, the horror of the trial itself, or the sweet thought of death he experiences just at the moment he passes out.

Reader Success Strategy or **Reading Tip,** page 189
Students should outline the passage beginning with "He who has never . . ." (line 63) to ". . . arrested his attention" (line 70).

Reading Check, page 189
The narrator is in prison and is trying to remember what has happened since he heard the judge deliver his death sentence and swooned.

Pause & Reflect, page 191
1. Students should cross out the phrase *believes he will be pardoned.*
2. Words and phrases to underline: "bore me in silence down—down—still down" (lines 79–80), "interminableness of the descent" (line 81), "had outrun, in their descent, the limits of the limitless" (lines 85–86).

Mark It Up, page 193
Details to circle: "wild desperation at heart" (line 115–116), "My worst thoughts, then, were confirmed" (lines 116–117), "blackness of eternal night" (line 117), "I struggled for breath" (line 118), "oppress and stifle me" (line 119), "intolerably close" (line 120).

Read Aloud, page 193
Students should check the phrase *being buried alive.*

Reading Check, page 195
The narrator slowly walks along the walls of his dungeon until he has almost reached the piece of serge fabric that he had hung earlier to mark his beginning point. While he is trying to do this, he slips and falls and is too tired to get up again.

Pause & Reflect, page 195 *(Plus)*
1. He tries to walk around the inside of it, marking his starting point with a piece of cloth so he will know when he has gone all the way around.
2. Students may predict that he will be tortured, left to starve, or bitten by rats. Accept any reasonable responses.
3. Students may say he would see an empty cell, instruments of torture, rats, or the bones of previous occupants of the dungeon. Accept any reasonable responses.

Pause & Reflect, page 195 *(AS, EL)*
1. Students may predict that he will be tortured, left to starve, or bitten by rats. Accept any reasonable responses.
2. Students may say he would see an empty cell, instruments of torture, rats, or the bones of previous occupants of the dungeon. Accept any reasonable responses.

Read Aloud, page 197
He pulls off a piece of cement and drops it into the pit. He hears it hit the sides of the pit and then splash when it reaches the bottom.

Pause & Reflect, page 199 *(Plus)*
1. They want to keep him alive so that he can suffer the torture and death they have in mind for him.
2. He falls down just before he reaches the pit. Students should circle lines 207–210 ("I had advanced . . . on my face") and lines 214–222 ("It was this . . . at the moment").
3. Students may say *yes,* because one of the torturers goes out of the dungeon right after the narrator discovers the pit, because they bring him bread and water while he is asleep, and because they seem to enjoy the suffering of their victims.

Students may say *no*, because it is too dark in the dungeon to see anything and because the dungeon is designed so that the prisoner will die without the torturers' having to be present.

Pause & Reflect, page 199 *(AS, EL)*
1. They want to keep him alive so that he can suffer the torture and death they have in mind for him.
2. He falls down just before he reaches the pit. Students should circle lines 207–210 ("I had advanced . . . on my face") and lines 214–222 ("It was this . . . at the moment").

Reader Success Strategy or **Reading Tip,** page 201
Invite students to share their diagrams with the class and discuss what information from the text they used to make them.

Reading Check, page 201
In his "confusion of mind" he missed the fact that he had reversed his direction and retraced his steps rather than continuing forward.

Pause & Reflect, page 203 *(Plus)*
1. Students should cross out the sentence *The floor is made of wood.*
2. He falls asleep after going almost completely around the dungeon. Then, when he wakes up, he goes the wrong way and doesn't reach the cloth marker until he has gone around the dungeon a second time. Students may cite lines 274–283.
3. They tied him to a wooden frame so that he could move only his head and his left arm.

Pause & Reflect, page 203 *(AS, EL)*
They tied him to a wooden frame so that he could move only his head and his left arm.

Reader Success Strategy, page 205
Possible responses: glittering crescent of steel, razor, tapering, hissed

Reading Check, page 205
The tormentors had planned to have the narrator die in the pit. When that plan fails, they watch him carefully and continue with a plan that keeps increasing the torment. First, they cleverly drug him and tie him to the wooden frame so that he can barely move. Then they give him spicy meat to eat but no water, so that he gets very thirsty. Next, they let rats in to distract him so that the shock of the descending pendulum frightens him to yet another point of emotional agony.

Read Aloud, page 205
The details appeal to one's sense of smell.

Reading Check, page 207
The narrator calls himself an idiot because he cannot hold a thought long enough to understand what it is or means.

Pause & Reflect, page 207
1. The rats could bite him easily, since he can hardly move.
2. Students may say that the pendulum is like the scythe of Time, that it moves excruciatingly slowly, that it is shaped like a crescent, that it hisses as it moves, that it is razor sharp, and that the sharp steel has a sharp smell. Accept any responses supported by the text.
3. Students should circle the phrase *the blade cutting his robe.*

Mark It Up, page 209
Some students may say that the author uses the word to build suspense. Others may say that repeating the word shows the repetitive, relentless movement of the blade toward the narrator's chest. Still others may say that the repetition of the word shows the narrator's state of mind—his obsession with the approach of the pendulum.

Pause & Reflect, page 211 *(Plus)*
1. It is one single belt.
2. Students may say that they would try to untie themselves, to shake the wooden frame out of the path of the blade, or to find some way to stop the blade. Accept any reasonable responses.

Pause & Reflect, page 211 *(AS, EL)*
Students may say that they would try to untie themselves, to shake the wooden frame out of the path of the blade, or to find some way to stop the blade. Accept any reasonable responses.

Pause & Reflect, page 213
1. He rubs meat on the strap so that the rats will chew it apart.
2. Possible details to circle include: "swarming with rats" (lines 474–475), "wild, bold, ravenous" (line 475), "their red eyes glaring" (lines 475–476), "sharp fangs" (line 484), "shrank alarmedly back" (lines 489–490), "fresh troops" (line 495), "leaped in hundreds" (line 496), "writhed upon my throat" (line 500), "cold lips" (line 501), and "thronging pressure" (line 502).
3. Some students may say they would not be able to control their feelings of disgust. Others may say they would do as the narrator does in order to get free.

Reading Check, page 215
The walls become hot and they close in on him. Outlines of unreal, demon-like figures are now gleaming on them.

Reader Success Strategy or **Reading Tip,** page 217
Sample headline: Inquisition Prisoner Saved Just in Time by French Army

Read Aloud, page 217
Students will most likely say he sees the bodies or skeletons of previous victims of the pit. Some students may say he sees the rats, waiting to eat him or feeding on a corpse. Others may say he sees some new aspect of the pit itself such as sharpened stakes mounted in the sides. Accept any reasonable responses.

Pause & Reflect, page 219 *(Plus)*
1. They become hot and they close in on him. Details to circle include the "sulphurous light," the fissure at the base of the walls, the glowing figures on the walls, the "vapor of heated iron," "fiery destruction," the change in the cell's form, the change in the walls' angles, the lozenge shape that grows flatter, "burning iron," "closing walls," and "seared and writhing body."
2. Some students may answer *yes,* because of the historical reality of the Inquisition, General Lasalle, and the French army's capture of Toledo. Students may also argue that the dramatic turn of events is consistent with the rest of the story.
   Other students may answer *no,* because the rescue just happens to come at the very moment the narrator is falling into the pit. Some students may add that the story hasn't prepared the reader to think that the narrator is someone who would be rescued by a French general.

Pause & Reflect, page 219 *(AS, EL)*
Some students may answer *yes,* because of the historical reality of the Inquisition, General Lasalle, and the French army's capture of Toledo. Students may also argue that the dramatic turn of events is consistent with the rest of the story. Other students may answer *no,* because the rescue just happens to come at the very moment the narrator is falling into the pit. Some students may add that the story hasn't prepared the reader to think that the narrator is someone who would be rescued by a French general.

Challenge, page 219
Examples of vivid descriptive language include lines 105–120 (the dungeon), lines 161–184 (the dungeon), lines 211–227 (the pit), lines 317–325 (the pendulum), lines 342–355 (the pendulum), lines 400–414 (the pendulum), lines 488–508 (the rats), lines 543–563 (the fiery walls), and lines 574–597 (the closing walls). Students will most likely say that the vivid language Poe uses builds a horrifying and suspenseful mood.

Active Reading SkillBuilder, page 220
Sample responses are given.

Characters
"I saw the lips of the black-robed judges. They appeared to me white—whiter than the sheet upon which I trace these words—and thin even to grotesqueness" (lines 15–18)
"I trembled at the sound of my own voice, and had become in every respect a fitting subject for the species of torture which awaited me." (lines 240–242)

Events
"tall figures that lifted and bore me in silence down—down—still down" (lines 79–80)
"I tore a part of the hem from the robe and placed the fragment at full length, and at right angles to the wall.
In groping my way around the prison I could not fail to encounter this rag upon completing the circuit." (lines 175–179)
"the remnant of the torn hem of my robe became entangled between my legs. I stepped on it, and fell violently on my face." (lines 208–210)

Setting
"The ground was moist and slippery." (line 181)
"I had fallen at the very brink of a circular pit . . . I succeeded in dislodging a small fragment, and let it fall into the abyss." (lines 220–224)
"The general shape of the prison was square." (lines 289–290)

Literary Analysis SkillBuilder, page 221
Sample events are given in sequential order below.
Narrator sentenced (page 186)/low suspense
Awakens in dungeon (page 190)/higher suspense
Moves around the cell (page 192)/low suspense
Almost falls into the pit (page 196)/high suspense
Manages to get back to the wall (page 198)/low suspense
Realizes he is tied down and a pendulum is dropping closer to him (page 204)/high suspense
Plans to escape (page 210)/higher suspense
The pendulum cuts through the rope (page 212)/highest suspense
Slides away from the pendulum (212)/low suspense
Realizes the room is closing in on him (page 216)/high suspense
Stops struggling and gives in to the inevitable (page 216)/highest suspense

The walls stop moving and then spread out (page 218)/low suspense

Words to Know SkillBuilder, page 222
A. 1. discordant
2. imperceptible
3. lethargy
4. lucid
5. relapse
6. eloquent
7. resolution
B. 1. surreptitiously
2. enclose
3. unachievable
4. assumption
5. hazardous
6. powerful
7. greed
8. obstinacy
C. Accept diary entries that accurately use at least five Words to Know.

from **Night,** page 223
Connect to Your Life, page 224
A sample response is provided.
How I Learned About the Holocaust: When I did a report on World War II in 8th grade
How I Felt About It: I was very upset and couldn't understand how something like that could happen.
Reading Check, page 226
Wiesel is concerned that since his father has aged so much in the camp, he might be selected as a "weak one."
Pause & Reflect, page 227 *(Plus)*
1. Students should star lines 18–20 ("Whenever he found . . . good for the crematory").
2. Move about so you get some color in your cheeks. Run as fast as you can. Don't look at the SS, but run looking straight ahead of you.
3. because his father is old and thin
4. Most students will respond that they would feel upset, sad, and scared and that they would be worried about the fate of their family members. A few might feel that they would be very cool and focused on beating the odds.

Pause & Reflect, page 227 *(AS, EL)*
1. Students should star lines 18–20 ("Whenever he found . . . good for the crematory").
2. Move about so you get some color in your cheeks. Run as fast as you can. Don't look at the SS, but run looking straight ahead of you.

Reader Success Strategy or **Reading Tip,** page 228
Possible response:
Before: nervous, frightened, terrified, apprehensive
After: relieved, joyful at not being selected himself, and that his father wasn't selected either
Reading Check, page 228
He ran very fast and was not selected.
Pause & Reflect, page 229
1. He worries that he is too thin and too weak (lines 95–99).
2. Each man is forced to run naked before the SS. Wiesel survives the cut, along with his friends Yossi and Tibi. At least one of the older men saw his number being written down for selection.

3. Possible answers: He does not want to face the fact that one of his men will die. Although the head of the block is in a position of power, he feels powerless because he knows he cannot help the man.

Reading Check, page 230
The head of the block shuts himself in his room because he feels so awful that some of the men were selected and he can't help them.

Pause & Reflect, page 231 *(Plus)*
  1. They are surprised because no one noticed the father's number being recorded.
  2. Possible completions: it was all he had to pass on to his son; he does not want to admit that his father might die.
  3. Wiesel hates the block and thinks it is an evil place—like hell, especially because of the events that are about to take place there.
  4. Because of the tone of the excerpt, students may predict that Wiesel's father will somehow survive the selection. A few students may respond that Wiesel's father will die.

Pause & Reflect, page 231 *(AS, EL)*
  1. They are surprised because no one noticed the father's number being recorded.
  2. Possible completions: it was all he had to pass on to his son; he does not want to admit that his father might die.
  3. Because of the tone of the excerpt, students may predict that Wiesel's father will somehow survive the selection. A few students may respond that Wiesel's father will die.

Pause & Reflect, page 232
  1. Most students will find this scene touching and positive.
  2. Possible answers: The other men liked young Wiesel and his father and knew how sad the boy would be if his father were killed. They feel sorry for him and want to do what they can to support him and comfort him.

Challenge, page 232 *(Plus)*
Students may describe Wiesel's tone as objective, understated, and matter-of-fact. Students may cite lines 70–75 or lines 200–206. Others may also note Wiesel's touches of sarcasm, as in line 1 and lines 64–65.

Challenge, page 232 *(AS, EL)*
Sample response:
Passage on pages 229–231: Weisel's tone is reporter-like and very matter-of-fact. His imagery is plain and simple, and so are the words he uses. He includes a lot of dialogue. This style does several things. First, it makes it possible to read about horrifying events without getting too upset or distracted to understand what is going on. Second, it makes events and feelings very clear and real for the reader. The dialogue makes the story seem very realistic, too. Third, his style reinforces how stark and bare life was in the camp.

Active Reading SkillBuilder, page 233
Sample responses are given.
Event/conversation: The head of the block tells prisoners about the selection and how to improve their chances. He ends by saying, "And, the essential thing, don't be afraid!" (page 227)
Reaction: It is almost inconceivable that such a thing would occur. And it is even more amazing that somehow they were expected to be brave and show no fear—they were still human and lived each moment in fear.

Event/conversation: Elie Wiesel discovers that his father also passed the selection. "How we breathed again, now!" (page 229)
Reaction: All that Elie and his father had were each other.
Event/conversation: Elie Wiesel discovers that his father's number actually had been written down (page 230).
Reaction: It was a horrible and frightening experience for both Elie and his father.
Reflections: Students' reflections will vary considerably. Most will feel horrified or repulsed by the Holocaust. Many students may feel deeply moved by Wiesel's excerpt; some may be touched by the dignity and courage shown by Wiesel and others imprisoned in the concentration camp. Some students may be descendants of survivors; these students as well as others may describe an overwhelming sense of sadness and despair. Accept all responses that demonstrate an understanding of what happened and why Elie Wiesel writes about his experiences.

Literary Analysis SkillBuilder, page 234
Sample responses are given.
Passage beginning: "There were three SS officers standing around the notorious Dr. Mengele, who had received us at Birkenau." (pages 227–228)
Word choice: notorious, ordinary prisoners, perfect physical condition [of Kapos], too thin, too weak, good for the furnace
Sentence length, structure, and variety: variety of sentence lengths; most of the sentences have a simple structure
Tone: fear, suspense, joy
Imagery: "with an attempt at a smile"; "As if this were a game!"; "foremen, all in perfect physical condition"; "I ran without looking back"; "I thought I had been running for years"
Dialogue: "Ready?"; "We can begin!"; "Was I written down?"; "No . . . In any case, he couldn't have written you down, you were running too fast. . . ."
Follow Up: Many students may feel that the simple sentence structure and tone encourages them to read quickly to find out what happens and that the style reinforces how quickly the event occurred. So much of Wiesel's fate rested on those few minutes, and this event is only one of many such events—one set of a few minutes—of countless others during Wiesel's time in the concentration camp.

Words to Know SkillBuilder, page 235
A. 1. din
  2. emaciated
  3. interminable
  4. stature
  5. notorious
B. Accept visual images that accurately use at least one Word to Know.

The Artilleryman's Vision/look at this), page 236
Connect to Your Life, page 237
Sample response: killing, tanks, bombs, hatred, enemy
Reading Check, page 239
The smoke from the explosions has temporarily concealed the targets, so the gunners are waiting for clearer visibility.
Pause & Reflect, page 240 *(Plus, AS)*
  1. Students may star details such as "the shells exploding leaving small white clouds" (line 8) and "the young colonel . . . with brandish'd sword" (line 14). Accept any reasonable responses.

2. Sample response: The speaker sometimes felt pleasure and excitement in shooting at the enemy during the war, and these feelings come back in his dream. He recognizes that there is something evil and insane about enjoying violence.

3. Students should circle "Feels excited during battle" and "Notices what happens around him."

Pause & Reflect, page 240 *(EL)*
1. Students may star details such as "the shells exploding leaving small white clouds" (line 8) and "the young colonel . . . with brandish'd sword" (line 14). Accept any reasonable responses.
2. Students should circle "Feels excited during battle" and "Notices what happens around him."

Pause & Reflect, page 241 *(Plus)*
1. He was shot with a 75-millimeter cannon.
2. Students will most likely say that the speaker regrets the death of his friend. A few students may argue that the speaker's tone and choice of words are a bit callous or that he doesn't seem very sincere.
3. These lines describe placing the body of the dead man in a coffin and shipping it to his family.

Pause & Reflect, page 241 *(AS)*
1. Students will most likely say that the speaker regrets the death of his friend. A few students may argue that the speaker's tone and choice of words are a bit callous or that he doesn't seem very sincere.
2. These lines describe placing the body of the dead man in a coffin and shipping it to his family.

Pause & Reflect, page 241 *(EL)*
Students will most likely say that the speaker regrets the death of his friend. A few students may argue that the speaker's tone and choice of words are a bit callous or that he doesn't seem very sincere.

Challenge, page 241 *(Plus)*
Students may say the Whitman poem is more effective because it has lots of realistic detail, because it shows us directly what happens during a battle, because of the powerful contrast between the battlefield and the peaceful domestic scene, and because it shows the long-term effects of war. Others may say the Cummings poem is more effective because the speaker is a believable character, because the poem focuses more specifically on the terrible result of war—death, because it shows grief, and because of the dark humor of comparing the coffin to a piece of mail. Students may also point out that Whitman's style has an almost dream-like quality—just like a vision—and that Cummings' style reflects the disjointed, chaotic experience of war.

Challenge, page 241 *(AS, EL)*
For examples of breaking the "rules" most students will cite the lack of end rhyme and the lack of a complete stop until the end in the Whitman poem and instances of broken lines, lack of capitalization, and irregular punctuation in the Cummings poem. Accept all reasonable examples. Students may say the Whitman poem is more effective because it has lots of realistic detail, because it shows us directly what happens during a battle, because of the powerful contrast between the battlefield and the peaceful domestic scene, and because it shows the long-term effects of war. Others may say the Cummings poem is more effective because the speaker is a believable character, because the poem focuses more specifically on the terrible

result of war—death, because it shows grief, and because of the dark humor of comparing the coffin to a piece of mail. Students may also point out that Whitman's style has an almost dream-like quality—just like a vision—and that Cummings' style reflects the disjointed, chaotic experience of war.

Active Reading SkillBuilder, page 242
Similarities: Both speakers experienced battle. Both speakers express connection to others—the speaker of "The Artilleryman's Vision" has a wife and a child, the speaker of "look at this" has a close friend.
Differences: Only the first speaker describes the battle in great detail. The speaker of "The Artilleryman's Vision" is cold and indifferent to the victims of war, the speaker of "look at this" is moved by the death of his friend.

Literary Analysis SkillBuilder, page 243
Sample responses are given.
"The Artilleryman's Vision"
Tone: serious
Diction: "I hear the great shells shrieking as they pass"
Diction: "the scenes at the batteries rise in detail before me"
Tone: proud
Diction: "the pride of the men in their pieces"
Diction: "the young colonel leads himself this time with brandish'd sword" ("look at this")
Tone: shocked
Diction: "a 75 done this nobody would have believed"
Tone: sad
Diction: "this was my particular pal"
Diction: "we was buddies"
Tone: bitter
Diction: "send him home . . . (collect")

from **The Tragedy of Julius Caesar,** page 244
Connect to Your Life, page 245
A sample response is provided.
What Makes Your Friendships Work?: kindness; things in common; caring; helping
What Is Hard About Friendship?: disliking things your friend likes; competition; changes in life; strong differences in opinions
Key to the Play, page 245
A sample response is provided on the student page.
Jot It Down, page 249
Possible response: Flavius is furious at the workers who are dressed in their best attire, not in their working clothes.
Reader Success Strategy or **Reading Tip,** page 251
Students should outline the portion of the speech that starts with "Knew you not Pompey?" (line 39), and ends with "Made in her concave shores?" (line 49).
Read Aloud, page 251
The repeated phrase is "do you now."
Reading Check, page 253
Flavius sarcastically tells the workers to collect all those like them who honor Caesar, go to the Tiber River, and weep until the river overflows.
Pause & Reflect, page 253
1. Possible response: The crowd is changeable in its choice of popular heroes. It is not constant in its affections.
2. Possible response: Flavius thinks of Caesar as a threat whose growing popularity must be stopped.

3. Possible predictions: The tribunes might be arrested and put to death by those loyal to Caesar. The tribunes might be protected from harm by those opposed to Caesar.

Read Aloud, page 255
Possible response: Antony regards Caesar as an absolute ruler whose word is not to be questioned.

Pause & Reflect, page 257 *(Plus)*
1. Many students will evaluate Caesar as comfortable in his role as leader. These students may circle lines 3–4 and lines 6–9 in which Caesar issues commands to Calpurnia and Antony. Students who feel that Caesar is not comfortable as a leader may circle line 24 in which he hurriedly dismisses the Soothsayer without probing him for more information.
2. Many students will say that they would ask for more details to try to find out who their enemies are and what they might intend to do.

Pause & Reflect, page 257 *(AS, EL)*
Caesar dismisses the soothsayer as a "dreamer." He does not take him seriously.

Pause & Reflect, page 259
1. Possible response: Brutus is worried about Caesar's growing popularity.
2. Students should check "that the people really want Brutus to be their leader."
3. Yes, because a true friend knows what you are really like deep down. No, because even a true friend may be blind to your innermost qualities.

Read Aloud, page 261
Caesar; honor

Pause & Reflect, page 263
1. pulling him (Caesar) from the Tiber River when he was exhausted and almost drowned
2. Students might circle details such as "he did shake," "His coward lips did from their color fly," "that same eye . . . did lose his luster," "I did hear him groan," and "that tongue . . . cried, 'Give me some drink, Titinius, as a sick girl.'"

Reader Success Strategy or **Reading Tip,** page 263
Students should note the differences in the two men, but also understand that they both do not want to see Caesar become king. A sample response is provided.
Cassius: "I was born free as Caesar"; "we petty men walk under his huge legs and peep about"; "a lean and hungry look"; "seldom he smiles"
Brutus: "I love the name of honor more than I fear death"; "What you have said I will consider".
Both: "rather be a villager than to repute himself a son of Rome under these hard conditions as this time is like to lay upon us"

Reading Check, page 265
Students will most likely respond that Cassius first points out that it is the Romans' fault that they are inferior to Caesar, and that it is an outrage that Roman commoners and nobles celebrate only Caesar. Cassius knows that Brutus, a noble, is firm about keeping the Republic, so he then cleverly appeals to Brutus's pride in his ancestors by reminding him of one in particular who would never have tolerated Caesar's ambitions to be king.

Pause & Reflect, page 265
1. Possible response: Cassius reinforces his taunt that Caesar, not Brutus, is the only man in Rome.

2. Many students will say that they would feel compelled to imitate their ancestor's example.
3. Possible prediction: Brutus might be prepared to kill Caesar.

Reading Check, page 267
Caesar fears Cassius because Cassius is extremely smart and "has a hungry look," meaning he is driven and envies Caesar. He is the type of man who might try to overthrow Caesar.

Pause & Reflect, page 269 *(Plus)*
1. Possible response: Caesar distrusts Cassius because he looks skinny, discontented, and envious.
2. Students should star lines 203–204 ("He loves no plays . . . no music").
3. Possible response: Good, because Caesar is correct in his assessment that Cassius is not at "heart's ease" and is therefore "very dangerous."

Pause & Reflect, page 269 *(AS, EL)*
Students should star lines 203–204 ("He loves no plays . . . no music").

Mark It Up, page 271
Students may circle "the rabblement," "chapped hands," "sweaty nightcaps," and "stinking breath."

Reading Check, page 271
Casca reports that the bad breath from the shouting crowd choked Caesar and caused him to swoon.

Reading Check, page 273
The women show they adore Caesar by calling "Alas, good soul!" and forgiving him.

Pause & Reflect, page 273
1. He fell down in a faint, foaming at the mouth.
2. Possible responses: Yes, because, according to Casca, Caesar's refusal of the coronet was merely a crowd-pleasing gesture. No, because Caesar may have been sincere in his refusal of the coronet, but Casca is biased against him and misinterprets his motives.

Challenge, page 273
Possible response: The crowd is highly emotional, fickle, and easy to manipulate. Flavius and Marullus make the crowd feel guilty for celebrating Caesar and forgetting Pompey. Later, the crowd's adulation of Caesar grows stronger each time he refuses the crown. But the crowd turns against him when he suffers an epileptic seizure.

Pause & Reflect, page 275
1. Possible response: Cassius thinks that Brutus is noble but foolish to let himself be swayed against Caesar.
2. Cassius plans to place forged letters—praising Brutus and hinting at Caesar's ambition—where Brutus will be sure to find them.

Challenge, page 275 *(Plus)*
Possible response: Brutus is meditative (lines 37–42), honorable (lines 85–89), and patriotic (lines 171–175). Cassius is proud (lines 93–96), envious (lines 125–131), sarcastic (lines 255–256), and manipulative (lines 308–322). Brutus opposes Caesar out of love for Rome; Cassius opposes Caesar out of envy. Most students will say that they admire Brutus more because of his unselfish motives.

Challenge, page 275 *(AS, EL)*
Brutus opposes Caesar out of love for Rome; Cassius opposes Caesar out of envy. Most students will say that they admire Brutus more because of his unselfish motives.

Reader Success Strategy, page 277

Students should highlight lines 11 through 13, beginning with "Either there is . . . (line 11), and ending with ". . . to send destruction" (line 13), and lines 28–32, beginning with "When these prodigies . . ." (line 28), and ending with ". . . that they point upon" (line 32).

English Learner Support: Language, page 277

Students should highlight lines 11 through 13, beginning with "Either there is . . . (line 11), and ending with ". . . to send destruction" (line 13), and lines 28–32, beginning with "When these prodigies . . ." (line 28), and ending with ". . . that they point upon" (line 32).

Pause & Reflect, page 279

1. Students should cross out the phrase "a lark eating an owl."
2. Possible prediction: That terrible event might be the murder of Caesar or civil war in Rome.

Reader Success Strategy or **Reading Tip,** page 281

Casca believes: that the storm is a terrible display of the gods to frighten people.

Cassius believes: that the storm is a sign from the gods that Romans must overthrow the dictator Caesar. It is a warning that the gods are unhappy with the current situation.

Read Aloud, page 281

Caesar

Read Aloud, page 283

Cassius considers suicide to be honorable. Suicide shows that a person's spirit is strong enough to choose death rather than a shameful life.

Pause & Reflect, page 285 *(Plus)*

1. Students should circle the words *unafraid and defiant.*
2. Possible response: By being weak and fearful, the Romans have given Caesar the opportunity to assume absolute power.

Pause & Reflect, page 285 *(AS, EL)*

Casca has agreed to join Cassius in his plot against Caesar.

Reading Check, page 285

Some students may recall that in Scene 2, Cassius planned to leave letters at Brutus' home that appear to be from citizens of Rome concerned that Caesar really wants to be king. Now he has also decided to leave notes in more prominent places such as on the judge's seat and on the statue of Brutus' ancestor. In all, he wants these notes to influence Brutus to join the conspiracy against Caesar.

Pause & Reflect, page 287

1. Possible response: The people respect Brutus for his honor and virtue; therefore, they will judge the conspirators favorably if Brutus is with them.
2. Possible response: Yes, because Cassius seems to be a good organizer and is the mastermind of the conspiracy. No, because without Brutus, who has a reputation for honor, the conspirators cannot justify the murder of Caesar to the common people.

Challenge, page 287 *(Plus)*

Possible response: The main external conflict in Act One pits Cassius and the other conspirators against Julius Caesar. The main internal conflict involves Brutus. He loves Caesar yet fears he is a threat to the freedom of Rome. Since Brutus lives for honor, he is tormented about what he should do to save Rome from Caesar. Most students will say that Brutus' internal conflict will be most important as the play develops. If he sides with the conspirators, then he must strike down the man he loves. If he does nothing, then he is acting dishonorably toward his country.

Challenge, page 287 *(AS, EL)*

Accept starred evidence that logically supports the two conflicts. Most students will say that Brutus' internal conflict will be most important as the play develops. If he sides with the conspirators, then he must strike down the man he loves. If he does nothing, then he is acting dishonorably toward his country.

Active Reading SkillBuilder, page 288

Anti-Caesar: Flavius, Marullus, Cassius, Brutus, Casca, Cinna

Neutral: Calpurnia, Cicero

Literary Analysis SkillBuilder, page 289

Students will choose different passages to exemplify blank verse. A sample response is given from scene 1, lines 76–77.

Blank-Verse Passage

Whŏ élse wŏuld sóar ăbóve thĕ víew ŏf mén
Ănd kéep ŭs áll ĭn sérvile féarfŭlness.

Follow Up: Students may say that Shakespeare had the commoners speak in prose because he wanted to differentiate them from the nobility—he did not want them to sound poetic or exceptional.

A White Heron, page 290

Connect to Your Life, page 291

A sample response is provided on the student page. Students will most likely rate commitments to friends, sports, school, pets, and hobbies. Accept any reasonable responses.

Key to the Story, page 291

Sample response: I think taxidermy is a good thing, for the most part. If the animals are already dead and they will be preserved to help people learn about them—for example in museum displays—then I think that is all right. If people kill animals just to make trophies out of them, especially if they are rare or endangered, then I think that is a bad practice and should not be allowed.

Reading Check, page 293

Sylvia came from a manufacturing town to live at her grandmother's farm. She loves the farm and being close to nature, and spends much of her time wandering about outside.

Pause & Reflect, page 294 *(Plus)*

1. Sylvia came from the city to her grandmother's farm. She loves being close to nature as she is shy and fearful of people.
2. shy, often alone, nature-lover
3. She loves the woods and the creatures that live there. Supporting details may vary, but should include the following ideas: Sylvia described the woods as a "beautiful place" and says she "never should wish to go home"; she wades in the brook and listens to the thrushes "with a heart that beats fast with pleasure"; being in the woods late "made her feel as if she were a part of the gray shadows and the moving leaves."

Pause & Reflect, page 294 *(AS, EL)*

1. shy, often alone, nature-lover
2. She loves the woods and the creatures that live there. Supporting details may vary, but should include the following ideas: Sylvia described the woods as a "beautiful place" and says she "never should wish to go home"; she wades in the brook and listens to the thrushes "with a heart that beats fast with pleasure"; being in the woods late "made her feel as if she were a part of the gray shadows and the moving leaves."

Reading Check, page 295
The stranger is hunting birds.
Pause & Reflect, page 297 (Plus)
1. The stranger is a young man who hunts birds. He is outgoing, direct, friendly, easy-going, and focused on obtaining his goal.
2. Sylvia is worried because the young man is a stranger to the area and he carries a gun. She senses that he might bring harm to the peaceful, gentle world she loves or to the creatures in it.
3. Students might comment about the last sentence in this part (line 172–173), wondering what the stranger is so eager to learn about.

Pause & Reflect, page 297 (AS, EL)
1. The stranger is a young man who hunts birds. He is outgoing, direct, friendly, easy-going, and focused on obtaining his goal.
2. Sylvia is worried because the young man is a stranger to the area and he carries a gun. She senses that he might bring harm to the peaceful, gentle world she loves or to the creatures in it.

Pause & Reflect, page 298 (Plus)
1. Opinions about the man's motives will vary. Some students may feel that the young man is trying to engage Sylvia's aid. Others may judge that the man is just expressing his dreams and desires.
2. The young man, an ornithologist, wants to study the heron and add the bird to his collection.
3. Possible answers: Sylvia knows that the white heron lives "where tall, nodding rushes grew," "in some bright green swamp grass, away over at the other side of the woods"; Sylvia knows that the bird can be found "not far beyond the salt marshes, and just this side of the sea itself."
4. Some students will respond that yes, they would help the man in order to get the money. They may cite the family's poverty as a reason for their choice. Others may say that no, they would not sacrifice the life of the heron to please the man or to get the ten dollars.

Pause & Reflect, page 298 (AS, EL)
1. Opinions about the man's motives will vary. Some students may feel that the young man is trying to engage Sylvia's aid. Others may judge that the man is just expressing his dreams and desires.
2. Possible answers: Sylvia knows that the white heron lives "where tall, nodding rushes grew," "in some bright green swamp grass, away over at the other side of the woods"; Sylvia knows that the bird can be found "not far beyond the salt marshes, and just this side of the sea itself."
3. Some students will respond that yes, they would help the man in order to get the money. They may cite the family's poverty as a reason for their choice. Others may say that no, they would not sacrifice the life of the heron to please the man or to get the ten dollars.

Reading Check, page 299
Sylvia doesn't like that he is carrying and using his gun.
Pause & Reflect, page 299 (Plus)
1. Sylvia is infatuated with the young man, but has some reservations about him because he is a hunter. To support this interpretation, students may circle the following details: "Sylvia kept him company, having lost her first fear of the friendly lad" (lines 228–230); "Sylvia would have liked him

vastly better . . . he seemed to like so much" (lines 238–240); "Sylvia still watched the young man with loving admiration . . . stirred and swayed these young creatures" (lines 242–245); "Sylvia followed . . . her gray eyes dark with excitement" (lines 249–251).
2. She is too shy to talk. She doesn't want the young man to leave her.

Pause & Reflect, page 299 (AS, EL)
Sylvia is infatuated with the young man, but has some reservations about him because he is a hunter. To support this interpretation, students may circle the following details: "Sylvia kept him company, having lost her first fear of the friendly lad" (lines 228–230); "Sylvia would have liked him vastly better. . . he seemed to like so much" (lines 238–240); "Sylvia still watched the young man with loving admiration . . . stirred and swayed these young creatures" (lines 242–245); "Sylvia followed . . . her gray eyes dark with excitement" (lines 249–251).

Reader Success Strategy or **Reading Tip,** page 300
Students will most likely describe Sylvia as shy and quiet and loving nature, and then might feel that they now also think she is daring and brave and athletic.

Reader Success Strategy, page 301
Possible responses:
For sight: paling moonlight (line 301), small Sylvia (line 302), bare feet and fingers (line 304), monstrous ladder reaching up (lines 305–306), white oak tree (line 307), dark branches and green leaves (line 308), red squirrel (line 310), swaying oak limb (line 317), thin little fingers (line 321), lighter (325)
For hearing: scolded (line 310), twitter (line 324)
For touch: pinched and held like bird's claws (line 305), heavy and wet (line 309), felt her way (line 311), crept (line 317), reach far and hold fast (line 319), sharp dry twigs caught and held and scratched (line 320), the pitch made her . . . fingers clumsy and stiff (lines 321–322).

Reading Check, page 301
Sylvia makes a dangerous pass from the oak tree's swaying limb to the pine tree, by reaching and holding tight to a limb in the pine tree.

Pause & Reflect, page 302 (Plus)
1. Sylvia climbs the tree in order to locate the heron's nest. Students may cite lines 282–284 ("What fancied triumph and delight . . . make known the secret!").
2. Possible responses include: adventurous, daring, ambitious, nervous, delighted at the wondrous things I saw, driven to reach the top.
3. Because Sylvia is a nine-year-old girl, some students may say that climbing the huge old pine in order to help her grandmother and the man was a brave action. Others may note that she climbed the tree alone in the dark of night. These students may respond that to endanger her life for ten dollars and the attentions of a young man was a foolish thing to do.

Pause & Reflect, page 302 (AS, EL)
1. Sylvia climbs the tree in order to locate the heron's nest. Students may cite lines 282–284 ("What fancied triumph and delight . . . make known the secret!").
2. Possible responses include: adventurous, daring, ambitious, nervous, delighted at the wondrous things I saw, driven to reach the top.

Reader Success Strategy or **Reading Tip,** page 302
Possible responses: the sea with sun making a golden dazzle
over it (lines 345–346), two hawks (lines 347–348), woodlands
and farms reaching far into the distance (lines 355–356),
church steeples and white villages (lines 356–357), white sails
of ships out at sea (lines 359–360), purple, rose-colored, and
yellow clouds (lines 360–361), the green marsh set among the
shining birches and dark hemlocks (lines 365–366), the white
spot of the heron coming up from the dead hemlock (lines
367–369), the white heron flying past with steady sweep
of wing, outstretched slender neck and crested head (lines
369–371), the white heron perched on the pine bough crying
back to his mate in the nest (lines 374–375), a company of
shouting catbirds comes to the tree (lines 377–378), the white
heron goes back like an arrow to his nest in the green world
beneath (lines 380–382).

Pause & Reflect, page 303 *(Plus)*
 1. Students should list three of the following items: the sea,
    the dawning sun, two hawks, woodlands and farmlands,
    church steeples, villages, the green marsh, birds, the white
    heron, the location of the heron's nest in the dead
    hemlock, catbirds.
 2. Possible descriptions of Sylvia's feelings include: satisfied,
    in awe, excited.
 3. The "secret" that Sylvia now understands is where the
    white heron has hidden its nest.
 4. Some students may predict that she will tell the man
    where to find the white heron because she wants the ten
    dollars and because she wants the man to like her. Other
    students may predict that Sylvia will keep the heron's
    secret because she wants to protect the bird and because
    she does not want the man to leave her.

Pause & Reflect, page 303 *(AS, EL)*
 1. Possible descriptions of Sylvia's feelings include: satisfied,
    in awe, excited.
 2. The "secret" that Sylvia now understands is where the
    white heron has hidden its nest.

Reading Check, page 303
She rebukes, or scolds, Sylvia because she was worried
because Sylvia was apparently away from home overnight and
has now come back dirty and disheveled.

Pause & Reflect, page 304
 1. Most students will respond that Sylvia keeps the white
    heron's secret out of friendship and loyalty to the bird,
    citing lines 413–418 to support this answer.
 2. Some students will say that Sylvia does eventually regret
    her decision because she misses the company of the
    young man. Other students may respond that Sylvia does
    not regret her decision because she has saved the heron's
    life. In addition, she is happy living in the woods with the
    creatures of the forest as her friends.
 3. Most students will say that they would have acted as Sylvia
    did. A few students may say that because the man is an
    ornithologist, rather than solely a hunter, they would tell
    where the heron could be found. These students may
    argue that the studies done by an ornithologist would be
    of long-term value to the species. Accept all reasonable
    responses.

Challenge, page 304 *(Plus)*
Passages students may cite include lines 297–300 ("Alas, if the
great wave . . . dumb life of the forest!") and lines 410–411

(No, she must . . . and makes her dumb"). Students might say
that the direct comments call attention to ideas or issues the
writer feels strongly about. Others may respond that these
questions and comments help to focus the reader's attention
on the theme of what matters most.

Challenge, page 304 *(AS, EL)*
Passages students may cite include lines 297–300 ("Alas, if the
great wave . . . dumb life of the forest!") and lines 410–411
(No, she must . . . and makes her dumb"). Students might say
that the direct comments call attention to ideas or issues the
writer feels strongly about. Others may respond that these
questions and comments help to focus the reader's attention
on the theme of what matters most. Some students may feel
that the narrator's comments are distracting; others may like
them and feel it makes it feel more like the story is being told
to them.

Active Reading SkillBuilder, page 305
Sample responses are provided.
Questions/Answers
 • What does the white heron symbolize?/It may symbolize
   power and the wonder of nature. (lines 202–205,
   377–382)
 • Why does the man befriend Sylvia?/He needs a place to
   stay while he hunts (lines 99–103, 136–147). He wants
   Sylvia to lead him to the white heron (lines 172–173,
   213–217, 396–398).

Literary Analysis SkillBuilder, page 306
Sample responses are provided.
Symbol: white heron
What You Think It Means: beauty, the preciousness
of life, the wonder of nature
Evidence You Find in the Story: Sylvia's reaction to seeing
the bird ("her heart gave a wild beat") and her desire to save it
from being killed; the ornithologist's eagerness to find it
Symbol: old pine tree
What You Think It Means: freedom, adventure, longevity,
strength
Evidence You Find in the Story: It is the "last of its
generation" and serves as a "landmark for sea and shore";
Sylvia believes she could see the ocean and the world if she
climbed the "monstrous ladder reaching up, up"; it is compared
to the mainmast of a ship.
Follow Up: Many students will think that Jewett's use of
symbols is effective; some may say that the detailed description
of the pine tree adds depth and variety to its power as a
symbol.

Words to Know SkillBuilder, page 307
A. 1. discreetly
    2. ponderous
    3. traverse
    4. squalor
    5. elusive
B. 1. ponderous
    2. discreetly
    3. squalor
    4. elusive
    5. traverse
C. Accept entries that accurately use at least two Words
    to Know.

Birches, page 308

Connect to Your Life, page 309

Sample response: When I was very little I liked to paint. I loved to squish the colors all around on the paper and make strange shapes. Now I still paint, but I've had some lessons. I still squish the paint around sometimes, but I also have more knowledge and control over what I'm doing. I still love it, though.

Key to the Poem, page 309

Sample response: running very fast; flying a kite; having hot cocoa when it is very cold; sleeping late

Pause & Reflect, page 311

1. Students should circle the word *forever*.
2. They give off colors and rhythmical sounds.

Reader Success Strategy, page 311

A sample response is provided.

Section 1: The speaker sees bent birches and likes to think a boy did it. But he knows it was probably an icestorm.

Section 2: The boy is a country boy and he learned to ride the birches. It is probably the speaker when he was young.

Section 3: He did used to swing on birches and wishes he could again, to get away from life. Not because he wants to die, but because you can feel like you're going almost to heaven and then maybe you could start over again, fresh, when you got back.

Pause & Reflect, page 312 (Plus)

1. Students should circle the phrase *to amuse himself.*
2. Students should circle the phrase *Timing and skill.* Possible response: because you need poise to climb to the very top of a birch tree before you kick out your feet and swing from it.
3. Students should select an activity that they enjoyed and that required discipline and skill to do well.

Pause & Reflect, page 312 (AS)

1. Students should circle the phrase *to amuse himself.*
2. Students should circle the phrase *Timing and skill.*

Pause & Reflect, page 312 (EL)

Students should circle the phrase *to amuse himself.*

Reading Check, page 312

The speaker fears that something could happen that might cause his premature death; he wants to be clear that he is not asking to die.

Pause & Reflect, page 313

1. Students should circle the phrase *to escape troubles for a while.*
2. Students should circle "your face burns and tickles" and "one eye is weeping / From a twig's having lashed across it open."
3. The speaker enjoys living on earth. Love makes life on earth worthwhile despite pain and troubles. The speaker does not want to leave the earth forever.

Challenge, page 313

Students may mark lines 5–13, lines 17–20, lines 32–40, and lines 41–49. Students may say that the birch trees symbolize a temporary escape from the harsh realities of life. Like the speaker, the trees are burdened—"loaded with ice." Yet they also afford opportunities for a boy to swing on them—to forget his troubles for a while and lose himself in the world of disciplined play. The symbol helps to express the message that it is important to strike a balance between joy and sorrow, play and work.

Active Reading SkillBuilder, page 314

Sample responses are provided.

Lines 1–20

Images of Sight: birches bending across lines of straighter trees, birches turning many colors and shedding crystal shells that resemble heaps of broken glass

Images of Sound or Touch: birches loaded with ice clicking and cracking, the sun's warmth, crystal shells shattering on the snow-crust, girls drying their hair in the sun

Lines 21–40

Images of Sight: a boy riding his father's birches, a boy carefully climbing a tree and then swinging out

Images of Sound or Touch: feet swishing

Lines 41–59

Images of Sight: black branches, snow-white trunk

Images of Sound or Touch: face burning and tickling with cobwebs, eye weeping from a twig's lash

Literary Analysis SkillBuilder, page 315

Sample responses are provided.

Figurative Language: "Such heaps of broken glass to sweep away" (line 12)

Figure of Speech: metaphor

Things Compared: ice pellets and pieces of glass

Figurative Language: "trailing their leaves on the ground/Like girls on hands and knees that throw their hair/Before them over their heads to dry in the sun." (lines 18–20)

Figure of Speech: simile

Things Compared: the leaves of birch trees and the hair of girls

Figurative Language: "With the same pains you use to fill a cup/Up to the brim, and even above the brim" (lines 37–38).

Figure of Speech: metaphor

Things Compared: climbing to the top of a tree and filling a cup to its brim

from Antigone, page 316

Connect to Your Life, page 317

Students should give each item on the list a ranking of 1 to 6.

Jot It Down, page 321

Creon plans to dishonor Polyneices' corpse by leaving it unburied for birds of prey to devour.

Read Aloud, page 323

Ismene is *fearful;* Antigone is *brave.*

Reader Success Strategy, page 323

Students should highlight lines 37–41, beginning with "Oedipus died . . ." and ending with "Each killed by the other's sword."

Reading Check, page 323

Ismene thinks Antigone's plan is dangerous because it interferes with the law.

Jot It Down, page 325

Antigone loves her dead brother deeply and feels a holy obligation to bring peace to his spirit.

Reader Success Strategy, page 325

Students should underline once statements beginning with "You may do as you like, . . ."(line 61), and ending with " . . . brother I love"(line 65); and underline twice statements beginning with "But I am doing . . ." (line 73), and ending with " . . . should not be tried at all." (line 77).

Reading Check, page 325

Antigone tells Ismene not to keep her plan a secret because she is aware that once it becomes known that Antigone broke the law by burying Polyneices' body, Ismene could be hated, and worse, punished for not having told the authorities.

Pause & Reflect, page 327 *(Plus)*

1. Students should cross out the phrase "respect for the laws of the state."
2. Possible response: Antigone feels she must obey the laws of the gods and bury her brother; Ismene, however, feels that she must obey Creon's law that forbids the burial.
3. Some students may say that Ismene is more sensible because she is cautious and refuses to endanger her life. Other students may say that from the gods' perspective Antigone is more sensible because she respects their laws.

Pause & Reflect, page 327 *(AS, EL)*

1. Students should cross out the phrase "respect for the laws of the state."
2. Some students may say that Ismene is more sensible because she is cautious and refuses to endanger her life. Other students may say that from the gods' perspective Antigone is more sensible because she respects their laws.

Challenge, page 327

Possible response: Ismene is fearful of authority and realizes her own limitations; Antigone, however, is strong-willed, passionate, devoted to her dead brother, and determined to follow her own conscience even if she must violate civil laws. Students may mark many details in the Prologue, especially lines 28–35 and lines 58–63.

Pause & Reflect, page 329

1. Possible response: The king of the gods punishes boastful behavior.
2. Students should circle the phrase "Face to face in matchless rage."
3. Possible response: *Yes,* because Thebes has survived a terrible assault by Polyneices and the Argive forces. *No,* because Antigone is determined to defy the new king of Thebes.

Read Aloud, page 331

Yes, because Polyneices was a traitor and, therefore, has no right to be buried with honor by the city he sought to destroy. *No,* because Creon rules only the living, not the dead. He is assuming authority that belongs only to the gods.

Pause & Reflect, page 333

1. Students should circle the phrase *loyalty to the state.*
2. Possible response: Creon seems to have strong principles. He values duty to the state above all. Still, he seems somewhat proud and inflexible. He may be trying too hard to assert his authority and look powerful. What is to be gained from trying to punish a dead man? Students may underline several details, including those in lines 19–27 ("Nevertheless, I say to you . . . an enemy of the people.") and lines 44–47 ("As long as I am king . . . when he is dead").

Reading Check, page 333

The sentry doesn't want to report to Creon at all and he is afraid of being punished just for bringing the unwanted news.

Jot It Down, page 335

Possible response: Creon feels threatened because his first decree as king has been broken almost at once. He realizes he must act quickly to bring the culprits to justice; otherwise, the citizens might perceive him as a weak ruler.

Reading Check, page 335

In panic, the guards immediately begin protecting themselves by accusing one another of having covered Polyneices' body with dust. Some students will likely say that they also probably accused one another of not properly guarding the body so that no one could interfere with it.

Read Aloud, page 337

Students should check the phrases *is hot-tempered* and *assumes he knows how the gods think.*

Reading Check, page 337

Creon assumes that the people who have been conspiring against him bribed one of his own guards to cover Polyneices' body or to not notice when they did it.

Reading Check, page 337

Creon commands the sentry to find the "man" who buried Polyneices or lose his own life.

Reading Check, page 339

The sentry asserts himself by suggesting that perhaps Creon's conscience distresses him because of his decision to treat Polyneices' body in such a manner. The sentry also protests that Creon is wrong in his judgment that he is guilty of accepting a bribe.

Pause & Reflect, page 339

1. Possible response: Creon assumes the sentry has taken a bribe from those who want to destroy the city. Students may circle lines 115–121 ("These are the men . . . and all for money!"), line 129 ("The dearest profit . . . too dear"), and line 137 ("Sold your soul . . . done").
2. Possible predictions: Creon will sentence her to death for breaking the law; Creon will spare her life because she is his niece.

Challenge, page 339

Line 78 ("And the man who dared to do this?") is rich in dramatic irony because the reader knows that a woman—not a man—has defied Creon's law. Students may also mark lines 112–116, in which Creon assumes that anarchists have bribed the sentry. Students will probably feel that the use of irony makes Creon look foolish.

Pause & Reflect, page 341

1. The Chorus views humans as the greatest wonder of the world, gifted with the intelligence that controls all other animals.
2. The only limitation is death.
3. Possible response: At this point in the play, the Chorus feels that Creon is right to uphold the laws that preserve the city.

Challenge, page 341 *(Plus)*

The conflict between Antigone and Ismene as to how to respond to Creon's law is external. Ismene also feels some internal conflict in that she admires her sister's loyalty to their dead brother but feels afraid to follow her example. She does promise, however, not to betray her sister. The conflict between the brothers Eteocles and Polyneices, described in the Parodos, is external. Creon's opening speech suggests that later in the play he might have an internal conflict between his personal feelings and his duty toward the state. Creon's conflict with the sentry is external. A conflict might develop between Antigone and Creon as to which laws are more important: human laws or those of the gods. This conflict might be resolved if Creon were to have a change of heart.

Challenge, page 341 (AS, EL)

Early on there are conflicts between Antigone and Ismene and between the brothers Eteocles and Polyneices, as described in the Parodos. A conflict will most likely develop between Antigone and Creon. Students will probably recognize that this will become the main conflict. It might be resolved if Creon were to have a change of heart.

Active Reading SkillBuilder, page 342

Answers should include some of the following points:

1. (Prologue, lines 28–35) Antigone is indignant and determined to do something for her brother, despite the threat of being stoned; Ismene thinks her sister is mad and sees herself as helpless.

2. (Prologue, lines 55–61) Antigone loves her brother dearly; she believes that the gods' laws are greater than human laws and dictate that her brother's body should be buried.

3. (Parados, lines 21–26) Zeus was punishing arrogance.

4. (Scene 1, lines 18–30) Creon says the state deserves the highest loyalty. What he says sounds admirable, but one suspects that Creon, representing the state, will make rules that protect his position, rather than serve the people who make up the state.

5. (Scene 1, lines 31–42) One suspects Creon of making an example of Polyneices as a warning to others not to challenge the edicts of a sitting king (i.e., himself). On the other hand, one can say that Creon is simply arrogant, assuming that he alone knows what is right.

6. (Scene 1, lines 117–122) Creon assumes that those who disobeyed him were bribed to do so by others desiring the overthrow of his government.

7. (Ode 1) The ode says that humans have achieved control of all of nature except for death and fate; the tragic limitation is that human intelligence can work evil as well as good. When laws are kept, a city stands proud; when laws are broken, the city falls. An anarchist is an enemy of the people, here represented by the chorus.

Literary Analysis SkillBuilder, page 343

Sample responses are provided.

Lines: "With hearts for dancing we'll take leave of war." (Parodos, line 41)

Responses: The citizens of Thebes did not support Polyneices, and they want to celebrate this time of peace.

Lines: "What are the new complexities/That shifting Fate has woven for him?/What is his counsel?" (Scene 1, lines 4–6)

Responses: As the Choragus introduces Creon, he raises the questions that are key to the play. The audience wonders what Fate has in store for the new king of Thebes.

Words to Know SkillBuilder, page 344

A. 1. well, it helps; lithe
2. top-grade filets; defile
3. actress ate dozens; sated
4. the dictator; edict
5. super verses; perverse

B. 1. C
2. A
3. E
4. B
5. D

from The Acts of King Arthur, page 345

Connect to Your Life, page 346

Sample response: armor; dragons, damsels; quests

Pause & Reflect, page 348

1. Students should cross out the last phrase, *sinners waiting for punishment.*

2. The knights told exaggerated stories of heroic deeds; Students may underline lines 23–25 ("it was the custom for the defeated . . . overcome them") and lines 30–33 ("knights who lately claimed . . . notice of value") to support their answer.

3. Some students will respond that yes, they would like to attend such a feast because they would be interested in seeing a castle and observing real medieval knights, hearing their stories, and tasting the different foods. Others may respond that they would not like to attend such a feast because it would be crowded, messy, and smoky.

Reader Success Strategy, page 349

Some possible responses: *humble, famous, great, immaculate, delicate white hands, recognizes people, observant, impatient, chuckled, nervously, amazement, fighting man, no time or inclination for love, shame, dog-weary, lost, loneliness, king's beloved hand, passionate, dizzied, blundered, weeping.*

Reading Check, page 349

Lancelot dozes and studies his hands while people praise him.

Reading Check, page 350

Lancelot is bored because is a humble man and is embarrassed and tired of listening to people over-praise him. Also, since they were his exploits, he already knows all about them.

Reading Check, page 350

Little girls were whipped and had to wear braces on their necks to force them to learn to walk with a high head on a swan-like neck.

Pause & Reflect, page 351 (Plus)

1. Possible answer: He is embarrassed by the exaggeration of his accomplishments.

2. Some students might respond that Lancelot is a favorite of the king and queen, and that the speakers want to be in their good graces. Students might add that the speakers also want to boost their own status by associating with Lancelot. To support their answer, they may cite line 35 and lines 40–47. Other students might say that the speakers admire Lancelot's skill, strength, and cunning and they want others to share their feelings. These students might cite lines 50–55 ("There is a seat of worth . . . its unchallenged tenant"). Still others might cite lines 40–43 as evidence that the speakers exaggerate Lancelot's exploits in order to save face and make themselves look less like failures.

3. People were trained to move and act in certain ways, based on their position in society.

4. Students will most likely respond that Lancelot and Arthur leave the hall suddenly because they are tired and bored.

Pause & Reflect, page 351 (AS, EL)

1. Possible answer: He is embarrassed by the exaggeration of his accomplishments.

2. Students will most likely respond that Lancelot and Arthur leave the hall suddenly because they are tired and bored.

Reader Success Strategy, page 352
Students should follow the dialogue through this section to
Guinevere's farewell "Forgive me, my lords." (line 234)

Reading Check, page 353
Lancelot changes the subject because he doesn't want to talk
with Guinevere anymore about the women he has met on his
quests.

Pause & Reflect, page 354
1. Students should realize that, no, Lancelot does not answer
   the queen truthfully. Instead, he looks nervously away and
   avoids answering the question directly, offering generalizations
   about "young girls" and their habit of exaggerating.
2. Lancelot is passionately in love with Guinevere. Students
   should star lines 182–185 and lines 202–203.
3. Students should circle the following statements: *She is
   jealous of his attentions to other women; she is in love
   with him.*

Reading Check, page 355
Students may suggest that Lancelot feels lost because
Guinevere has just left the room and he realizes that he has
feelings for her, his king's wife.

Pause & Reflect, page 355
1. Students will most likely respond that because Lancelot
   was so in love with Guinevere, his spirit (or soul) reached
   out to follow her. Some students might wonder if there
   was not some kind of magic taking place that caused him
   to have such an out-of-body experience.
2. His experience makes him feel "dog-weary, tired,"
   "haggard," and disoriented. Students will most likely
   underline lines 244–246, 259, and 275–277.

Pause & Reflect, page 356
1. Students with prior knowledge of the relationship between
   Lancelot and Guinevere will not find the events at all
   surprising. Many other students will say that no, they were
   not surprised by the events, citing Guinevere's questions
   about the women Lancelot encountered on his quest,
   Lancelot's reaction to Guinevere's touch, and his out-of-
   body experience as reasons for their feelings. Others may
   say that yes, they are surprised by the turn of events
   because both Lancelot and Guinevere have such sterling
   reputations—Guinevere is the beloved wife of King Arthur,
   and Lancelot is his most-trusted friend.
2. Lancelot weeps because he knows he has betrayed his
   best friend and king by embracing and kissing Guinevere.
   He realizes that their mutual attraction can only lead to
   trouble and disgrace for them all.

Challenge, page 356
Steinbeck develops the relationship between Lancelot and
Guinevere by subtly revealing the characters' feelings for each
other. Guinevere is jealous when she hears that Lancelot may
have been in the company of other women, especially other
queens. Lancelot feels a "searing shock" of longing course
through his body when the queen merely touches his arm. His
spirit or soul seems to follow Guinevere to her room, while his
body is still with Arthur. These feelings hint at the intensity of
their passion for each other.

Active Reading SkillBuilder, page 357
Sample responses are provided.

Inferences About Lancelot
His Attitude Toward His Fame
Clues
"monotony of his victories" (line 39)
"dozed and wished to be otherwhere" (lines 46–47)
"deeds exalted beyond his recognition" (lines 47–48)
"Truthfully, I don't know." (line 152)
Inferences
He is bored by stories of his great deeds; fame doesn't interest
him; he is not proud or boastful; he is truthful.
His Feelings About Guinevere
Clues
"Lancelot looked nervously away." (line 163)
"searing shock [at her touch] . . . mouth opened in amazement
at a hollow ache" (lines 182–184)
"His mouth was dry." (line 188)
"a perfume which sent a shivering excitement coursing through
his body" (lines 238–240)
". . . he saw himself leap up and follow her, although he did not
move" (lines 243–244)
Guinevere senses that he is following her, too. (lines 280–288)
". . . the room was bleak, and the glory was gone from it . . . Sir
Lancelot was dog-weary, tired almost to weeping" (lines
245–246)
". . . he felt lost, and a cold knife of loneliness pressed against
his heart" (lines 254–255)
"Their bodies locked . . . each devoured the other . . . Lancelot,
[as he leaves her] dizzied, . . . blundered down the stairs . . .
weeping bitterly." (lines 293–298)
Inferences
They are in love; he desires her desperately but fights his
feelings; Guinevere tempts him intentionally. She is jealous and
so he is reluctant to tell her of women he meets on his travels;
he would rather be on the road, where he can serve her without
inner conflict.
Other Aspects of His Life
Clues
"I can fight, travel, live on berries, fight again, go without
sleeping, and come out fresh and fierce . . ." (lines 262–264)
"my liege lord, my liege friend" (lines 273–274)
Inferences
Lancelot is a man of strength and action. He is proud to be a
knight. He loves Arthur and wants to be loyal to him.

Literary Analysis SkillBuilder, page 358
Sample responses are provided.

Descriptive Detail
tight focus; Steinbeck describes the crowds approaching
Winchester, the feast hall, and Arthur's chambers in vivid detail;
he also uses imagery: "at the long trestle boards the people
were as fitted as toes in a tight shoe." He reveals obscure
details of medieval life, as in his description of ladies' training.

Dialogue
There is no dialogue as the castle scene is set, but the scene in
Arthur's chamber is almost entirely dialogue. The dialogue has a
significant role in conveying the personalities and conflicts of
the characters.

Characterization
Steinbeck's Arthur, Guinevere, and, especially, Lancelot, are
rounded characters; through description and dialogue Steinbeck
reveals their private thoughts and inner conflicts as well as their
public images.

Diction

Steinbeck uses formal language structures, complex vocabulary, and many long sentences, especially in describing public scenes. Yet at times his diction is simple and intimate: "Lancelot chuckled." Steinbeck's diction in dialogue is less formal than in descriptive passages.

Tone

intimate, compassionate; Steinbeck understands some of the less-pleasant aspects of medieval life and sensitively imagines what might take place in the personal lives of the legendary Arthurian characters.

Words to Know SkillBuilder, page 359

A.
1. disparagement
2. decorous
3. carriage
4. vagrant
5. penitence
6. reprisal
7. intemperate
8. fallible
9. haggard
10. exalt

B. Accept diary entries that accurately use at least four Words to Know.

Academic and Informational Reading Answer Key

Reading a Magazine Article, page 362
Mark It Up

1. youth sports rage
2. The caption might lead readers to believe that parents can behave inappropriately at youth sports games.
3. "Silent Sunday" is a day when spectators are not allowed to cheer or talk until the game is over.
4. The photos provide vivid examples of angry parents and kids playing sports. They help the reader imagine the topic.
5. The box contains information about ways that coaches and leagues are trying to improve spectator behavior at youth sporting events.

Reading a Textbook, page 364
Mark It Up

1. Napoleon's rise to power
2. Students should circle the list of Terms & Names at the top right: *Napoleon Bonaparte, coup d'état, plebiscite, lycée, concordat, Napoleonic Code,* and *Battle of Trafalgar.*
3. Students should draw a box around the following sentence: "A military genius, Napoleon Bonaparte seized power in France and made himself emperor."
4. Answers will vary. Students might note that Napoleon had a certain magnetism, he was an inspirational speaker, and he was generous to his troops.
5. Napoleon became a hero by saving delegates to the National Convention from an attack by royalist rebels.

Reading a Graph, page 366
Mark It Up

1. "Daily High Temperature Dec.1–Dec. 14"
2. temperatures in degrees Fahrenheit
3. dates in December
4. December 4

Reading a Map, page 367
Mark It Up

1. to show the population distribution of Australia
2. Melbourne and Sydney
3. Tasmania
4. kilometers

Reading a Diagram, page 368
Mark It Up

1. The diagram shows the changing states of water during the water cycle.
2. clouds, rain, and dew
3. Condensed water vapor becomes liquid water.
4. Students should trace the large arrow at the top of the diagram that extends from right to left.
5. During sublimation, heat absorption causes ice to become liquid water, which then evaporates and becomes water vapor.

Main Idea and Supporting Details, page 370
Mark It Up

1. Students should circle the main idea: "When Elizabeth I inherited the English throne in 1558, she quickly began making changes within the country."
2. Students should underline the three sentences that follow the main idea.

Problem and Solution, page 371
Mark It Up

1. Students should underline the proposed solution: "Forming a community anti-noise group can be useful in the battle for peace and quiet."
2. Students should circle one of the following details: "According to hearing experts, noise in excess of 85 decibels can cause hearing loss if exposure is long enough"; "Hair dryers and lawn mowers commonly reach levels of 90 decibels"; "Noise pollution is not just an annoyance—it can actually be dangerous."
3. Responses will vary. Some students will think the proposed solution will help resolve a genuine problem. Others might question whether the solution will be effective, or whether action to reduce noise pollution is really needed.

Sequence, page 372
Mark It Up

1. Students should circle the following words or phrases: *as a boy, At 16, The next day, for the first time in 10 years, since the time of the Romans, lasted only 10 years,* and *dates.*
2. Students should underline the following words or phrases: *at the beginning of his military career, after becoming a soldier, gradually, after many military successes, the next day, after failing to defeat Napoleon, for the first time in 10 years, since the time of the Romans, lasted only 10 years, after an escape from Elba,* and *again banished.*
3. Events that students should add to the timeline include the following: 1795—Defended the revolutionary convention of 1795; 1799—Seized power; 1802—Signed peace treaty with Britain, Austria, and Russia; 1804—Became emperor; 1814—Exiled to Elba; 1815—Defeated at Battle of Waterloo; 1821—Died in exile.

Cause and Effect, page 374
Mark It Up

1. Students should circle the following words and phrases: *as a result, also a cause, can also be a reason,* and *consequently.*
2. Students should underline the following clause: *Wood storks prefer somewhat dry weather . . .*
3. Students should list at least three of the following causes: drought, unusually wet weather, changing weather, and varying water levels.

Comparison and Contrast, page 376
Mark It Up

1. Students should circle the following signal words and phrases: *also, similar in age, similarly,* and *both.*
2. Students should underline the following: *in contrast, while, major structural differences as well,* and *on the other hand.*
3. Students should add at least one of the following to the Egypt circle: greater height; smooth sides rising to a point;

served as royal burial chambers. Students should add at least one of the following to the area of overlap: built in the middle of cities; took years to build. Students should add at least one of the following to the Americas circle: less height; receding steps; used as temples.

Argument, page 378
Mark It Up
1. Students should circle the following: *evidence is mounting, so I think,* and *the experts have a point.*
2. Students should underline the following: *I've learned a lot* and *I think.*
3. Students should list some of the following arguments in favor of working part-time: earning money to defray expenses, building good work habits, and getting experience in an industry. Students should list some of the following arguments against working part-time: lowered academic performance, reduced participation in extra-curricular activities, and increased use of drugs and alcohol.

Social Studies, page 380
Mark It Up
1. Students should circle the following sentence: "Indo-European peoples migrated into Europe, India and Southwest Asia and interacted with peoples living there."
2. Students should place a check mark next to the following terms: *Indo-Europeans, steppes, migration, Aryans.*
3. Students should list at least three of the following languages: English, Spanish, Persian, and Hindi; Celtic, Germanic, and Italic languages.
4. By studying how languages spread, historians can trace paths of the migration and determine where various tribes settled.
5. Students should underline the following sentence: "Speakers of a language that developed into most of today's eastern European languages."

Science, page 382
Mark It Up
1. Students should underline the two key ideas, "Marine organisms are an important . . ." and "While most marine life need many of the same nutrients . . ." The Key Ideas head is located in the top right corner.
2. Students should underline the sentence "Phytoplankton are typically single-celled plants that float freely in the ocean's surface waters."
3. ocean currents, temperature, and the amount of nutrients available
4. Answers will vary. The photograph shows what diatoms look like and illustrates their diversity—many different shapes and sizes. Diatoms are one-celled creatures. They are microscopic in size.

Mathematics, page 384
Mark It Up
1. Students should circle "The Distributive Property."
2. Students should place a check mark by the two learning goals under "What you should learn" in the top left margin.
3. Students should underline the following sentences: "Example 1 suggests the distributive property. In the equation above, the factor . . ."

4. Students should draw a box around the rectangle at the bottom of the page titled "The Distributive Property."
5. The worked-out solution shows how to find the area of a rectangle when you are missing the complete measurement for one side.

Reading an Application, page 386
Mark It Up
1. Students should circle the question "Are you a U.S. citizen? (circle one) Y/N."
2. Applicants under 18 need a work permit.
3. Employers should be listed in chronological order, beginning with the current or most recent.
4. Employers that don't fit on the application should be listed on a separate piece of paper that is attached to the application.
5. C

Reading a Public Notice, page 388
Mark It Up
1. Sunnyvale, California, Department of Public Works
2. The notice is for Sunnyvale drivers and people who live near the work zones.
3. The notice is intended to give drivers and residents advance notice of road closings.
4. The city wants residents to follow detours and be patient during construction.
5. Students should place a star next to the last paragraph of the notice, which explains where people can get more information.
6. D

Reading a Web Page, page 390
Mark It Up
1. Students should circle the URL <http://www.pbs.org/newhour> at the top of the screen.
2. RealVideo Segments
3. Clicking on "Lt. Governor Mary Fallin" would probably take you to an interview with or a statement from Oklahoma's lieutenant governor about the situation with tornadoes in her state.
4. Students should circle the link "The Wichita Eagle – Daily Newspaper."
5. C

Reading Technical Directions, page 392
Mark It Up
1. This page explains how to zoom in on a graph created on a TI-82 graphing calculator.
2. Students should underline the following sentence: "To select an item, you may either press the number to the left of the item, or you may press until the item number is highlighted and then press *ENTER.*
3. 2
4. WINDOW
5. B

Product Information: Safety Guidelines, page 394
Mark It Up
1. Students should circle the word *drownings*.
2. When not in use, a pool should be covered.
3. Students should circle the e-mail address in the paragraph labeled D: info@cpsc.gov.
4. B

Reading a Museum Schedule, page 395
Mark It Up
1. Students should underline the following exhibits: O. Orkin Insect Zoo, Butterfly Habitat Garden, Tarantula Exhibit.
2. Students should circle 10 A.M. to 8:00 P.M.
3. Tuesday–Friday
4. A